MOVING MOUNTAINS

MOVING MOUNTAINS

How One Woman
and Her Community
Won Justice from Big Coal

PENNY LOEB

THE UNIVERSITY PRESS OF KENTUCKY

Publication of this volume was made possible in part by
a grant from the National Endowment for the Humanities.

The University Press of Kentucky
Scholarly publisher for the Commonwealth,
serving Bellarmine University, Berea College, Centre
College of Kentucky, Eastern Kentucky University,
The Filson Historical Society, Georgetown College,
Kentucky Historical Society, Kentucky State University,
Morehead State University, Murray State University,
Northern Kentucky University, Transylvania University,
University of Kentucky, University of Louisville,
and Western Kentucky University.
All rights reserved.

Editorial and Sales Offices: The University Press of Kentucky
663 South Limestone Street, Lexington, Kentucky 40508-4008
http//www.kentuckypress.com/

     11 10 09 08 07   5 4 3 2 1

Map by Terry D. Hounshell

Library of Congress Cataloging-in-Publication Data

Loeb, Penny.
  Moving mountains : how one woman and her community won justice from
big coal / Penny Loeb.
    p. cm.
  Includes bibliographical references and index.
  ISBN 978-0-8131-2441-4 (hardcover : alk. paper)
  1. Bragg, Patricia, b. 1968?—Trials, litigation, etc. 2. United States. Army. Corps of
Engineers—Trials, litigation, etc. 3. Groundwater—Pollution—Law and legislation—West
Virginia—Pie. 4. Coal mines and mining—Law and legislation—West Virginia—Pie.
5. Mining permits—West Virginia—Criminal provisions. I. Title.
  KF228.B733L64 2007
  344.75404'65—dc22

                           2007014648

Manufactured in the United States of America.

Member of the Association of
American University Presses

For Chris

Author's Note

This is a work of nonfiction. No names have been changed. Most of the quotations were heard by me, transcribed from a videotape, or repeated to me by a reliable person. In some instances, I cite quotations from people described in historical works. The thoughts attributed to various people have been approved by the people. Every possible effort has been made to verify the words I quote with the individuals who spoke them. Dozens of people mentioned in the book have read either the entire manuscript or the parts pertaining to them. All scenes described were witnessed by me, viewed on videotape, or related by someone present. I have striven to make this an accurate and factual account.

Contents

Contents

Preface

One day early in April 1997, I rounded the last turn to Blair, West Virginia. Straight ahead a dragline shovel—twenty stories high—loomed on the edge of a sheared hill, seeming to be about to topple on the blue mobile home across the road. In nine years in the coalfields, I never saw a more startling sight than on that day.

I came to West Virginia's southern coalfields from the Washington, D.C., area with the sensibilities of an East Coast resident. My purpose was to write an investigative article on mountaintop removal for U.S. News & World Report. What I saw in Blair that day and the moonscapes of former mountains that I viewed flying over the coalfields seemed outrageous. How could anyone do that to the environment?

Though the story did not grow out of my own interests in alternate energy, that background gave me a unique perspective. I had been young when President Jimmy Carter wrapped himself in a sweater and asked Americans to become energy-independent. After my mother's heating-oil bill hit $1,500 in 1977, I took a course in alternate energy. She and I both built solar houses, and I added a wind generator. Since then I've had two other houses with different types of solar heat. But one of the things I learned in the alternate-energy course was that if nuclear power was deemed too dangerous and oil ran out, coal would always be there. No mention was made of the danger to miners, to people living near the mines, or to the environment.

Unavoidably, I brought my environmental sensibilities to the coalfields. It was probably the same prism through which national environmental groups and their members viewed mountaintop removal as it became a national sensation. Soon, though, I met Patricia Bragg, Vicky Moore, Elaine Purkey, and Bob Schultz and slowly came to see coal mining through the eyes of those who lived in the coalfields, who had to confront the problems of mining while realizing that coal was their only ticket to economic survival.

Early on, I learned that deep mining could do as much damage as mountaintop removal, though in different ways. I also realized that the struggle for proper, less-damaging mining could not be separated from other hardships of the coalfields. Those who lived there wanted politicians they could trust, a government that fixed their problems, and new industries that would loosen the stranglehold of coal. So, on finishing the U.S. News article, I set out to learn about these other aspects of the coalfields.

When I met West Virginia University law professor Pat McGinley late in February 1997, on my first reporting trip to West Virginia, he handed me the recently released paperback edition of *A Civil Action* by Jonathan Harr. Pretty quickly, I decided to turn my magazine article into a book. At that point, there was no lawsuit, and I was unsure how to shape a book. Early in September 1997, a newly minted lawyer, Joe Lovett, called me at U.S. News. A man from Blair named James Weekley had walked into his office and handed him my article. The lawsuit was born.

Where the case would lead, no one knew. But I made the commitment to follow it and witness as much action as possible. And my story would be as much through the eyes of those in the coalfields as from the perspective of the lawyers. I greatly admired nonfiction writers Tracy Kidder, Samuel Freedman, and, naturally, *A Civil Action* author Harr. Like novelists, they brought the reader into the events that unfolded. I would try my best to produce half as good a book as my models.

Criticism of coal—and awareness of mountaintop removal—has increased in the past decade as coal-fired power plants have been blamed for damaging the climate. But conditions now are not nearly as bad as when I first arrived in the coalfields in 1997. I have chosen to point out the positive gains of the citizens' struggle and the lawsuits. I learned that the struggle for equality with the mines is intertwined with the sometimes backward economy and politics of the coalfields, but my book tells how battles of the past decade have begun to enlighten the coalfields. Understanding what has been accomplished will help others who enter the ongoing struggle for better mining.

While this book provides a narrative of the fight for equality with coal companies, the successes and failures follow patterns of organizing identified by scholars in the 1980s and 1990s. Key among these is Stephen L. Fisher's thoughtful analysis in the conclusion of his anthology *Fighting Back in Appalachia*. In the past half century, activism in Appalachia has expanded from single-issue battles over such injustices as strip mining to broader empowerment of the citizens themselves. Just how lawyers, legislators, and national environmental groups help, or even occasionally hinder, empowerment of coalfield residents is another question asked by sociologists. Hopefully, my book will bring fresh insights into various reasons for the success or failure of activism.

Although the lawsuit that bears Patricia Bragg's name ended in late 1999, circumstances slowed the publication of this book. And it is well that they did. Not until early 2006 did one last piece of the story come full circle to conclusion. On January 2, 2006, the explosion of the Sago deep mine took the lives of twelve miners and focused the eyes of the world on West Virginia and the dangers of mining. It also brought perspective to the struggle over mountaintop removal, for much more of West Virginia's coal is below the ground than is on the mountains.

The intervening years have also revealed the continuing impact of the Bragg case. And I've been privileged to see how the lives of the people in my book have evolved. I have enjoyed watching Vicky Moore's sons and Patricia Bragg's daughters grow up and seeing Joe Lovett move on to other cases, Bob Schultz's sons get good jobs, and Arley Johnson progress to other inspiring pursuits.

Because my focus has been Patricia Bragg's community of Pie, as well as Blair, and Mingo, Logan, and Boone counties, I have not followed the past few years' growth of Coal River Mountain Watch along the Coal River in northeastern Boone County and southwestern Raleigh County. Other writers, including Peter Slavin, Bryan McNeill, and Michael Shnayerson, know that area far better than I, and it is for them to tell those stories. Mining issues in Kentucky and Tennessee are considerably different from those in West Virginia. Two recent books, Erik Reece's *Lost Mountain* and the anthology *Missing Mountains* by a group of Kentucky writers, tell the story of that state.

Acknowledgments

Unfortunately, more than a dozen people whom I came to know during those nine years have died. They are Bill Cook, Laura Forman, Ray George, Brother Goodman, Phyllis Griffith, Judge Charles H. Haden II, Peggy Hatfield, Patricia McGinley, Jim Miller, Hughie Moore, Leff Moore, Sibby Weekley, and Tracy Wriston.

Finally, I thank Joyce Harrison and the University Press of Kentucky for taking a chance on this book.

Recurring People and Organizations

People

Abraham, Rick. A coal operator and political leader in Logan County.

Ailes, John. The director of mining and reclamation, West Virginia Division of Environmental Protection, 1992–2001; special assistant to the secretary of the Department of Environmental Protection, 2001–4; consultant, Bailey & Glasser law firm, 2004–present.

Bragg, Patricia (Trish). A housewife from Pie, West Virginia, who began fighting for better mining practices when a deep mine dried up water wells in her community at the end of 1994. When an Arch Coal mine put a valley fill at the end of the hollow by her house, she became the named plaintiff in Bragg v. Robertson.

Cook, Bill. The mine inspector who handled Dickie Judy's blasting complaints.

Crum, Matthew. The director of mining and reclamation, West Virginia Department of Environmental Protection, June 2001–August 2003.

Gardner, Blair. The vice president for legal affairs of Arch Coal, 1986–2001; a member of Jackson Kelly law firm, 2001–present.

Haden, Charles H., II. The chief judge of the federal district court in Charleston who presided over Bragg v. Robertson.

Hamilton, Chris. The vice president of West Virginia Coal Association.

Hecker, Jim. The environmental enforcement director of Trial Lawyers for Public Justice. He assisted on Bragg v. Robertson.

Jackson, Lloyd. The state senator who chaired the Committee on the Impact, one of the committees of the Governor's Task Force on Mountaintop Mining and Related Mining Methods. Jackson crafted Senate Bill 681 for the 1999 legislature.

Johnson, Arley. A state delegate who supported blasting legislation proposed by the West Virginia Organizing Project.

Judy, Dickie. A resident of Foster who fought for a decade to control the blasting from a Massey Energy mine above the dream home he had built.

Lovett, Joe. The attorney who brought the Bragg v. Robertson case over valley fills as his very first case.

McGinley, Pat. A law professor at the University of West Virginia who was a cocounsel on Bragg v. Robertson. He was also the lawyer representing the Moores in a case against Arch Coal.

Moore, Vicky. A young housewife in Blair, West Virginia, who, starting in 1994, fought dust and blasting from the Arch Coal mountaintop-removal mine hovering over her community.

Purkey, Elaine. An organizer for the West Virginia Organizing Project, the wife of a union miner, a folksinger, and a grandmother.

Raney, Bill. The president of the West Virginia Coal Association.

Sammons, Terry. An attorney who represented the West Virginia Coal Association in Bragg v. Robertson negotiations.

Schultz, Bob. A miner who worked at the mine in Blair for nearly three decades until it closed because of Bragg v. Robertson.

Simpkins, Freda. A retired teacher and cable-TV-company owner from Beech Creek, West Virginia, whose well dried up, probably because of blasting from a nearby mountaintop-removal mine. As a member of the West Virginia Organizing Project, she helped fellow members lobby for better blasting laws.

Weekley, James. A resident of Pigeonroost Branch in Blair who walked into Joe Lovett's law office with a magazine article that led Joe to bring the Bragg v. Robertson case.

Weise, Suzanne. A cocounsel on Bragg v. Robertson who also represented the Moores against Arch Coal. Married to Pat McGinley.

Williams, Freda. A seventysomething daughter of a union miner who fought in the Battle of Blair Mountain. She has fought for better mining regulations for over a decade as a member of both the West Virginia Organizing Project and Coal River Mountain Watch.

Organizations and Their Officials

Division of Environmental Protection (DEP). A West Virginia state body responsible for oversight of all mining in the state. Promoted to cabinet status in 2001 and name changed to Department of Environmental Protection.

Directors:
John E. Caffrey
David Callaghan
Mike Castle
Eli McCoy
Michael Miano

Secretaries (after DEP became a cabinet organization):
Michael Callaghan
Stephanie Timmermeyer

Other DEP Staff:
John Ailes
Larry Alt
Bill Cook
Matthew Crum
Ed Griffith
Wendy Radcliff
Harold Ward
Darcy White

Environmental Protection Agency (EPA). A national agency.
W. Michael McCabe
Dan Sweeney

Office of Surface Mining, Reclamation, and Enforcement (OSM). A federal government organization, under the Department of the Interior.
Roger Calhoun
Kathy Karpan

Ohio Valley Environmental Coalition (OVEC). An independent activist organization.
Dan Kash

Southern Empowerment Project (SEP). An independent activist organization.

Trial Lawyers for Public Justice (TLJP). A charitable organization of lawyers.
Jim Hecker
Peter Perlman

United Mine Workers of America (UMWA). The primary labor union for mining employees. West Virginia Organizing Project (WVOP). An independent activist organization.

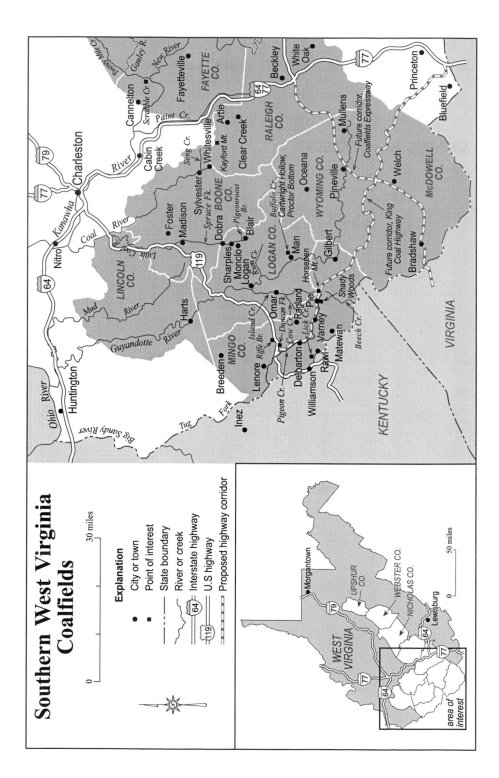

Southern West Virginia
Coalfields

Explanation

- City or town
- Point of interest

--- State boundary
River or creek
64 Interstate highway
119 U.S highway
Proposed highway corridor

0 ___ 30 miles

0 ___ 50 miles

Chapter 1

Awakening to Injustice

A long time ago, Patricia Bragg's grandmother had told her, "You got to fight for what you believe in." They were words that Patricia never forgot. But she never thought she'd have to live by them. Not till a cold day near Christmas in 1994.

All through the summer, Trish, as her friends called her, had watched a new house rise at the edge of her garden. She and her husband, Dewey, a disabled miner, knew they could never afford anything better than their green-shingled rambler tucked under the mountain.

Trish had known Susan Curry, the new homeowner, since she was fourteen. Now Susan was an elementary schoolteacher, with a husband and a baby. As Susan's tan clapboard home rose, all fresh with new lumber and possibilities, Trish joined Susan in plotting the decorating scheme.

It became their dollhouse: Trish the little girl dreaming, Susan the fortunate doll. Walls were painted in the palette of country decorating magazines: china blue, pink, peach, forest green. Teddy-bear wallpaper trimmed the kitchen, while stuffed bears sat on the cupboard tops. Often the phone would ring in one of the houses: "Come down and see." Or "What do you think of this?" During the summer, Trish's mother had come from North Carolina after her husband died. Additional loads of laundry had required more water. So Dewey ran a water line from the old well on Susan's property.

Christmas was nearing by the time the paint had dried and carpeting was complete. Moving day dawned blue and cold. Trish and Dewey helped Susan and her husband, Roy, carry in boxes and furniture, and late in the afternoon friends arrived for the housewarming. One by one, they were given the grand tour, exclaiming in admiration as Susan and Trish showed them the homey details so carefully chosen.

Someone needed a glass of water, so Roy grabbed a glass from a kitch-

Trish, Dewey, and Kayla Bragg lived in this house in 1994 when an Arch Coal mine dried up their neighbors' wells.

en cabinet and held it under the faucet. But no water came out. He rushed back to the living room. Trish called Dewey, who had gone home, put off by the crowd of people. Dewey came over and used electrical testers on the pump, which was working fine. Out the door they went to the well. Dewey threw a rock down, and what came back was that hollow sound of emptiness.

The group stood in puzzled silence for a moment. Many were miners or retired miners. One mentioned deep mining. Dewey explained: "The longwall machines are huge. They keep going straight forward. Through anything in their path." *Anything* included aquifers—the channels that carry water underground.

Yes, one person recalled. A few miles down the road at the Shady Woods community, about thirty people had lost their water the year before. Now what water could be had from the community well wasn't fit for drinking. A deep mine was blamed there, too.

Such a crisis on moving-in day overcame Susan. She began to sob.

Trish hugged her. Later Susan would compose a letter to state mining regulators, trying in her reserved manner to say how she felt that day: "I hope you understand how I feel: It's not right to have a brand new home and not have any water."

———

Trish had come to Pie, in West Virginia's southern coalfields, nineteen years earlier, as a seventeen-year-old bride. She had grown up poor in Mooresville, North Carolina, near Charlotte. Rich in love for her parents and brother and sister, Trish didn't realize how deprived she was until years later in a teaching exercise. Step forward, the social scientist told the group of about fifty, if you had more than three books as a child; step forward if your family subscribed to a magazine; and so on. At the end, everyone except Trish and one other person had stepped forward again and again. The two of them stood alone where they had begun, the most deprived of all.

When Trish was fifteen, Dewey Bragg, a lanky coal miner from Pie, thirteen years older, came to visit one of his sisters, who lived next to Trish. He was smitten, and Trish glowed from the warmth of his devotion. Dewey had nine brothers and sisters, and Trish, on her first visit to West Virginia, was overwhelmed by so many relatives. That first night, Trish slept on the porch. As she drifted off to sleep, she looked up at the modest mountains embracing her and saw God in their majesty. Into her slumber came a new feeling of peace. Pie was now her home.

Dewey and Trish married in June of her seventeenth year. The next spring, Trish's mother-in-law took her for walks along the hillsides, pointing out ramps and other wild plants that could be picked and cooked for dinner. She and Dewey planted their first garden. Eager to prove herself a good homemaker, she set about canning her mother-in-law's sauerkraut recipe. Only she didn't realize Dewey's mother left the lids loose. Trish awoke at 3:00 a.m. to a steady pop pop pop in the cellar. Pressure had exploded the tops off the jars, coating the cellar with a tangy mess. Over the years, Trish became a skilled cook and canner. Dewey and Trish's summer crops fed the couple throughout the winter, as did the deer meat Dewey brought home in the fall.

The Christian religion of the Appalachian hills drew her in. Soon she began teaching Sunday School at the Pie Church of God. Little by little, she adopted the hollows' heritage and traditions and came to feel obligated to protect them.

Pie stretches three miles along Pigeon Creek and Route 52 in Mingo County, from the base of Horsepen Mountain to the gas wells at Grants Branch. The origin of its name is a bit hazy, but a postmaster in 1933 explained that "the word Pie was included in the list of suggested names sent to the POD because there lived here one Leander Blankenship who really likes pie, regardless of kind."

Most of the men worked in mines in surrounding communities; Pie itself was never a coal company town. From the 1950s to the 1970s, it was a favored community to live in—rural, clean, and a good place for kids. Telephones didn't arrive until 1959, and there was never a grand supermarket, but people competed for the most attractive yards and picnicked with friends.

Although the name Pie still appears on the state map and on a green road sign, the post office disappeared in the early 1990s, along with a dozen houses in an entire section of the community. The company that owned the houses had evicted residents because a deep mine was coming underneath. Now Pie residents have an address of Delbarton, twelve miles away.

As she reached her midthirties, Trish often described herself as "that little fat lady" or sometimes "a housewife from Pie." She had blond hair and a smooth face that could glow with joy or flatten into steely anger. Dewey was tall and laconic. Though he worked hard in the mines, he had never fully recovered from his stint in Vietnam. In comparison to other states, West Virginia regularly sends one of the largest percentages of its youth off to war. Crowds made Dewey uncomfortable; if there were many visitors, he would leave the house to roam the nearby hills. He was a good husband and a good father to Kayla and Connie, born eleven years apart. Trish was devoted to him.

Dewey was laid off from the mines in the early 1990s, and the family went on welfare. Eventually, Dewey started receiving about thirteen hundred dollars a month in pension and disability benefits. In 1993 they bought the little green house along Nighway Branch, which joins Pigeon Creek. In the winter they burned coal and oil, which gave them soot and petroleum smells as well as warmth. To save delivery costs, Dewey used a borrowed pickup truck to bring the coal and barrels of oil home. A brand new house was beyond their wildest imagination.

———

That afternoon of Susan and Roy's housewarming, Dewey took care of the immediate crisis. He ran a line from his well over to theirs. It was a stop-gap, not a real solution.

Unbeknownst to Susan and Trish, underground mines had been advancing toward their homes all year. They were the kind of mines that Dewey had worked in, run mostly by machines that move efficiently through five-foot-high coal seams. The aquifer near Susan's well had been pierced, sending the water elsewhere in the underground network of rock fissures. Their liquid lifeline had vanished.

At the time, public water and sewer service was just a dream for Pie. Some of the more populous parts of the coalfields had public water by the mid-1990s. But rural areas had trouble finding the tens of millions of dollars to serve widely scattered communities. Federal grants for water and sewers in rural areas had dried up in the 1980s. Loans were available from a variety of federal and state agencies, but patching together enough money was difficult before a central board was created in 1994. Without public water, and without a functioning well, those who could buy bottled water did. Others would hunt for a spring—or the outflow from an old deep mine full of water—and fill dozens of plastic jugs.

After Christmas presents had been opened and New Year's festivities had come and gone, Trish and Susan started looking for a way to restore water to the community. By now they had discovered that a couple of dozen neighbors were having problems with the underground mine. If they hadn't lost their water completely, it had turned brown or orange and had a terrible taste. The Hatfields, who lived along highway 52 near the mouth of Trish's hollow at Nighway Branch, lost their water and then watched as parts of their house started buckling into the ground. The longwall mine (a type of mine in which collapse of the mine roof is an expected feature) was cracking the ground beneath their house. To compensate for the water loss, the mine company supplied a four-hundred-gallon water tank called a water buffalo and had it filled every few days.

Trish and Susan thought that if they just called the coal company, it would fix the problems. With some difficulty, they discovered that the company was named Mingo Logan and that it was a subsidiary of Arch Coal of St. Louis. What they didn't know at the time was that the mine, named Mountaineer, would be the highest-producing coal mine in the state and one of the top twenty nationwide.

Audrey Carter (right) and Vicky Moore look at the water buffalo, used to provide water when Arch Coal's deep mine dried up the well at Herbie and Deb Hatfield's house in Pie.

The coal company did send men to investigate. Mingo Logan even had a solution—but it came with a price. The company would drill two dozen replacement wells for the community. But homeowners would have to sign agreements promising not to sue the coal company for future damages. This just wasn't right, Trish thought. She and Susan refused to sign and advised their neighbors not to sign.

As the weeks dragged on, Trish became angrier. A neighbor suggested she call the state mine inspectors. She discovered an office for West Virginia's DEP (Division of Environmental Protection) in Logan, about twenty miles north. Susan's mailbox began filling with official manila envelopes. Soon, Trish thought, we'll need filing boxes. To Trish, the copies of inspection reports that DEP must send to the complainant weren't any help. The inspectors didn't think the mines had taken the water. Trish was becoming frustrated. Her own well was fine, water clear and abundant. But just because she had water didn't mean she shouldn't fight so the rest of her people had good water.

One night a few weeks later, Trish stopped at the convenience store near the top of Horsepen Mountain, the only shop within ten miles. "I hear some people been losing water down by you," owner Willis Chafin said to Trish. A little surprised, Trish nodded. Chafin had a suggestion: Call the WVOP (West Virginia Organizing Project) in Logan. A new group, it was helping people who had problems with the mines.

Susan called the WVOP office and spoke with organizer Elaine Purkey. "You need to organize a house meeting," she told Susan. "Call me when you're ready, and I'll come and meet with the people." Elaine met with Susan twice to organize the house meeting, and Susan told her about Trish. Then one day in early spring, Susan greeted Elaine and helped her carry a box of papers into her house. Elaine was in her midforties and had a friendly face. She cocked her head toward Trish's house. "Is that where your mouthy neighbor lives?"

"Yes," Susan replied. "She's really angry about what's happened to everyone. If she knew what to do, she wouldn't care to take up for the rest of them."

"Well," Elaine said, "let's see what I can teach her."

About two dozen of Trish and Susan's neighbors had gathered in Susan's living room. Elmer Goodman, a retired miner in his seventies, was there, as tall as his wife was petite. Trish called him Brother Goodman and loved his little jokes. Barb Harris, who lived near the mouth of the hollow, had come too. Slim and fortyish, she drove heavy equipment at a surface mine about forty miles north of Pie. She also had lost her water.

Half-eaten cake and other sweets sat on coffee tables when Elaine arrived. She began by handing out copies of WVOP's *Mountain Monitor*. The lead headline read: "WVOP dominates DEP town meeting." Trish and her friends glanced through the article. Trish noticed that WVOP had met with DEP director David Callaghan in October. Their letter to him had expressed concern about dust and noise from coal trucks, large surface mines too close to homes, and, most importantly, well damage from surface mine blasting and underground mines.

"I know you all are wondering about me," Elaine began. "And you don't trust me yet. That's okay. I don't blame you after all you've been through. It's true I get paid to do this. But I got this job because of the work I did in the Pittson coal strike of 1989. My husband's a union miner, and he and I helped lead the strike over health benefits.

"I'm not from Charleston. I was born and raised in Harts in Lincoln County. My daddy worked for the C&O Railroad, and my husband's a third generation underground coal miner. We have three daughters. I was raised poor, and I'm still poor. But one thing I never had to do was go without water. I can't imagine how you all are feeling right now."

One man suddenly recognized Elaine. "You sing," he said. "I heard you on the radio."

Elaine smiled proudly. "I was performing on a local radio show—that's where you heard me. When I started working on the Pittson strike, I started writing and singing labor songs."

Trish's face was stern as she watched Elaine from a corner of the room. Occasionally, she took notes. Finally she challenged Elaine: "How much will it cost for you to help us?"

"Nothing," Elaine responded calmly. "I told you, I am an organizer for the West Virginia Organizing Project. We write our work up in grants and get money to teach regular people like you all to pretty much do what we do. We are a membership organization. Our dues are based on one's ability to pay. If you can't afford the dues, you give us your time and energy and become a member that way."

Barb raised her hand. "Will you help us pay for a lawyer?"

"WVOP doesn't do lawsuits," Elaine explained. "We believe in giving people the power to change their own lives through organizing to confront the powers that be and forcing them to do what's best for the people—not for big business."

"Does that usually work?" Barb asked.

"Government officials and public officials are scared to death of a group of citizens knocking on their doors with enough confidence and knowledge to tell their story and make demands."

"But how do we know who to talk to and what to say?" Barb wondered, puzzled.

"It's my job to teach you," Elaine said, then paused, searching. "That is, once we figure out who's got the power to give us what we want. Who that is, that's our first task to figure out."

Finally Trish was ready to join in. She moved closer to the center of the room: "Why can't you do it for us?"

"That's not what I get paid to do," Elaine countered. "My job is to empower citizens to speak for themselves. I don't know your story. I don't know how you feel. Nobody can tell your story as well as you can. And I tell you right now, I won't make your plan for you. You have to make your own plan 'cause you are the only ones who know what you are willing to put on the line. If you don't work, I don't work." Elaine looked around the room and added, with emphasis: "I don't live here, it's not my problem, it's yours."

Trish wasn't convinced. "What if we make a plan, and you don't agree with it?"

"Then I'll tell you what I think based on my experience," Elaine explained patiently. "If you want to continue with your plan, it's my job to help you. If the plan is mine and you don't agree with it, you're not going to work hard on it." Elaine smiled. "And we will always have a plan B, and if possible, a plan C."

Brother Goodman raised his hand, nearly dumping his plate of cake, and asked plaintively: "What can we do? I don't have any water. The state tells us the mines didn't do it."

"The surface mining law says they have to replace your wells," Elaine reassured him. "We have to force them to do it.

"Don't get me wrong, mining has made a good living for me and my family. But my husband would be the first to tell you what they are doing now is just plain wrong. They're tearing down your homes with blasting, and they are stealing your water. We have to do something, and we have to do it now."

Trish squared her shoulders and looked at Elaine. "How do we know you're not connected with the government?"

Elaine just looked at Trish. "You don't have to trust me," she said. "I know it's really hard right now. But what else do you have?"

Trish was silent for a minute, then her shoulders relaxed. "Okay," she told Elaine, "You've convinced me for now. I've got a mouth, now you teach it what to say."

"That's a challenge I want to accept," Elaine smiled, then turned back to the table where Susan, Barb, and a half dozen others were filling out membership forms for WVOP and handing in payment. Trish hung back; she didn't have money for a membership. Besides, she still wasn't sure how much she wanted to be involved with this organization—and that bossy organizer.

Actually, Elaine wasn't sure about Trish either. She thought she had a smart attitude and a big mouth. But they soon got down to the business of organizing. Differences melted away, replaced by a close bond. Not long after that first meeting at Susan's house, Elaine and Trish and Kayla, who was seven at the time, went to dinner after a conference on water at DEP. "I wish I could join WVOP," Trish told Elaine. Kayla piped up, "Me, too." As Trish searched her wallet, Elaine pulled a few dollar bills from her purse. Trish and Kayla were now members of WVOP.

WVOP's philosophy was different from that of service groups, which help connect the poor and minorities to social services. WVOP, which was formed in 1991, did not give handouts, not money, not goods. Nor was it an environmental group, though the media would tag it as such over the next few years. Instead, WVOP taught people how to help themselves and their neighbors. In fact, staff were not even permitted to speak for members when the press came looking for interviews.

Following a pattern similar to the one developed by Saul Alinsky in Chicago in the early 1940s, WVOP encouraged members to decide on problems that could be solved and then design an approach. Usually it included negotiation, action, pressure, and resolution. Alinsky's philosophy infuses many social-justice movements, from the struggle of low-income-housing tenants to that of the United Farm Workers. The groups choose winnable issues, often using small victories as building blocks to a bigger goal. "How the hell do we get people to participate in their lives and government?" Alinsky asked. "The real democratic program is . . . a healthy, active, participating, interested, self-confident people who, though their participation and interest, become informed, educated, and above all develop faith in themselves, their fellow man and the future."

Some writers, especially during the 1960s, have questioned whether the people of Appalachia are capable of working together for the betterment of themselves. This was the view expressed by Jack E. Weller in *Yesterday's People*. Weller had spent thirteen years as a missionary in Whitesville, in Boone County, West Virginia, about sixty miles northeast of Pie. In the same vein, Harry M. Caudill's *Night Comes to the Cumberlands* focused on Kentucky, describing descendants of white Europeans who were sometimes violent and whose education and socialization had been stunted by the coal-company domination.

More recently, Appalachian studies scholars have become increasingly critical of the typecasting perpetuated by the Caudill and Weller books.

"In the 1980s and 1990s, an impressive array of scholarly studies have laid the groundwork for transforming the way we understand and think about the Appalachian region," wrote Stephen Fisher in the introduction to *Fighting Back in Appalachia.* "They explain how, why and for whose benefit the damaging and misleading stereotypes of Appalachians were developed. They document how the economic problems faced by many in Appalachia are a result not of isolation and lack of economic development, but of the type of modernization that has occurred there." People needed to get on equal footing with coal.

That wasn't easy. Mining regulations were as difficult as calculus for the average citizen. Coalfield residents became increasingly angry as they tried to understand what regulations required and which agency enforced them. Their frustration with the mines became misdirected toward mine regulators who tried to help but found their hands tied as well. When WVOP opened its doors in the coalfields, it was immediately entrusted with a vital mission, yet one that sometimes seemed nearly impossible.

WVOP had spent its early years, from 1991 until 1994, gathering mining regulations and learning who was who at the state and federal regulatory agencies. The group had won significant victories, including re-routing coal trucks away from communities and stopping one mine because the coal trucks would have overwhelmed the narrow road through the community. So when Elaine met with Trish and Susan in the spring of 1995, the office files were already brimming with complaints to DEP and hydrology reports on the more than a dozen underground mines near Pigeon Creek.

Ten years older than Trish and already a grandmother by the time they met, Elaine, with her husband, Bethel, had led the 1989 UMWA (United Mine Workers of America) strike against the Pittson mine, which lay between Logan and Man—a fight over health-care benefits that was the last successful union action against the mines. Years earlier, as a high school student, Elaine had won the week in Washington fellowship awarded by West Virginia Congressman Ken Hechler, one of the state's best-loved public officials. By the time she met Trish, she had already set off on the precarious path of trying to control mining abuses while understanding that the nation's need for West Virginia coal would probably keep the mines open.

———

On May 25, 1995, Trish, Susan, Brother Goodman, and more than a dozen neighbors—and even Dewey—were off to an 8:00 a.m. picket line at DEP's headquarters in Nitro at the western edge of the Charleston suburbs. Tucked in the shadow of the monstrous cooling towers of the John Amos coal-fueled power plant, Nitro was said to have been named after the nitroglycerine once manufactured there.

The group had created clever slogans for their placards, including "Don't Take the Sweetest Slice of Pie." Elaine watched from the sidelines, since WVOP staff were prohibited from participating in members' undertakings. Signs held high, the group intimidated DEP staff inside. One secretary wondered if she should call the police. Wendy Radcliff, the first-ever DEP environmental (people's) advocate, quickly quelled that thought. "This is their building too," she said. "We will put them in the board room and treat them like royalty." Over the coming years, Wendy became one of WVOP's strongest allies.

On this trip, Trish and her friends didn't get to see any of the top DEP officials. They were able to set appointments for a future meeting, however. And before they left, they took their empty jugs and collected many gallons of clean water from the water cooler near the first-floor cubicles. They climbed in their cars feeling a bit triumphant.

When WVOP had realized it would have to deal with DEP—quite possibly for years—members decided to try to cultivate a cooperative spirit. It was one of the group's best decisions, Elaine realized as the years went by. That was not to say that WVOP members couldn't protest DEP rulings or picket. But they invited top DEP officials to meetings at homes or public auditoriums in the coalfields. There they calmly laid out their problems—and asked what DEP proposed as solutions.

Early on, Elaine and WVOP members had noticed two DEP mining officials who seemed as sympathetic as government officials could be. Mining director John Ailes, who turned fifty in 1994, had been with the agency in its various forms since graduating from West Virginia University in 1973 with a degree in forestry. His great-grandfather, John Jacob Cornwell, had been governor from 1917 through 1920. As a young boy, Ailes's job had been to pick up his great-grandfather, then blind, and walk him home from lunch. Ailes's uncle, Stephen Ailes, was secretary of the army under President Lyndon Johnson, and this was one reason Ailes served in the Army National Guard for more than twenty years. A short

Trish Bragg speaks at a West Virginia Organizing Project get-to-know-you meeting with the state Division of Environmental Protection. Mining chief John Ailes is second from right. DEP director Mike Castle is on his right. Elaine Purkey is on the lower left, seated next to WVOP organizer Ashley Cochrane.

man with a wad of tobacco stuffed in his cheek, Ailes had an easy manner and moved smoothly between coal barons, legislators, and citizens.

Ed Griffith, a little younger than Ailes and with the slim build of a constant smoker, came from humbler beginnings. He and his wife, Phyliss, a miner's daughter, lived about sixty miles east of Pie in Princeton. Like Ailes, Griffith was a career DEP official. By the mid-1990s, he had become head of DEP's three southern offices in Logan, Oak Hill, and Welch. From the start, WVOP found him a friend, but extremely cautious. He would take strong enforcement action only if he was absolutely sure a law had been broken and he was supported by the DEP director. Although the state had a progressive Democratic governor in 1995, both Ailes and Griffith had survived repressive Republican administrations by picking their battles carefully. One or the other, or sometimes both of them, attended many meetings between WVOP and DEP directors.

A month after the demonstration at DEP, on June 22, the new DEP director met with WVOP in the coalfields. Eli McCoy, a career environmental regulator, was the most environment- and citizen-friendly of the seven DEP directors Trish would come to know. In the following months, he would even call her from his car phone just to be sure improvements were progressing. Before the meeting, when Trish and her friends researched McCoy's biography, They discovered he was a native of Delbarton, not far from Pie.

This first meeting, at Southern West Virginia Community College in Logan, was just a get-to-know-you event, where they introduced WVOP to McCoy and listened to his thoughts. They told him they weren't against mining—they just wanted it done without harming homes or people. "We believe that if we establish a productive relationship with Mr. McCoy from the beginning, we can have access to him in the future to deal with particular problems," stated the plan for the meeting. Food was served, as it usually was at WVOP meetings with government officials.

The tough questions came at the next meeting with McCoy, Sunday afternoon, July 9. Trish, Susan, and their friends prepared as if to defend a dissertation. They knew the laws inside out. The first of Susan's nine questions asked: "Will you implement subsidence and water replacement regulations which comply with the Energy Policy Act of 1992 immediately?" Two of the questions dealt with the possibility of public water for houses along Pigeon Creek—something coal companies wanted so they could keep mining under communities. Susan asked, "Will you assure us that if a water system is installed, groundwater will continue to be protected, and well owners may continue to use their wells?"

On July 14, Trish and Susan wrote McCoy, thanking him for coming to Mingo County for a meeting on a Sunday afternoon. Thank yous became a hallmark of WVOP's procedure. They were a respectful nicety John Ailes and other public officials appreciated, especially compared to the stridency of some mining critics. The letter confirmed what McCoy had committed to, including enforcement of the 1992 law requiring water replacement (West Virginia was the first state to enact that requirement). Trish and Susan also asked for the status of four requests he did not commit to; among them were finding a way to get money for public water from the coal companies and from a federal program for cleaning up abandoned mines. These would be ways to gain needed benefits without increasing the tax burden of local residents.

Answers came at a meeting with the group on Trish's birthday, August

9. McCoy agreed that the water-replacement waivers that Mingo Logan had asked residents to sign were not legally binding. The mine must dig them new wells, no strings attached. Residents were free to complain all they wanted about future mining. McCoy also promised to halt any new permits on the other side of Pigeon Creek until public water was assured.

The community soon got more good news. County officials had determined that 65 percent of the homes along Pigeon Creek had lost their water from the mines that honeycombed the area. In June 1996 the county gave the go-ahead for public water and began raising funds for the $5.8 million price tag.

For the time being, problems seemed to have subsided.

————

The summer of 1995 was a whirlwind of new experiences for Trish, coming at a time when her entire being seemed to soak up every drop of knowledge. Sensing a leader in the making, Elaine sent Trish off for a week of training at SEP (the Southern Empowerment Project) in Tennessee, an umbrella group and informal parent to several dozen citizens' groups. At WVOP's annual meeting in September 1995, Trish was elected vice chairperson.

The federal Welfare Reform Act helped set Trish's course the next year. With Dewey disabled, the family had been on welfare for a couple of years. Now the government wanted welfare clients to join the workforce. Dewey couldn't work, so Trish had to get a job. At first the welfare office gave her a make-work position cooking and answering phones at the Gilbert firehouse. Trish, with her empowered attitude, didn't take this long. The social services office thought she was too old to go to college. Trish did not agree. She wouldn't back down until she was allowed to take the skills tests. When she got the second-highest score, the woman in charge of educational development told her she could be anything she wanted: administrator, teacher, psychologist.

But where could she find money for college? Through SEP and WVOP, she learned about various organizations that pay tuition for older students. Elaine wouldn't let Trish give up, having always regretted that she herself didn't have the opportunity to go to college.

In January 1997 Connie, Trish's older daughter, started attending Southern West Virginia Community College in Williamson. By the fall semester, Trish had gathered enough scholarships to enroll as a full-time student too. Scared and shy, Trish asked Connie to help her register for classes. She had never been inside a college. The mass of teenagers frightened her at first; she sought protection by taking three classes with her daughter. But soon Connie joked that her mother had more friends at her table in the cafeteria than Connie had.

The students might be young, but they would come in Monday morning wasted from a weekend of partying. Trish studied until midnight. Her papers and quizzes frequently received A or 90 percent. But when she opened her first semester grades, she began to weep. Seeking out Connie, she thrust the report at her. "I got a 40," she moaned. Connie took the paper, read it, and started to laugh. "No, Mom," she said. "You have a 4.0. That's a perfect grade average."

As Trish's confidence grew, she began to aim higher. She allowed herself to imagine earning a bachelor's degree, then a master's, and perhaps even a doctorate. If she became a college graduate, she would join an elite minority, since only 7 percent of the residents of Mingo County had a bachelor's degree in 1990.

By the summer of 1997, Trish's involvement with WVOP had waned. Elaine had left after a new coordinator was hired, and Trish didn't hit it off with him. Gradually, she withdrew, though she had been elected secretary of SEP and continued to travel to Tennessee for those meetings. Trish's days were filled with college, keeping her house *Good Housekeeping* tidy, caring for Kayla and Dewey, and teaching Sunday School at her church. Connie had married and moved to North Carolina, where jobs were easier to find.

It was a mine—actually two mines—that jolted Trish back into action.

Chapter 2

Slicing Mountains

A new kind of mining was coming three-quarters of a mile behind Trish's house—coming, too, a few miles down the road behind Kayla's school in Varney. What gave West Virginia its nickname—The Mountain State—was being inexorably altered: hills that had stood for millions of years were becoming extinct.

The mountains surrounding Pie are part of a densely packed jumble of peaks in an area about 75 miles wide and stretching 150 miles south and west from Charleston into Kentucky, Virginia, and Tennessee. They were formed just as the first beta version of dinosaurs was released on earth—in the Permian Period, 290 to 240 million years ago. In geological revolution, continents rose from the placid and shallow seas of Carboniferous times. In the tumult, deposits of coal and sandstone and shale were thrust upward, forming the central and southern Appalachians. Over millions of years, water melted from the Ice Age chiseled their peaks. These are not the long, smooth walls of the Blue Ridge Mountains as viewed from Interstate 81 in Virginia, or the tall craggy peaks of the Rockies. Quite modest, coalfield mountains rarely surpass three thousand feet above sea level, and they are barely one thousand feet above the communities. From an airplane, the mountains look like green cones randomly plopped on the earth.

The coal was created out of decomposed plants in swampy land. Layer upon layer of mud and sand from draining streams covered the organic material, and heat and pressure transformed it into coal. Forty-three of the state's fifty-five counties have minable coal seams, most of them lying in the mountains like fudge icing between cake layers. Although there are 117 identified seams, only 62 are said to be accessible with today's technology.

For a century, coal in the lower seams had been scooped out by dig-

A scene of mountaintop removal in West Virginia.

ging deep into the ground. Now nearly one-third of West Virginia's coal is mined on the surface of the mountains, instead of underneath them. Much of that surface mining—more accurately mountaintop removal— slices off several hundred feet of the mountaintops, uncovering entire seams of coal. In the southern coalfields, 40 percent of the coal is taken from the tops of the mountains. So if you fly over southern West Virginia, pancakes, in the tan of bare soil and the green of new grass, interrupt the rhythm of the peaks.

Because mountaintop removal can capture a dozen or more seams in one mountain, it is considered the most efficient method of mining. Between 1982 and 1997, about 270 square miles of southern West Virginia had been mined, either by removing the mountaintops or by taking sections off the sides of the mountains. The dump trucks and shovels that do the work are monsters, often bigger than houses, hulking on the hills as if history had gone into reverse and giant animals were reappearing.

At some mines, the mountains are partially restored with the material removed. Others have been left fairly flat. Either way, the laws of physics are undeniable. The loose rock removed from the mountain takes up more space than what had been compressed over millennia. At least 20 percent of the rubble is left over, even after restoration, and it has to go somewhere.

The easiest dumping place is the narrow valleys, the hollows, which lie between the scrunched-together folds of mountains. The streams that start at the heads of the hollows are buried as well. "Valley fills" these are called, and a small fill may stretch a few hundred feet and contain 2 million cubic yards of rock and dirt. A large fill can bury a mile or two of stream beneath 30 million or more cubic yards of material. A sediment pond at the bottom of a fill is supposed to catch runoff. By the end of 1997, 157 miles of stream had been covered by valley fills in the southern West Virginia coalfields. Fills had been created since the early 1980s, but their size has increased by about 72 percent since the mid-1980s, and the length of streams covered has more than tripled.

The mountains in Pie and other parts of the southern West Virginia coalfields are sought after for yet another reason. They have coal with the highest energy value and the lowest sulfur content in the nation. The 1990 revisions to the Clean Air Act required power plants to reduce sulfur dioxide emissions, so the coal in these mountains became especially precious. America powers itself largely with coal, which is the fuel for as much as 50 percent of all electricity production. West Virginia is the second-largest coal state, producing an average 175 million tons a year in the late 1990s. After supplying its own generators, West Virginia sends much of its coal to Virginia, Georgia, and other southern states, with a small amount exported as metallurgical coal. The nation would go dark if it were not for Pie and the other squares of the quilt of the mountains.

———

An Arch Coal subsidiary now had a mountaintop-removal mine, and its new permit called for a valley fill behind Trish's house. An even more immediate concern was the White Flame Energy mine planned for the mountain right behind the grade school in Varney, where her daughters had been educated. Trish's distress overcame her doubts about the WVOP coordinator who had replaced Elaine.

So when the Division of Environmental Protection held a public hearing about the mine at the Varney grade school in November 1997, Trish was there, along with Susan and other neighbors who had won the battle for public water. Wearing coats on the chill night, they crowded around

A valley fill being created at Arch Coal's Catenary Coal Samples mine: (top left) The beginning of the valley fill. (bottom left) The fill from a distance; eventually most of the valley was filled. (top right) Trees are stripped before rocks are dumped.

(bottom right) The dragline that accomplishes the earthmoving. This one at Samples is one of the largest in the nation.

A new valley fill for the White Flame mine up a hollow near Varney, with its sediment pond.

maps of the mine laid out on the cafeteria tables in this room that did double duty as cafeteria and gym. Larry Alt, the DEP permit supervisor in the Logan office, presided, as he did at most hearings on new permits. As usual, he wore the DEP uniform of olive-green pants and tan shirt with a DEP patch on the right upper arm. He set up a microphone and two speakers that looked old enough to have presided over sock hops. A cassette tape recorder placed on the table nearby provided the official record.

"The reason for this meeting tonight," Alt told the group, "Is a disturbance by surface mining within one hundred feet of public roads."

From her seat in the middle of the front row, Trish asked, "Can we make comments if we don't like the permit?"

"The comment period for that closed three months ago," Alt responded. Once again, as many times before, a mine had been approved without local residents realizing that the mountains surrounding their homes were about to be altered. Coal companies were required to publish legal ads in local newspapers. But the associated maps were usually hard to read and locations were vaguely stated. Even if coalfield residents saw the ads, they had a hard time figuring out what to do next. Nonetheless, this group was going to voice their concerns.

"How close to the school will they be?" one woman asked.

"Half a mile up the hill," Alt responded.

From a seat at a table on one side of the room, a man in his late thirties rose, looking agitated. "Have you ever had problems with blasting from other mines?" Danny Hobbs asked. Hobbs worked on a surface mine about forty miles north and already knew the answer.

"Yeah, we've had some problems," Alt answered.

"How do you feel about fly rock in the school yard?" Hobbs asked, referring to large loose rocks that occasionally fly off mine sites during blasts. One had gone through a house about forty miles north of Pie.

At this point, a heavyset woman DEP inspector, bulging out of her uniform, stepped to the microphone.

"I don't think it will happen," Darcy White told Hobbs. "We don't need to be in a back and forth: What do you think will happen over that blast or that dust?"

Hobbs was perturbed. "You can get up and draw on that map until you fall dead. 'Til it happens, what's a goin'—?"

White walked over to where Hobbs was sitting and put her head within a foot of his face. She wagged her finger at him. Hobbs appeared ready to punch her. "I will hold you personally responsible for damages at this school," he said.

Such acrimonious charges had become common at hearings on mountaintop removal mines, as residents worried about damages. Alt attempted to regain control. "You who signed up, I will call you to the microphone." He looked around the room and called, "Patricia."

Trish took the microphone. "There's no guarantee there won't be any damage. You've got people right here that can tell you the mines won't mind hurting your property, or hurting your children. I don't think any mine should be this close to a school despite what Darcy says."

As Trish sat down, she noticed a slim man in his thirties watching her. Wearing a field jacket, a blue oxford shirt, and khakis, Joe Lovett was attending his first permit hearing. He was astounded.

————

By late 1997, Trish realized that problems with coal mines troubled dozens of communities. WVOP had been helping some of them, so Trish was aware of the issues. National media had discovered mountaintop removal and deep mining as well.

When *Inside Edition* began researching a show on huge deep mines like Mingo Logan, Trish sent a memo to WVOP members: "We have endured many hardships from mining and we need national attention brought to this matter." She included a sentiment that had become WVOP's mantra: "We must express that we are not against coal mining, for mining is our main industry here in W.V. We need mining to be done responsibly. Most of us realize this will never happen without existing laws being enforced."

Soon Trish would travel far from Pie to help other WVOP members—and try to make DEP enforce its regulations. The first permit hearing she attended as part of this broader focus was in December 1997, at the elementary school in Sharples, about thirty-five miles northeast of Pie. Trish sat on the hard wooden bleachers listening to a half dozen residents of Blair tell what the mountaintop-removal mine had done to their community over the previous four years. Now the coal company wanted to mine another thirty-one hundred acres—nearly five square miles—of mountain. A glimpse at Blair and its history explains why residents were so alarmed by the proposed mining.

———

Back in early June 1994, as Vicky and Tommy Moore returned home to Blair, they were greeted by flames that shot through the dusk. Oh, my God, thought Vicky, is it our house? They had spent the afternoon at Tommy's grandmother's little farm, five miles away in Sharples. Their young sons, Dustin and Levi, were in the backseat. As they rounded the last hairpin curve of Route 17, Vicky exhaled. The fire was at the house next door, about two hundred feet from their robin's-egg-blue mobile home.

The owners of that house had been among the first to sell out to the land company of Ashland Coal, which was mining the mountain six hundred feet away. Over the next few years, more than half of the Moores' neighbors sold. Little Blair turned from postcard-pretty to blackened shells as most of the empty houses were torched.

Tommy and Vicky had met in high school and married soon after their graduation in 1988. Tommy was Vicky's first love; he was solid as a linebacker but gentle as a kitten and one to shrug off trouble with barely

A house burns in Blair in April 1997.

a notice. Tommy's father had been a labor relations specialist with Peabody Coal, and the family had lived in Illinois, Kentucky, and Ohio, but summer vacations with his grandparents nurtured in Tommy a love of the tiny communities tucked between the mountains. So when his parents divorced in his ninth-grade year, he went to live with his grandparents and enrolled at Sharples High School.

Vicky was born in Washington state and moved a dozen times before her father retired from the army and the family settled near Logan, ten miles to the south. She went to high school in Logan but came to Sharples High School sometimes with her father, who taught ROTC. Vivacious, Vicky would clutch her hands to her neck charmingly when she laughed. Vicky and Tommy married soon after high school graduation in 1988 and moved to Blair in 1990, buying the home that had been Tommy's great-uncle's. A broad birch tree shaded the yard, where Vicky later planted a Mother's Day gift of tulips.

Vicky came to treasure the closeness of the community. She dreamed of using savings from Tommy's job as a bulldozer operator at the mines to build a fine home someday, replacing the mobile home on the land bordering Spruce Fork. Vicky's childhood had been a blur of consecutive

Dustin, Vicky, Tommy, and Levi Moore in the summer of 1997. Photograph by Charlie Archambault for U.S. News & World Report.

homes; the family had never paused in one place long enough to hold onto friends or neighbors. She wanted a place like Tommy's grandmother's, filled with decades of memories of children, grandchildren, and great-grandchildren.

———

The southern part of West Virginia is a quilt of tiny places, the blocks stitched by the coal companies. The quilt was sewn quickly, by many hands, in the first two decades of the twentieth century. Coal had been discovered in the knotted hills that only the hardiest pioneers penetrated. In the 1880s and 1890s, rights to the coal and timber in the southern coalfields were snatched up by speculators, who paid a few thousand dollars for a hundred or more acres, a significant amount of money at the time. In some cases, the mineral barons straightened out boundaries and granted clear title for surface rights, since various land offices had often given the same piece of land to several different settlers. However, stories abound of fraudulent deeds, signed with X's by landowners who could not read. The ownership pattern was never successfully challenged in court, and today descendants live on land that lies on top of millions of dollars worth of coal sold by their ancestors.

Companies needed workers, so they brought them from Ellis Island and southern black communities. In the early years of the twentieth century, more than three-fourths of the miners lived in towns built by coal companies, communities bustling with activity but shrouded by the grime and harshness of life in the mines. Many places bear the names of the coal company owners, slapped on in haste when the Postal Service required designations for mail delivery. The L.C. Blair family of Philadelphia invested a lot of money in the area. Nearby Monclo was named for two principals in the Boone County Coal Corporation: William Clothier of the prominent Philadelphia family and a Mr. Montgomery. The late Sam Rogers, who researched the origins of community names for the *Logan Banner,* wrote: "I take offense in the fact that certain communities or other entities are named for people that only took, and some are still taking, from us mountain folks. But, you know, they seem to expect it, and we let it happen."

Coal company towns were designed by the principles of speed and geography. Homes and stores were erected swiftly, not necessarily soundly. The confines of the hollows between the mountains often restricted communities to a straight street along a stream, and houses were frequently layered in rows up the hillsides. Sometimes the creek itself was the road, since there was no other space for a flat passage. Often railroads for carrying coal squeezed along the hollows as well.

Blair was different. Route 17 along Spruce Fork curved toward Blair in a mile of natural delight. Uninhibited trees crowded close to the pavement, linking branches in a canopy across the road. Species were as abundant as crayons in a deluxe box: tall, straight tulip poplars, delicate dogwoods, sycamores dressed in patches of light and dark, elegant white birches, shaggy-barked black birches, unmistakable big-leaf magnolias, and even the pushy Chinese invader tree of heaven.

Modest mountains hugged the southeast side of the road like sheltering curtains. Driving from the north, one came upon the community after a ninety-degree turn to the right; the land spread out to a thousand-foot-wide apron between creek and road. Houses and churches lined the sides of Route 17 for three miles, all the way to Aleshire Hollow. The road

A summer afternoon in Dehue in 1997. A typical coal town, it has only this one street, with houses facing the railroad. Rum Creek runs roughly parallel to the street behind the houses. (These houses are now gone, having made way for a Massey Energy preparation plant.)

curved and swayed between mountains and river in such a serene symphony that one almost imagined the hand of a master landscape designer.

In the early 1990s, the town carried itself with the quiet refinement of an elderly lady. Its heydays were past, the times when it had four gas stations and six stores, a passenger train to Charleston, a hotel, and several schools. Smaller hamlets, its suburbs, had been fueled by mines that flourished in the 1940s and then shut down abruptly in the early 1950s, flinging many men off to auto and steel plants in Ohio and Michigan. Other mines opened, and Blair thrived again until better roads made it easier to get to bigger stores in larger towns. No longer was it a stop on the main road between Logan and Charleston; the four-lane highway fifteen miles to the west had opened up the coalfields but moved Blair out of the limelight. Nonetheless, its residents, many of them retired, lived quiet lives nourished by their gardens, their families, and their memories.

———

Coming into Blair in 1998. Second on the left is the house of Mushie Bella, one of the Moores' neighbors. Straight ahead is the mountaintop removal above the Moores' home.

Vicky didn't know anything about coal mining when her family moved to West Virginia. Even after she married, it seemed a beneficent industry since it employed Tommy's father and Tommy, too. That was before she tried to stop the dust.

Mining began on the mountains above Blair in the mid-1980s, and by the time of the first fire in 1994, it had spread over nearly seven thousand acres. The Dal-Tex mine was one of the largest mountaintop mines in the nation. Nearly five hundred feet would be removed from the mountain beside the Moores' home, and mining was expected to continue for sixteen years.

The first hint Vicky Moore had of the mine was the blasting. One day around Christmas in 1993, she heard a loud noise like a big boom; something jarred the house and scared Dustin. "What was that?" she asked Tommy when he came home from work. He explained that it was a blast to break up the rock and earth covering the coal. In a few months, the blasts became fairly regular, a couple of times a day. Pictures fell off the

Mountaintop removal above Blair in spring 1997. Photograph by Charlie Archambault for U.S. News & World Report.

wall, the glass cracking on impact. Vicky's collection of red birds, inherited from her grandmother, was knocked off its shelf by a blast and shattered. Vicky gathered up the pieces and put them in a box.

Up on the hill, the crew would spend most of a day designing blasts. Dozens and dozens of holes were drilled in a rectangular pattern, as if for a giant Peg-Board. The holes were loaded with ammonium nitrate, the same material used for the 1995 Oklahoma City bombing. Only much more of it. A typical blast at Dal-Tex would use between 25,000 and 150,000 pounds of explosive; some employed as much as 500,000 pounds.

After a blast, a brownish cloud of dust floated onto the cluster of a dozen houses near the Moores', covering cars, porches, and house siding with grime. Vicky could feel it on her skin and in her eyes, could even taste it. Soon Vicky and her neighbors Charles "Mushie" Bella Jr. and Johnnie and Brenda Rollins became comrades in adversity. Mushie was a retired miner who had built one of the two new houses at the north edge of the community; Johnnie worked for a contractor who reclaimed land after mining.

The dust cloud thickened when the dragline, a twenty-story-high shovel, arrived in July 1996 and began its job of scooping rock and dirt away from coal seams. Like the lingering haze in photographs of old factory towns, this dust was constant. The machine frequently perched on the edge of the hill above Vicky's home, making her worry that it would fall off the hill. At night, with lights on its boom, it looked like a giant Ferris wheel.

Nighttime brought yet another burden; it was when the fires occurred, and Tommy was afraid to leave their home unoccupied. In the early 1990s, there were about 230 homes in Blair. By the end of 1997, half had been sold to the coal company's land agent. Selling prices were determined more by the whim of the buyer and the obstinacy of the seller than by fair market value. In all, the coal company spent almost $6 million to remove possible complainers from the community. Frequently the houses burned as soon as the owners moved out. There were lots of rumors about who was doing the burning, but no one was ever arrested. Tommy Moore and Johnnie Rollins could drive a visitor down the road, pointing out remains as if the destroyed houses had been their friends: piles of blackened boards, a bathtub in white contrast, green weeds trying to hide the mess.

Upon selling, people had to sign two agreements. The first, much like the one Trish had quashed in Pie, required sellers to withdraw any complaints about the mine to DEP and not to complain in the future. The second prevented them from ever living in any of eleven small communities between the top of Blair Mountain, six miles south of the Moores' home, and Clothier, ten miles to the north. The coal company intended to mine that entire area and didn't want anyone around to complain. Life in the coalfields had always been at the will of the company. There were many communities that used to be—communities where people had packed up and moved to wherever the mine opened next. Blair was packing its suitcases. But the people weren't moving with the mine; they were moving away from it. With regret.

Vicky thought there must be a law against what was happening. It was just too wrong. Tommy called the mine. The miners had a job to do, but maybe they would be more careful if they knew what was happening down below. Instead, the mine manager purposely ignored the residents, the miners said later. Mushie Bella gained a good sense of the manager's attitudes through comments on the radio scanner: "Those people down there is causing us trouble again. The company has offered them enough money. It looks like them shitting people would get the hell out of there."

Stymied, Vicky began asking around the community. She was told to call DEP. She had to learn everything about mining laws. She would ask, "Are they allowed to do this to your house? Is dust allowed to fall on you?" To her it seemed illegal because the regulations say that nothing—no rocks, no coal, no debris—was allowed to fall from the mine onto private property. The mine had broken the law; the community was harmed; the mine should be punished. Vicky soon learned that the word *stop* doesn't seem to exist in mining regulations. Anyone who enters this regulatory morass quickly starts to see in shades of gray, rather than blacks and whites. *Less harm* is the closest anyone comes to *stop*.

From 1994 until the end of 1997, Vicky and her neighbors made 165 complaints to DEP about blasting and dust. Her calendars became diaries of daily tribulations. There, her careful rounded script recorded the time of a blast or a visit from a DEP inspector. Vicky came to feel as if she knew the mining laws and regulations better than the DEP inspectors.

Within the confines of the regulations, some DEP officials did try to find ways to lessen the impact of the blasts and the dust. But the coal company dragged its feet. After three notices of violation for dust, it was ordered to add dust-control measures to its mining plan. The mine objected to some of the alleged violations, sending its lawyers to appeal to the Surface Mine Board. In an agency made up of departments and boards that, like odd-shaped puzzle pieces, don't seem to belong together, the Surface Mine Board was one of the oddest items. The seven members ruled in near anonymity on appeals of DEP actions. They had the reputation of being industry sidekicks.

The first hearing before the Surface Mine Board was in April 1996, and Vicky and her neighbors were granted permission to intervene. Angry, she wondered why she had to help DEP fight the mine. She and several neighbors arrived at the DEP headquarters in Nitro early the morning of the hearing. Vicky was scared. She looked around the small conference room. There were no windows, since the room was in the center of the warehouse-sized DEP headquarters. Instead, there were photos of the state's scenic vistas. Lord, she thought, *I will have to act like a lawyer and stand up to all these lawyers from the coal company.*

Since the state has no regulations on dust near mines, DEP had proposed an unusual way to measure dust. Dal-Tex would install air monitors to measure the amount of dust particles ten microns or smaller (known as PM-10), the kind found to impede breathing. Vicky had studied how DEP set a limit of twenty-five micrograms of PM-10 in any ten minutes and had decided that was too much. But most of the board, which generally issued pro-mining decisions, ignored her. One member, a lawyer perceived as siding with citizens, agreed with Vicky on one point. The DEP had exempted Dal-Tex from the rule that allowed the mine to be shut down after three of the same kind of violations in a year. The citizen-friendly member pointed out that with the exemption the mine could have an infinite number of dust violations as long as it paid a two-thousand-dollar fine for each one. As Vicky predicted, the dust kept coming after the monitors were installed. In February 1997 DEP finally ordered the mine to stop blasting when the wind blew over Blair. Dal-Tex officials protested, saying that the monitors were picking up pollen and mold spores—not dust from the mine.

The one thing DEP did not do was shut down the mine. It was one of those might-have-beens that would haunt DEP official John Ailes in years to come. In the summer of 1997, he admitted publicly that the dust problems at Blair should never have happened.

It was too late, though, for Vicky and Tommy. In October 1996 the dust became too bad for Dustin's asthma, and they moved to Tommy's grandmother's farm. But something made them keep their mobile home and their acre of land on the riverbank. Mushie Bella sold and moved out the Monday before Thanksgiving in 1997. His house was soon rented to a Dal-Tex miner. He was never content in the more populous Danville and returned often to visit. The Rollinses left the week before Christmas the same year. Their house vanished shortly after New Year's, leveled by a bulldozer, not an arsonist's torch.

––––––––

Blair was historic as well. It was the site of a bitter two-year battle to unionize the southern coalfields, which ended in bloodshed and defeat on September 4, 1921.

The United Mine Workers of America had gained a foothold in Paint Creek and Cabin Creek, southeast of Charleston, by 1913. Nonetheless, Logan and Mingo county mines mostly remained steadfastly anti-union, despite a surge in union membership at mines elsewhere during peak production during World War I. After the war's end, the coal companies with UMWA contracts actually encouraged the union's foray into the southern coalfields, as the companies feared that non-union mines could undercut their prices.

As Lon Savage recounted in *Thunder in the Mountains: The West Virginia Mine War, 1920–21,* by May 1920, three thousand miners in those southern counties had joined the union, only to be tossed out of their homes by Baldwin-Felts detectives—hired thugs who had terrorized unionization attempts across the country. The miners had a friend in Matewan Police Chief Sid Hatfield, who went after the detectives for illegally carrying weapons. When the detectives countered with a warrant for Hatfield's arrest, tempers boiled, and a gun battle left the Matewan mayor and Al Felts and six other detectives dead on May 19, 1920. A grand jury indicted Hatfield for the Baldwin-Felts murders.

Though Hatfield was acquitted, miners continued to agitate, despite the presence of federal troops. Early in 1921, President Warren G. Harding denied Governor Ephraim F. Morgan's request for martial law. So merchants and other community leaders formed a citizens' militia. When they stormed a tent colony and killed a miner, the union miners southeast of Charleston made plans to march to Mingo County, their only route over

Blair Mountain. A few weeks later came the event that steeled their resolve: On August 1, 1921, Sid Hatfield was killed on the steps of the McDowell County courthouse in Welch.

More than eight thousand miners set off from Lens Creek, about forty miles north of Blair, three weeks later, trudging along a dusty path—the only route to Mingo County. Several thousand more joined along the way, many wrapping red bandanas round their necks (the origin, according to UMWA lore, of the nickname "redneck"). First, though, they would have to cross about twenty miles of Logan Country, ruled by Sheriff Don Chafin, who was amply supported by the coal companies. According to press reports, he had vowed: "No armed mob will cross Logan County."

Now, President Harding appeared ready to send in troops. The threat of federal intervention persuaded union leaders to hire a taxi and cut the march off twenty-five miles away in Madison. Most miners were satisfied and started to journey home. A few hundred, however, soldiered on and soon joined up with the hundreds of miners who lived along Spruce Fork on the way to Blair. They had already cut phone and electric lines and were ready to do battle.

Sheriff Chafin quickly led his troops over the mountain from Logan and stormed a coal camp. Word of the slaughter rapidly reached Charleston, and miners turned in their tracks and rushed to join the rebellion. When the battle erupted on August 31, more than ten thousand fighters were scattered over Blair Mountain.

On September 1, President Harding made good on his promise. Biplanes bombed the miners. Union leaders convinced miners that they did not want to fight the U.S. government. More than one thousand people were indicted. And UMWA membership in District 17 shrank from 42,000 before the march to 512 in 1930. It was not until the Roosevelt administration that the UMWA was reborn and flourished for nearly fifty years.

———

Looking back, it's easy to see why Blair—not Pie—would become the focus of the world media. The sight of the mountains sliced down and the twenty-story dragline appearing ready to topple onto the road was the starkest image of mountaintop removal in the coalfields. Add in houses burning, with rumors of coal company involvement—and a historic battle—and the media couldn't resist. Even this early December night in

1997 when Trish watched the Dal-Tex permit hearing from the bleachers, the first signs of Blair's notoriety were evident.

It was another permit hearing, and the bleachers were packed with local residents, including men from the mine and their wives, a few citizens from other mining communities, several lawyers, a few representatives of environmental groups, and a handful of reporters. At one end of the bleachers sat a man in a suit with a young face contradicted by a helmet of thick silver hair. This was Blair Gardner, Arch Coal's vice president for legal affairs, who had come from St. Louis. Arch Coal had become the mine's parent company in the summer of 1997. Vicky Moore sat in the front row, slight apprehension weighing against her eagerness.

Much energy and passion were pitched at the coal company and DEP. But whatever was said came too late in the process to have much impact. Even questions asked at a hearing went unanswered, since DEP officials were not allowed to respond to speakers.

About a dozen people came to the mike. Arch officials had been spreading concern among miners that citizens like Vicky Moore might prevent them from mining. Early on, an imposing man in his late forties stood up as a representative of the Tug Valley Chamber of Commerce and the Tug Valley Mining Institute in Mingo County. There are laws to control strip mining, he said, and people can sue if rocks land in their yards. Jobs are what's most important. "I'm tired of seeing youth of West Virginia go to North Carolina or South Carolina to get a job." He paused for a hearty round of applause before continuing. "When I was in high school, everyone took Route 23 north or Route 52 north to Detroit. Bet everyone here has a relative living in Michigan or North or South Carolina. Sure it's about economic development. Do you know how much dust or flying rock you have in a ghost town? Give them this permit so that my kids and their kids can work."

When it was Vicky's turn, she turned the microphone toward the audience. Her right hand made exclamation points; her left arm was a shelf for a stack of documents. "We have a right to live here without the blasting, without the dust." Without fear, she confronted the incendiary issue. "We are not here to shut that strip mine down. And another thing, I know this coal company is giving a lot of men a lot of jobs. And they are hard to come by and they make good money and have good insurance. My husband works his butt off, too, and he does reclaiming work. Someone asked me ain't I cutting off the hand that feeds us. I said no. God gave me my child to take care of him best I know how."

There were chuckles as she attacked the enforcement system. "I have got papers here. I don't even know how many violations this coal company has got. But if you look at these papers, they are either extended or terminated. How can you terminate a violation? They've already broke the law, that's why they got the violation. What if I come in your yard and throw rocks, and I hit somebody or it hits your car or something. Do you think that they're going to let me say I didn't mean to? No, they can get me probably for attempted murder. But for the coal company it is under a $5,000 fine."

Trish had never met Vicky, though Vicky had joined WVOP about a year earlier. As she watched, Trish thought, *What passion that young woman has.* Trish even got a little angry at the audience when Vicky had to deflect a few nasty comments from the bleachers. When the hearing ended, she went over to Vicky. If she had known her better, she would have hugged her. "It is really great to hear someone say what we feel," she said. They had become comrades in struggle. What Trish didn't know yet was that she soon would become as well known as Blair.

Chapter 3

A Miner's Life

The mines around Blair, first those underground, and then the surface mine that opened in the 1970s, had provided a good living at union wages for more than one thousand miners. In addition, hundreds of people worked for suppliers of machinery and other items that made the mines run. And local groceries and gas stations depended on the miners. In late 1997 the Dal-Tex mine at Blair employed more than four hundred miners. Most worked on the mountaintop, but a smaller group with specialized skills worked at the preparation plant. Bob Schultz was one of the latter group, and he was also one of the people longest employed by the series of owners of the mine.

In the coalfields of the 1980s and 1990s, a miner's job earned about the best pay to be had, sometimes as much as lawyers and bank presidents received. Many large mines were still union, guaranteeing complete health care and good pensions. And one of the very best mines to work at was the Dal-Tex mine in Blair and Sharples.

Bob Schultz started work at the mine August 5, 1971, less than two months out of high school. Coal mining was the only career goal for young men of the area, as he was growing up. A sturdy block of a man, nearly six feet tall, Bob had no fear of hard work. He was born in Clarksburg, in the northern part of the state, but since the age of three, he had lived in the little community of Monclo, about a mile southwest of Sharples.

Bob's great-grandfather Schultz had come from Germany with the wave of immigrants. After working in a couple of chemical plants, he was drawn to the good pay in the mines at Monclo, and his son and his grandson followed. Bob's grandfather, Austin Shirley Schultz, had been involved in the Battle of Blair Mountain and has "redneck" on his tombstone.

A fierce distrust of mine management seemed to be bred into the min-

A typical coal preparation plant.

Bob Schultz at work at an Arch Coal mine.

ers of Monclo. Growing up, Bob heard stories of his grandfathers' love-hate relationship with the coal company. There was no unemployment in Monclo, because miners who didn't work were thrown out of their houses by the deputies. Bob's Grandpa Schultz hated coal companies until the day he died. He had been evicted from his house after the union battle and had to leave to work in Baltimore for a few years. After returning, he leased a garden spot from the company. When the men voted on unionizing in the 1930s, the mine superintendents got all the cards back and saw his name supporting the union. No more garden, the superintendents told him. He ignored them and gardened anyway.

Most of the miners lived in Monclo; the managers lived in larger homes in Sharples. Monclo remained a coal camp until Bob was about eight. The Schultz family had a four-room white frame house with an outhouse, next to the church. Anyone could be evicted from coal-company houses who didn't keep them neat or had rowdy children. Nonetheless, Bob and others who grew up there recall a busy and happy place. An African American community coexisted peacefully across the stream from the white area, with its own stores, beer joints, and church. Some larger coal camps in the first half of the century included a sizable community building, usually called "the Y." In Sharples, it housed a bowling alley and a theater and remained until the early 1970s. When the company houses in Monclo were sold in 1961, Schultz's father bought their house for two thousand dollars.

For children, Monclo was a good place to live, and weekends were special. Saturday mornings meant cartoons and Church of God hot dogs. Frances and William Starkey lived near the end of the Monclo hollow, raising six children while he pastored the Church of God and several other churches for forty-one years. Every Saturday, Frances and the other women in the church cooked big batches of hot dogs and chili with a unique Italian flavor, a recipe handed down from her Italian immigrant father who fought in the battle of Blair Mountain.

The Monclo community contributed to a great diversity of ancestry in the area. Early in the twentieth century, 35 percent of West Virginia miners were foreign-born. While Frances Starkey's father was Italian and Bob Schultz's great-grandfather was German, Gene Phillips's grandfather was Hungarian, drawn like the others by the promise of a good job in the mines around the time of World War I. Phillips, who was thirteen years older than Bob, recalled a hard life warmed by the closeness of the coal camp and the simple pleasures of making fun without fancy toys. It was a childhood that made him appreciate the gains of his adult life in the mines. Especially sweet was the day he moved his young family into the rustic lodge-style hilltop home that had once housed coal-company managers.

When Bob went to work in the mine, it was still owned by Boone County Coal Corporation, which had begun in 1911 and owned about thirty thousand acres. Vesta was the trade name of Boone County Coal, and the company's logo carried a picture of the Roman goddess of the hearth fire. The original investors had sold out by 1964, but the company continued for nearly another decade. Wages were so high then that in a few months a young miner would have enough money for a new car. Fast cars and pretty girls were about all the young men desired, so the mines were far more attractive than four years in college.

Bob spent his first five years underground, and it was there he first confronted death. One of his co-workers went down to unplug the power while Bob began hanging electric cable. He heard the crash of slate falling from the mine roof in the tunnel, rushed back, and found his friend buried. Eight other miners died in the years Schultz worked at the mine: two more underground and six on the surface. In 1958, when Bob was just a boy, his grandfather barely escaped death, along with twenty-three other miners when a dam broke and the water behind it, left from cleaning coal, filled the mine and trapped Bob's grandfather and the others. Fortunately, all were rescued, and a local UMWA member commemorated the rescue in a poem.

Thursday, May 8th, after dinner time,
24 men were trapped in a mine,
Of their jobs, these men were proud,
24 men in this little crowd.

Near the drift mouth there was a scramble,
Their friends and loved ones and their families,
With anxious faces and tear stained eyes;
While many a prayer went up to the vaulted skies.

I stood and watched as the waters rolled out;

I saw some weeping as I turned about;
Silent prayers were uttered deep within,
While we thought about the 24 men.

They had eaten their food and drank their drinks,
Now God had given them a time to think,
They thought of the present and they thought of the past,
And they began to wonder how long they would last.

It was the darkest day they ever knew,
They had to trust God to bring them through,
More than 13 hours they stayed this way,
Not knowing they would ever see the light of day.

Men work for a living and play a game to win,
But let me give you the names of the 24 men,
There was Flannery, Schultz and Dawson,
Bowen, Richards and Johnson.

In a place as black as night
Were also Hamilton and Willie White.
Just wait and I'll tell you more.
There was Bradley, Burgess and Gore.

They were fenced in like a chicken;
Here were Thompson, Phillips and Kitchen.
There sitting on the mine floor
Were Castle, Bob Turner and Carassco.

To rest this wasn't a pleasant place to choose,
For Ray Turner, Cottrill and Zickefoose.
These names were in a paper that came daily,
Including Baldwin, Collins and Fraley.

The grim reaper failed to work his sickle,
He also spared Leonard Nickles.

May we pause every now and then,
And thank God for the rescue of the 24 men.

Miners grow accustomed to danger and hardships, developing a
toughness that sometimes spills over into their personal lives. Bob soldiered on no matter what, not missing an entire day in twenty-five years.
A broken hand wasn't enough for sick leave, and he took off only four
hours when he got a piece of metal in his eye.

In 1977 Jim McGlothlin of United Corporation in Bristol, Virginia,
bought the mine, and for fifteen years it had about the best working conditions in the state. This was the heyday of coal, with southern-power-
plant contracts for fifty and sixty dollars a ton. Each month the miners got
bonuses, averaging two hundred dollars, based on the amount of coal
shipped. At the end of the year, McGlothlin gave them the sum of all the
monthly bonuses. There were Fourth of July picnics and trips to North
Carolina. One year Bob made eighty-one thousand dollars. Even more
important than the money, though, was the attitude of the management.
If a miner thought something hadn't been done quite right, he went to
McGlothlin and usually got the problem worked out.

McGlothlin, who had gotten into mining in 1970 in his hometown
of Grundy, Virginia, recalled his first weeks of ownership, a time when he
didn't follow any corporate plan—just did what he thought was just. At
one time the mine was shut down during a national strike, and Christmas
was approaching. McGlothlin's staff took a tractor trailer of fruits and
hams and coffee and invited the miners to join in, to have a Christmas.
"You aren't union," some of the miners countered. McGlothlin explained,
"We just want you to know we all want the same thing—to make a profit
and share the profits."

With the same compassionate management style, McGlothlin quickly
erased animosity between miners and management. One of his first moves
was to take down the sign in the office that told miners not to come in unless they were management. Early on he befriended Alan Workman, head
of the local union. McGlothlin listened to the union's complaints and
thought they made a lot of sense. He hired Workman to run the mine,
and Workman stayed on the job until McGlothlin sold the mine.

The miners laughed when McGlothlin said he would run 1 million tons of coal a month. In 1981 McGlothlin started the first mountaintop-removal section, known as 295. It was small by the standards of the late 1990s. Most remarkably, the valley fills were constructed entirely differently. Instead of dumping huge truckloads of rock and dirt over the side of the mountain, the company built the fills from the bottom up. It took longer but made for shorter fills, only about a quarter mile long.

"I have nothing but the fondest memories of the people at Sharples," McGlothlin said years later. "They just wanted to be part of the team. It was amazing to see the mine grow over the 15 years—it had been desolate, without hope." McGlothlin recalled fondly one Christmas when a miner gave him the arrowhead collection he had put together from the hills of the mine. Miners received a bonus when McGlothlin sold the mine.

McGlothlin's United Companies continued to own the coal under Blair, Sharples, and Monclo, as well as much of the surface land being mined, but he left the coal business in the late 1990s; most small coal companies could no longer compete with huge corporations. Still he adhered to the business philosophy that endeared the miners: "In business not only do we own it, the employees and people around us are part owners. We must give back to the community and recognize them as constituents. If we do that in business, we will be successful."

By the late 1980s, both Bob and Phillips were working in the coal preparation plant in Monclo, loading the black gold into trains of more than 100 cars two or three times a day. Conveyor belts carried the coal down to the plant, which looked a bit like an Erector set with a couple of silos and long chutes. The coal was cleaned and placed into two tall piles according to quality and sulfur content. Two bulldozers constantly rolled around the piles, pushing it into eleven underground tunnels. A lab worker determined what mix of coal would meet the regulatory limits for ash, and a computer told Phillips the correct mix of tunnels to use. They could load a 150-car train in four hours. One train went to an American Electric Power plant west of Charleston, while another went to a power plant in Georgia.

Bob had married Debra Runyon, whose father had run a company store in Monclo. Debra developed a career as a gospel singer, with recordings and numerous tours. They had two sons, Richard and Nicholas. In 1981 Bob and Debra built a modest house in Clothier, a small community a few miles from Sharples along Spruce Fork. The house had a bird bath and ample summer flowers in the front yard, which Bob tended. At Christmastime, decorations in a country theme of bows and wreaths sprouted throughout the house.

In April 1992 the era of corporate ownership began. Ashland Coal Inc., one of the biggest coal corporations in the state, bought the mining operations and coal leases for about $253 million. Miners' bonuses shrank, and more bosses appeared. Resentment built; the UMWA miners weren't satisfied with Ashland's pay and benefits. Finally, in May 1993, Dal-Tex was one of the mines that went on strike as negotiations on the UMWA nationwide contract stalled.

Every day angry strikers gathered with their signs at the bridge over Spruce Fork, between Sharples and Monclo. Up on the hill, Gene and Cheryl Phillips sat on their swing and videotaped the mine guards, and the guards aimed their cameras right back. Strikers scattered roofing nails along the sides of the road, causing many a flat tire for those who crossed the picket line. One day the miners managed to block sixteen tractor trailers and four ten-wheelers carrying fuel and supplies to the mine. There had been talk of violence, but some of the managers were friends of the strikers, and cooler heads prevailed.

In the end, the strikers had expended months of passion for virtually nothing. Because of the selective-strike provision, which the UMWA had approved in the mid-1980s, not all the mines in the country shut down. Ashland trained some workers from other parts of the company to run the heavy equipment and load the trains, so the mine never had to stop operating. The miners ended up with less than half of their demands satisfied, and their full dental coverage was reduced to merely checkups. The Sharples strike was the last in the southern West Virginia coalfields. Without realizing it at the time, Bob had witnessed the waning days of the UMWA's strength.

In the early 1990s, Monclo began changing. By 1994 most of the homes of the community, places where Bob had played with friends, were gone. When the mining expanded on the mountain above the community, the preparation plant was doubled in size, and in a few years a large electrical substation was built to power the mine and the plant. Soon the mile-long community was showered with dust and shaken by the blasts. Construction work frequently blocked the road, preventing residents from getting in and out of Monclo. Children had to climb through parked trains to reach school buses. Engine noise from trains and coal trucks kept residents awake all night. Most of the residents got fed up and sold to the coal company. Some received good prices of $70,000 or $80,000 for their homes, while others didn't get enough to buy a house elsewhere. A few moved near the Moores in Blair. When the land agent came to see Bob's father, his father wouldn't budge from his price, and he got $74,000. So he left the place he had lived in most of his life.

In July 1997 yet another change came to the community. The Dal-Tex mine was taken over by Arch Coal Inc. Actually, Ashland and the St. Louis–based Arch had been financially intertwined for nearly three decades, but Arch and Ashland Coal merged that year, and Arch managers moved in. Arch was now the third-largest coal company in the country. Considered one of the best-managed and most environmentally friendly of the coal companies, it had a storied history chronicled in Otto Scott's 1989 *Buried Treasure: The Story of Arch Mineral.*

Arch was born on June 20, 1969, 106 years after West Virginia itself was formed on the same date in 1863. Ashland Oil, which was named after the city of its headquarters in Kentucky, just across the West Virginia border, became a 50 percent owner of Arch. Merl Kelce, the largest individual shareholder, who had run Sinclair Coal, quickly knit together a group of coal leases and contracts that became the foundation of Arch: a mine in Alabama that had a contract with the Tennessee Valley Authority power plants, coal reserves leased in southern Illinois, and a share of the vast reserves of low-sulfur coal in Wyoming. He ordered five draglines, possibly the largest number ever owned by one company. Then he died on May 16, 1970.

After weaving through a few lawsuits, Arch emerged with the TVA contract intact and a new partner: the Hunt family of Texas, oilmen who had decided coal was the next big thing. Arch bought Southwestern Illinois Coal Company, a huge surface mine appropriately named Captain, with the largest shovel in the world: twenty-one stories high and capable of moving one hundred to two hundred tons of earth every thirty-eight seconds. Tom Hunt, following the family tradition of hands-on involvement, frequently went out on the mines and spent time with the miners who ran the shovels and drove the trucks. Arch did only surface mining, and the land mined in Illinois and Wyoming was fields or rolling hills, not the steep terrain of West Virginia. Coal prices quadrupled from $4.80 a ton in 1972 to nearly $17 a ton by 1975, just as the Wyoming mines began operation. Arch got a further boost with President Jimmy Carter's energy bill, which urged utilities to switch from oil to coal.

By the early 1980s, Arch began to look toward the low-sulfur and high-Btu coal of the Appalachians. Ronald Eugene (Gene) Samples, CEO of Consolidation Coal, came on board as Arch president in 1982. Samples, the son of a teacher who worked in the mines to make ends meet, had earned an engineering degree and worked his way up at Consolidation. Arch made its first move into Kentucky through acquisition of the Lynch District coal properties of U.S. Steel in Harlan County in 1983. Next it acquired Diamond Shamrock and four subsidiaries, including mines in Kentucky and the Amherst Coal Company in West Virginia, which had reserves that later became the Ruffner mine along Rum Creek over the mountain from Blair. These mines now offered recoverable coal reserves of 850 million tons, equal to nearly five years of West Virginia's total production. In 1989 Arch bought a mountaintop mine in eastern Kanawha County from coal baron and philanthropist Lawson Hamilton—and named it the Samples mine. By 1996 production had slowed in the Illinois mines, but the company's West Virginia operations yielded 11.2 million tons.

Arch may have been the young lion of the corporate world, but Bob Schultz and the other miners weren't impressed with Arch management. Their bonuses were eliminated, yet the top men in the company received bonuses based on annual production. Gone was the give-and-take with management that McGlothlin had encouraged. At one time there were forty-eight employees at the preparation plant, eight of them bosses. Bob saw a company top-heavy with highly paid management. Furthermore, most of the managers came from outside the area and didn't seem to have outstanding people skills. In the fall of 1997, Bob drove the three miles to the plant every morning just before 7:00 a.m., watching his heritage transform quickly, like a series of photos of the same place taken each decade and run at hyperspeed. In his heart, he sensed that even bigger changes lay ahead.

Chapter 4

The Lawyer

While Vicky testified that damp night in Sharples, a slim man, younger-looking than his age of thirty-eight, watched from near the stage. *This one was even wilder than that one in Varney,* Joe Lovett thought.

Three days into Joe's first week as a lawyer early in September of 1997, a gaunt man with a shock of gray hair walked into Joe's office at Mountain State Justice on the fifth floor of a nondescript office building in downtown Charleston. James Weekley and his wife, Sibby, who came with him, lived in Blair, and they had a problem with the Arch Coal mine.

Weekley spread a magazine photo in front of Joe. The mine at the edge of the mountain dwarfed the tiny houses huddled along Route 17. Weekley pointed to the right edge. There was Pigeonroost Hollow, where he lived. Soon the mine planned to fill most of it with a huge valley fill. What Weekley was upset about, though, was not the fill. The mine had blocked access to the hills and the stream where—though he did not own them—he had hunted and fished his entire life. Joe was astonished, and incensed, by his first look at mountaintop-removal mining.

Joe had grown up in Charleston, the son of a lawyer, but had never been to the coalfields. After college at Vanderbilt University, he studied agriculture at Virginia Polytechnic Institute for a time and became interested in organic farming For several months he worked at Potomac Vegetable Farm in Virginia near Washington, D.C., where three hundred acres at three farms were partially tilled with plows drawn by Belgians, the blond-colored gentle giants of draft horses. The horses and the rhythms of the earth pleased Joe, but he left Virginia Tech's program, realizing it was oriented too much toward corporate farming, and soon was employed at an organic farm and vineyard near Charlottesville, Virginia.

In 1987 he enrolled in graduate school at the University of Virginia. There he met Gretchen, a gentle woman who was studying for a degree in child psychology. They shared a commitment to the simple life: organic food and no television. Joe studied philosophy but left the program in 1992 without completing his doctoral dissertation. He enjoyed philosophy, an arcane pursuit in a time of ever-shortening attention spans and rapid-fire video images. Philosophy required the ability to grasp abstract theories, to concentrate until an entire thought is digested, and to weigh the pros and cons of one concept against another—all skills that would soon prove their value as his career took a new direction.

In 1992 he entered law school at the University of Pennsylvania. He had always contemplated environmental law, and in the back of his mind he sensed he should do public-interest work. He spent the two summers of law school working for Dan Hedges, a legendary legal crusader in Charleston.

Hedges had brought a series of public-interest cases in the 1970s and 1980s that resulted in sweeping reforms in nursing homes, Medicaid, and school funding. At one point he had all the prisons under a consent decree. One of Joe's tasks was to go around the state checking whether jails were in compliance. Hedges's legal crusades were propelled by his reverence for the state, which he knew so well that, as a youth, he was named a Knight of the Golden Horseshoe, an honor bestowed each year on the 221 eighth-graders who best appreciate the state's heritage and people. This love for their diminutive state seemed to be a character trait of a number of West Virginia leaders.

Joe's career choice was not an easy decision at one of the nation's leading law schools, where students were encouraged to go into corporate law. Joe realized the ramifications of his decision. His salary might never reach $100,000. He and Gretchen had married by now, and the birth of his first child coincided with his law school graduation. He would be practicing without a staff of secretaries and researchers. But he could be a hell-raiser, a rare opportunity for a lawyer in the mid-1990s.

Joe and Gretchen and their son moved to Charleston, where Joe had landed the prize job of clerking for Charles H. Haden II, chief judge of the federal district court. Haden, appointed by President Gerald Ford, was not known to favor environmental causes. The legal community viewed him as a conservative who often interpreted the law and regulations in favor of the powerful. During Joe's two-year tenure, he worked on an important Clean Water Act case. State agencies were required to determine the amount of contamination streams and rivers could contain from all sources of pollution and then adjust discharge limits for individual industries. Before Haden could rule, the state agreed to implement the law in West Virginia. Joe gained valuable experience for his career involving cases on environmental laws that would be tried in federal court.

With the changing regulations and tighter restrictions on government-funded legal services organizations, Dan Hedges had spun off a new public-interest law organization, Mountain State Justice, and Joe was eager to begin work in September 1997. He had planned to jump right into air pollution cases. Three major chemical complexes line the Kanawha River on both sides of Charleston, making it one of the least healthy cities in the nation. Instead, Joe met James Weekley.

James Weekley had lived all of his fifty-six years in Pigeonroost Hollow, where a two-mile-long stream joined Spruce Fork, about a half mile from the Moores' home. Weekley's ancestors, the Mullinses and the Burgesses, had been among the few adventurous pioneers who bullied their way through the dense forests and over the cantankerous mountains to settle along Spruce Fork in the early 1800s. N. Bayard Green, writing in *Mountain Heritage,* pictured life in the hollows: "It was not a gentle land, but it was rich. There was an ample water supply, and that water was clean. It was difficult to build a home in the thick forests, but when a home was finished, it was safe. . . . The very inaccessibility of the mountain-enclosed Guyan Valley no doubt attracted rugged individualists who wished to be undisturbed by near neighbors."

Weekley's father, Bill, had been a well-loved teacher in Blair. He took a personal interest in students, giving them rides home after football. He supplemented his teacher's salary with a job as a night watchman at one of the deep mines that dotted the area. James Weekley graduated from high school in Sharples and worked a couple of years in the deep mines. He also traveled around the coalfields building coal preparation plants, known as tipples. But mostly he worked as a logger in various parts of the state, including Blair. He had stopped working around 1990 after being convicted of possession of marijuana with intent to deliver and serving eleven months in jail, and the Weekleys now lived on disability benefits. In the late 1980s, he had built a yellow one-story home close to the house where he grew up, and where his mother still lived. It was a pleasant spot with a wide porch running the length of the house, the creek bubbling by, and humming-

The mine at Blair that Joe Lovett viewed from a nearby mountain in 1997.

birds whirring at the feeders. James and Sibby had four sons and two daughters.

The Weekleys had been bothered by the dust and had complained to the mine a number of times, but they didn't join with Vicky Moore and her neighbors. Weekley's greatest aggravation came when Dal-Tex closed off the road up the hollow to prepare for a valley fill. His niece's husband, an Ohio attorney, offered to help Weekley find a lawyer. He looked into the handful of Charleston poverty law groups and found Mountain State Justice.

A couple of weeks after their first meeting, Joe accepted Weekley's invitation to see the mine. Like many living in the coalfields, Weekley had an all-terrain vehicle. Joe gingerly climbed on behind, and they set off up the winding path to Weekley's "meditation rock." This was the same place Mushie Bella and the Moores and the Rollinses came to from the other side of the mountain. The three-foot-high rock stands in the shape of an anvil at the edge of the mountaintop. Sometimes there would be droppings and hoofprints nearby, recording a visit from the wild boars that roamed the mountains. From the rock, looking across Spruce Fork and the Five Block side of Blair to the mine, the view was a moonscape. Trucks and shovels busied themselves on a flat, barren land in the midst of green forests. In stark contrast, the virgin valley of Pigeonroost Hollow stretched like a green velvet quilt. Joe thought: *We can stop this.*

The stairs at 922 Quarrier Street were the minimalist colors of a Mondrian painting: white walls, steps with gray tops and black fronts, shiny black railings. Joe Lovett didn't trust the rickety elevator, so he took the stairs to the fifth-floor offices of Mountain State Justice. At the entrance, he passed a small poster, a jumble of white words on a red background: "100 years of Equal Justice Has Not Made It a Reality." In the fall of 1997, Joe hurried by, writing paragraphs of justice in his head.

After visiting Blair in September, Joe submerged himself in mining laws. He called every lawyer, every environmental agency official, every journalist he could find. His single-mindedness as an only child coalesced with the innocence and enthusiasm of his first job and his first case. Battle-worn activists, wondering how to reinvigorate the tired twenty-year-old mining law, had never even dreamed of such a fresh spirit.

The 1977 federal Surface Mining Control and Reclamation Act, or SMCRA, was born in discord. The law evolved for six years and was regrouped after two vetoes by President Gerald Ford. President Jimmy Carter finally signed it. The activists who helped pass the law were proud of their creation, yet saddened by its failings. The puzzle for Joe would be to pinpoint those enforcement failures that had actually broken the law.

Before SMCRA, most coal states had passed their own mining laws. West Virginia was the first to do so. The legislature fashioned a law in 1939 focusing on reclaiming land after surface mining, as much to protect deep mines as to protect the land. However, those first regulations had little effect as strip mining increased tenfold in four years. So a stronger West Virginia law was passed in 1945. But enforcement was absent. Then in 1963, the legislature actually weakened the law. No longer would coal operators have to map the area to be mined; and bonds to cover damages shrank from $500 an acre to $150 an acre.

The consequences of weak laws and lax enforcement hit home in the coalfields in the 1960s. During hard rains along Clear Creek in Raleigh County, rocks and dirt pushed off the mines invaded homes and even buried cars. With help from antipoverty workers, local resident Ellis Bailey joined neighbors and citizens from nearby counties and formed the Citizens Task Force on Surface Mining in 1967, which got the toughest law so far passed. Besides requiring proper reclamation, the law now prohibited mining on very steep slopes—areas impossible to restore. If mining damaged private property, owners could get triple damages. Still, though, enforcement was lax. In the next few years, 250,000 acres were surface mined, but only half were properly reclaimed.

In having their own way, the coal companies actually encouraged dissent. The movement to abolish strip mining had been growing across Appalachia for half a decade. Among the leaders in West Virginia were John D. Rockefeller, who was secretary of state; Ken Hechler, who represented the southern coalfields in Congress; and Si Galperin, a newly elected state senator from Charleston. In 1971 opponents came as close as they ever would to banning strip mining. With nearly one thousand abolitionists marching on the capitol, the legislature finally compromised and placed a two-year ban on stripping in the twenty-two counties that had no surface mining. That gave time for a study by the Stanford Research Institute. However, the study found that the 1967 law adequately controlled strip mining and that increased deep mining would not compensate for coal lost by prohibiting strip mining. Abolition bills died quickly in the 1972 legislature. After Rockefeller's defeat in the 1972 gubernatorial election, he, too, gave up attempts at abolishing surface mining.

But abolitionists across the Appalachian coalfields had already taken their fight to Congress. The Appalachian Group to Save the Land and the People had formed in 1965 to stop surface mining. A year later, the Congress of Appalachian Development formed in Bristol, Virginia, to promote public ownership of mineral resources and establish new towns along the Appalachian chain. Congress held the first hearings on strip mining in 1968. By 1970 abolition sentiment was so strong across Appalachian coalfields that the *New York Times* endorsed prohibition.

As Chad Montrie recounted in *To Save the Land and People*, Ken Hechler introduced the first abolition bill in Congress in February 1971. No new strip-mine permits would be granted, and existing permits would phase out over six months. Importantly, the bill would have established a program to reclaim abandoned strip mines. And it would have given citizens the power to sue regulatory agencies. Though the ban eventually died, these last two provisions survived and became key parts of SMCRA.

Alarmed by the strength of the abolitionist movement, the American

Ken Hechler (sitting in truck). The truck belongs to Larry Gibson, and the occasion was the summer 1999 March for the Mountains across West Virginia, led by Gibson.

Mining Congress moved from opposition to any law to support of federal regulation of surface mining. The UMWA worried, too. It did not want to lose what union jobs it had at strip mines. Yet, many miners lived near the mines and had to deal with the polluted runoff and the flooding. President Tony Boyle told Congress: "The cure should not be to forego further surface mining, but rather, to stop the adverse effect which it causes." In 1972 Boyle was ousted in a reform movement by Arnold Miller, a deep miner from West Virginia. Although he briefly supported abolition, Miller's UMWA position backed proper reclamation and opposed all badly done stripping.

In July 1972 both the House and the Senate reported out surface mining bills. But five long years passed before SMCRA was signed into law. In the interim, the beginning of the energy crisis strengthened the political position of the coal industry. Far fewer volunteers came to work and organize in the coalfields as funding for antipoverty programs shrank. The Sierra Club and other national environmental groups saw regulation as the only law Congress would accept. So gradually only Ken Hechler and diehard coalfield activists, including members of the Tennessee group Save Our Cumberland Mountains, were left supporting abolition of strip mining. In fact, Hechler blasted Washington environmental groups for "settling for the lowest common denominator." As debate continued for several years, he presciently told a hearing in July 1974, "They are displacing families and moving them out of those areas because everybody down slope from where there is mountaintop mining is threatened."

Congress actually passed surface mining regulation late in 1974 and again in 1975. All for naught. In vetoing the bills, President Ford charged that such measures would increase America's dependence on foreign oil in the midst of the energy crisis. Only after President Carter was elected, did a bill get White House support. While it was being debated, the coal industry, emboldened by the two vetoes, argued against imposing any regulation. But the remaining activists stood strong. And Rockefeller, now West Virginia's governor, supported regulation, as did the governor of Pennsylvania. Though Ken Hechler had left Congress for an unsuccessful 1976 primary campaign for West Virginia governor, he was at the Rose Garden signing of SMCRA and told Carter, "This will not work unless it is very strongly enforced."

Last-minute compromises, both good and bad, shaped the final bill. On the plus side, highwalls were banned. These are one-hundred-foot or higher vertical rock faces left when hills are scraped away to reach coal. Mountaintop-removal mining would be allowed—but only if the flattened land was put to commercial or residential uses. Diversifying the economy was essential in the coalfields, an area perennially ranked nearly last in income and educational attainment. However in 1977 no one imagined that the one-hundred-foot-high shovels operating in Ohio, Illinois, Wyoming, and other flatter states could ever be brought on the narrow, twisty roads to West Virginia and Kentucky. In fact, the largest mountaintop-removal mines today are four hundred times as large as those envisioned in 1977.

One of the most stringent provisions was the ban on dumping spoil dirt and rock blasted from mines on steep slopes, an important step for West Virginia. Hechler's original plan to restore abandoned mines became the Abandoned Mine Land program, funded by a tax of thirty-five cents on each ton of surface-mined coal and fifteen cents on each ton deep-mined. The provision for citizen lawsuits endured. And SMCRA established the Office of Surface Mining, Reclamation, and Enforcement (known as OSM) within the Department of the Interior. President Jimmy Carter signed SMCRA in the Rose Garden August 3, 1977.

OSM was staffed by a group of young, idealistic mine engineers and inspectors. They were going to change the world, clean up the coalfields. And for a few years, they did. OSM inspired unusual dedication and loyalty. Many OSM staff whom Joe met had been with the agency since its earliest years.

———

By 1997 the exponential growth of mountaintop-removal mining in West Virginia made the state a fitting site for celebration and reflection upon the twentieth anniversary of SMCRA at a celebration on Buffalo Creek August 2 and 3. Two weeks later, WVOP and Wendy Radcliff, the environmental advocate at DEP, hosted a three-day tour and symposium. They went to Blair, talked with Vicky and her neighbors, and inspected homes damaged by blasting along Beech Creek in Mingo County, over the mountain from Pie.

The tour wrapped up with an all-day symposium in Charleston on the past and future of SMCRA. Roger Calhoun of OSM was praised as the only regulator or legislator who bothered to attend the final day. He was proud of SMCRA's accomplishments: far fewer scars on the land and fertile farmland in the Midwest mining areas once again. Other speakers noted that OSM had too few staff and let state regulators give mines too many breaks.

A woman with the plain demeanor of a Quaker told the group about her nearly twenty years of battling the mines and DEP. Cindy Rank and her husband Paul had moved to Upshur County in the middle of the state a quarter of a century earlier. They had never seen strip mining. Within seven years, engineers came down her road looking for coal. She and her neighbors joined together and stopped that mine from developing. Little did she know that her battle had just begun. Soon she had two full-time jobs, one paying and one as a self-taught and unpaid student of SMCRA and state regulations. She became a leader of the West Virginia Highlands Conservancy, the state's largest environmental group. She was also quickly targeted by the coal industry as an outsider looking to shut down all strip mines.

Cindy considered SMCRA a good law. But she had watched high ideals twist into double knots as state regulators weakened phrase after phrase

Cindy Rank (right) on the way to an anti-mountaintop removal rally at the capitol.

of the law. To her SMCRA had become a hollow shell of its original intent. Even Cindy found it hard to keep up with the ways it was being watered down. And furthermore, she asked, had the mere presence of SMCRA made it seem like the problems were solved? Had problems that are not fully addressed by SMCRA—like dust and blasting—fallen by the wayside of regulatory controls? Had too heavy a burden been placed on coalfield residents? Cindy noted that SMCRA is so complicated that coalfield residents have trouble framing their complaints properly.

A tall, middle-aged law professor stood at the podium, punctuating his sentences with gestures. Pat McGinley, who served in the early 1970s as a lawyer for Pennsylvania's environmental strike force, had taught at the West Virginia University law school for nearly twenty years. In his spare time, he and his wife, Suzanne Weise, who was also a lawyer and could double for actress Julianne Moore, had taken cases for citizens and environmental groups. They had handled the dust problems in Monclo. More recently, Pat had a lawsuit over the state's undertaxation of coal reserves. He was also concerned that mines did not pay enough in bonds to reclaim land if the mines went bankrupt and were abandoned.

The idea behind SMCRA, Pat explained, was that the consequences of mining on the environment and the citizens would be considered by coal companies, investors, and regulators before mining began. In that mission, the law had fallen short. "The coal industry has the money," Pat said. "Citizens have the truth."

Even though citizens have the truth, making regulators hear the truth had become nearly impossible, Walt Morris pointed out. Morris had worked at OSM from 1979 until 1988. When he began practicing law in 1990, he planned to ram citizen complaints through OSM. After seven years, he had come to the sad realization that regulators usually found ways to ignore citizens. The only alternative, he said, was to sue the coal companies. Nonetheless, the citizen outrage should not lessen; in fact it should shout louder. However, citizens needed to become more professional and network with other groups. They needed to find experts who could provide scientific proof that regulations were ignored. "Now," Morris told the audience, "is the time to reenergize the citizens' movement of the 1970s."

––––––

Cindy Rank was one of the first people Joe called in his quest to understand mountaintop removal. She quickly agreed to help, and he came to trust her quiet wisdom.

Joe also reached out to every lawyer who had brought cases against coal companies. Only Pat McGinley and his wife, Suzanne Weise, agreed to help on the case. On October 25, 1997, the three embarked on a trip through the coalfields. As they drove south on the four-lane Route 119, known as Corridor G, toward Logan, the mountains drew closer and higher, the sky above the bright blue of fall, the sun pushing away the morning chill. In one day, they would confront just about every insult a mine can dump on its neighbors.

As they drove, Pat and Joe began to talk legal strategy. The case would be filed in federal court. Like most lawyers, they knew which judges would be most likely to rule favorably in which type of case. Robert C. Chambers, one of Pat's former law students and the much-respected Speaker of the House of Delegates, had just been appointed judge in the federal court in Huntington. Pat believed he would be a fair judge, and neither Pat nor Joe thought they had much of a chance before Joe's former boss, Judge Charles Haden II.

Soon they arrived at their first stop, Cartwright Hollow along Buffalo

Creek, where they would see their first valley fill. Their guide was Jack Caudill, a charter member of WVOP, a retired miner, and a Vietnam veteran. Caudill had helped lead the strike against the Pittson Coal Company. During the past summer, two washouts had flooded some of the homes in the hollow, and some residents blamed the valley fill.

As Pat parked their station wagon, Suzanne noticed a dozen chicken coops nearby, each with a rooster in a rainbow of black, red, and orange feathers. She wondered aloud if they were used for cockfighting. Cockfights were illegal, but they were still regular Saturday night pastimes. In the ragged communities at the end of some hollows, someone went door to door late in the week, collecting small bets made with the same quicksilver hope as in a lottery ticket purchase. Jack was ready, so everyone piled into his Blazer. As he edged up the hill, a Jeep driven by a mine worker came down the hill. The man asked Jack to stop. "What are you doing?" "Just driving," Jack said, his shoulders hunched and his voice barely above a whisper. "Turn around," the man commanded. "Okay, at the top of the hill." Jack continued to the top of the hill, around a right-hand turn, and along the side of the mountain, occasionally checking over his shoulder to be sure no one was following. Ten minutes later, they reached the valley fill.

"Look at that!" Pat exclaimed with boyish enthusiasm. The fill was a jumble of loose rocks and dirt, nearly black in color, about 300 feet wide at the top and 200 feet high. It covered at least 1,000 feet of stream and ended at a 75-foot-wide pond, which was supposed to catch the dirt that ran off the fill. Fresh green grass was newly planted on the surface of the mine above the fill, but the fill itself was bare. Joe, who had by now memorized the regulations on fill design, immediately looked for violations and found several. "They're supposed to put drains down these things on the sides." Joe commented. "Look what they've done there, just nothing."

Next, Jack took them to two communities along Rum Creek, which lies between Buffalo Creek and Blair. As they headed down the mountain, they came upon a five-hundred-foot-wide ribbon of newly planted bright green grass on the side of a mountain below an Arch Coal mine. In late June, a section of the mine had weakened during a heavy rain and slipped over the side, blocking the road with rubble for several miles. This was one of the few times DEP connected a mine with flooding and immediately issued a violation. The debris was so massive that Arch had to bring in its giant shovels to clear the road.

The valley fill that Joe, Pat, and Suzanne saw at the Arch Coal mine.

A half mile farther on, they saw charred remains of houses and trailers. This had been Yolyn, a community of about fifty homes and a post office. The land company had evicted the residents after the flood. The move was not for their safety, but because some of them had complained and because the mine was going to advance closer. At one spot, a television set and a sofa sat among the remains. Even a shaggy dog had been abandoned. "What's going to happen to these people?" Pat asked.

The next stop was a couple of miles down the creek in Chambers. For more than forty years, water for a half dozen houses had come from a nearby hillside, running in a narrow pipe to the community. That hillside and water supply were soon to be obliterated under a valley fill. Public water, which cost as much as eighty dollars a month, was residents' only alternative. Hughie Moore, a retired miner in his sixties, was upset that he had sold a one-third-acre lot near the water supply. The land agent had sat on Moore's porch and told him he could still ride his four-wheeler up the hollow and that the water supply would be protected. After Moore signed the intent-to-sell form, he looked at the company's mine permit and discovered that a valley fill would be placed on his land. He didn't want that; he even refused to accept the registered letter from the land company.

The remains of Yolyn after residents were evicted by a land company.

Hughie Moore, left, talks with Pat McGinley (center) as Suzanne Weise and a neighbor look on.

Hughie Moore and a neighbor invited everyone to ride with him up to look at the water supply. The land rose in a V from the sides of the stream, which ran year-round. A sign warning of blasting greeted them. The mine would be working on this mountain and valley for about seven years, they explained. As they stood near the water line, a noise like a gunshot shattered the air. "A blast," Moore's neighbor said. "They wait until they know DEP has gone home and let off bigger ones."

The sun set directly ahead of the car as Pat, Joe, and Suzanne left the community. But no one could see it through a thick cloud of orange dust that had sunk into the valley, puffing itself into every crevice. Even though the blast had been a half hour earlier, the dust still hung in the air.

"I've had enough," Pat told Joe and Suzanne.

"That's what they want people to think," Joe replied. "That there's no hope."

"Some lawyers, who were my students and who practice in Charleston now, should see this."

"If it's allowed to continue, it will become a national sacrifice area," Joe added.

"We need some more lawyers on the case," Pat said. "We will be up against 30 for the coal companies."

"It could be fun," Joe suggested. "I know it will have impact if we do it."

———

Joe had tracked down Dan Sweeney in the Region 3 office of EPA (Environmental Protection Agency) in Philadelphia. Sweeney was an expert on coal mining and the Clean Water Act. EPA officials had been watching the valley fills grow larger, and they were worried. Sweeney pointed Joe to Section 404 of the Clean Water Act, which allowed filling of streams if the fill was to be used for development, such as a shopping center or a housing development. In the labyrinth of environmental regulations, the administration of 404 fell to the U.S. Army Corps of Engineers.

Since 1986 the Corps had lumped all valley fills under Nationwide Permit 21. This allowed each fill to be rubber-stamped, without any significant examination. Joe found one West Virginia case dealing with Section 404, in 1989. The case was *West Virginia Coal Association v. Reilly* (Reilly was the EPA administrator), and in it federal district judge John Copenhaver had written: "The primary purpose of the fills and treatment ponds is to dispose of waste or spoil and treat sediment laden water, not to create dry land such as is needed for the construction of buildings or land development, as contemplated by the Army's definition."

At first, the importance of Copenhaver's comment escaped Joe. In Copenhaver's case, the Coal Association had claimed that the Corps had jurisdiction over the area between the toe of the fill and the bottom side of the sediment pond where water could discharge to the original stream. Copenhaver disagreed, ruling that the EPA had jurisdiction, under Section 402, which controls point-source pollutants into streams and rivers. Then, Joe discovered that a 1986 Memorandum of Understanding gave the Corps jurisdiction over fills under Section 404.

Now, Joe, wondered, did valley fills comply with Section 404? When Dan Sweeney didn't seem to have an answer, Joe pressed on. He asked officials at the Corps of Engineers. No one seemed very clear on the matter. Then he reread Copehnaver's opinion and finally understood the import of his rulings: *valley fills did not qualify as waste placed in order to develop land.* "Ah, ah!" he said aloud, jumping up and down in a rare burst of emotion. Now the case seemed so simple. It took nearly another year, though, to bring it to the point where Corps officials agreed under oath.

Chapter 5

Changing the Laws

As 1997 wound down, Trish Bragg and Vicky Moore continued their quest for help from the state and federal governments. Joe, too, turned to officialdom, but for a different reason. Thinking a stint as a part-time lawyer during the two-month legislative session would help him learn the laws and politics of the state, he became a staff attorney for the House Judiciary Committee. It would still be four months before he would meet Trish. In the interim, all three would step into the colorful, sometimes corrupt, world of politics that is unique to West Virginia.

Vicky and Trish began with a trip to Washington, D.C., in January 1998, hoping to call attention to their plight by speaking at a conference at the Office of Surface Mining. Trish was beside herself with joy as she climbed aboard the van for the long trip. For OSM and others, they were going to finally put human faces on the suffering and damage occurring in the coalfields.

They and several other members of the West Virginia Organizing Project, including Freda Simpkins, a retired teacher from Beech Creek (near Pie) who had lost her well to blasting, sat through hours of reports and statistics from coal and government officials. But when it came to their time to speak, they were snubbed. They had wanted to show a film about Larry Gibson's fight to save his home place atop Kayford Mountain from mountaintop removal. But the film miscued, and they weren't allowed to continue. Then their question-and-answer period was eliminated because lunchtime had arrived. Afterward, Vicky tried to tell OSM director Kathy Karpan of their problems. "I'm sorry," Karpan told her. "I don't speak Southern."

Tears of frustration streamed down Trish's face. Then she spotted the seal of the Department of the Interior on the podium. "At that moment," she wrote later in an unpublished letter, "I felt very much like that buffalo on that seal. Appalachians are close to extinction and definitely a dying breed. And if you continue to look the other way, Appalachian culture will soon be gone just as the great buffalo herds of the West. I have nothing against protecting our wildlife or marine life, but Appalachia has endangered wildlife, too. For that matter, we have water, air, homes, streams, land and the very quality of our lives being endangered in the coalfields. Oh, but there will be PROGRESS, PROGRESS, PROGRESS, or should I say $$$.

"Appalachians are labeled as passive, clannish people that are complicit in the backwoods of the mountains. They're suspicious of government and big industry. I say, why not? We have been for centuries abused, used, oppressed, but our concerns are seldom addressed by the powers that be. I find Appalachians are also passionate, hard working, courageous people with a deep love of family and their land. These family-oriented people have become frustrated with the total disrespect we receive from the nation we have lived, fought, and many times died for. Oh, did I mention Appalachians are also terrific fighters, stubborn, and determined people. My people do not back off when we have took all the abuse we can stand. That's where you find most of us now, on the front-line of a war for the salvation of Appalachian culture, and we will not back off, we will not compromise, but we will continue to speak about the tremendous destruction of our land and the way of life we hold so dear."

———

Stymied in Washington, Trish, Vicky, and WVOP turned next to the state legislature. They wanted stronger laws on blasting. Here a twist of fate brought a new person into the struggle, a person for whom the past had become the present.

When Arley Johnson noticed the small item in the *Huntington Herald Dispatch* about a forum on mountaintop removal, he immediately decided to go. Later, he would see this as one of those times God put a hand on his shoulder and steered him toward a new and better course.

The auditorium was half full when he arrived that night. Vicky and Tommy Moore were there, along with Pat McGinley, Suzanne Weise, and Joe Lovett. The stage was already decorated for Christmas, with three-foot-high red and white poinsettias as accent points.

Speakers included David Todd, Arch Coal's vice president for public relations; John Ailes, representing DEP; and Dan Kash, chairperson of OVEC (the Ohio Valley Environmental Coalition), the sponsor. Arley was friendly with Todd, since they served together on a committee for Marshall University. Todd read a portion of a statement that Interior secretary Bruce Babbitt had made when he visited Arch's Hobet 21 mine about twenty-five miles southwest of Charleston in August 1996: "In some ways it is a better landscape than it was before. It is a more diverse landscape, a savanna of forests and valleys, fields and open spaces. . . . It's an example we ought to hold up as a rebuke to those who say it's jobs versus environment. The answer this landscape shouts out is: We can have both." Arch Coal, Todd said, goes beyond what the law requires, reaping a slew of awards for outstanding reclamation of the land after mining.

John Ailes portrayed DEP as a stern enforcer of the laws. His body language, though, seemed to imply he had doubts. Ailes could seem like two different people when he spoke in public, depending on his audience. If he was speaking to friends, he seemed to relax and talk more openly. But when he seemed programmed by a script he did not endorse, the truth seemed to be trying to burst out of his body.

After an hour of presentations, the moderator allowed an hour of questions. There were four or five hands up when the question time permitted just one more. Perhaps fate laid a finger; perhaps Arley, being a member of the House of Delegates, would have been selected anyway. He stood, the lone African American in the audience. He had three requests: Would David Todd show him a mine? Would John Ailes explain the regulations? Would someone from OVEC take him to communities impacted by mining? The third request was granted first. He became the only state legislator who, on his own initiative, visited the people living near the mines. In a way, he was going home.

———

Arley's grandfather had been drawn out of Georgia to Logan County in the 1920s by the promise of the mines. For African Americans, more money could be made in the mines than as sharecroppers. Arley was born in April 1959, the sixth of nine children. His family lived in Proctor Bottom, a black and white community along Buffalo Creek, about ten miles east of Blair. The white communities in Logan County were not kind to blacks in the 1960s. "Nigger" was a name Arley often heard as he and his brothers and sisters trudged between home and school.

One day in April 1968, on a day off from school, Arley's mother commanded him to watch television. The images on the black-and-white screen burned into the young boy's brain. While he didn't know the man in the coffin, he saw famous people he did know: the president, the vice president, the Kennedys, Harry Belafonte. He thought this black man must be a king. And he wanted to know more. So he began research for school reports, learning that the man was not a real king, but Dr. Martin Luther King Jr. Soon he memorized King's "I Have A Dream" speech, reciting it often during King Day celebrations.

During Arley's childhood, deep mines dotted the fifteen-mile length of Buffalo Creek, with a preparation plant every few miles. Coal was washed before shipping, and the black water and coal washings had to be put somewhere. The favored place was in the valleys between the mountains. Pittson Coal, the nation's largest coal company at the time, had dumped coal waste up a hollow about three hundred feet from Buffalo Creek. Eventually, 135 million gallons of water pooled behind the makeshift dam. On the morning of February 26, 1972, the dam broke, and a huge wave of water rushed down the valley. By the time the wave reached the town of Man, a dozen miles south, 125 people were dead and four thousand homes had been destroyed.

The Johnson family survived; their two homes did not. Later Arley helped carry the bodies. As soon as the road was passable, Arley's mother decreed, much as she had ordered the children to watch the funeral, that the family would leave Buffalo Creek forever. They drove out over Blair Mountain to Charleston and on to Huntington. The flood etched two imprints on the psyche of the twelve-year-old boy. One, the disaster didn't have to happen; corporate greed had taken innocent lives. And two, life is short: time must not be wasted, and change cannot wait.

In his late teens, Arley became a man of the streets, dealing some drugs. It was a time when the pattern of his life was closer to that of the young Malcolm X than to that of Dr. King. But his early school years in the close-knit community of Proctor Bottom had given him a sound foundation. A naturally bright and inquisitive youth, he remained an honor student and entered Marshall University at eighteen. He majored in political science and minored in journalism. Eight days before his twenty-first birthday, Arley had another life-changing event. After a night of partying, he wandered into an all-night revival. He was entranced by the fire-breathing preacher, the rich music, the guttural sounds of the parishioners who declared themselves to God. He accepted the faith. As at other times in his life, he felt as if a hand were on his shoulder.

After graduation, Arley rose quickly in the business world, with jobs in sales and at a heavy-equipment dealership. In 1988 he made his first run for city council in Huntington and won. Another funeral, in 1968, had instilled in him a belief that someone in government could change the world. He had attended a memorial service for Robert F. Kennedy at the church in Proctor Bottom. Later he learned that this white man, who had several times brought hope and help to Logan County, had cared enough to try to make the world better for African Americans. In 1992 Arley took the bold move and ran not from the district with a majority African American population, but for one of the at-large seats. People said he'd lose. He won and became chairman of the city council.

He faced naysayers, too, in early 1994 when he declared for the House of Delegates. There were six in the race for three seats, with two incumbents. The district contained a piece of the adjacent county of Lincoln, the start of coal country, joining Logan County at its southeastern tip. A powerful political operative who had a grudge against Arley took fistfuls of flyers showing a picture of Arley and his wife and five children to the Lincoln County Courthouse, the stronghold of the power brokers. He thought they would refuse to vote for an African American. But Arley, who transforms strangers into friends with a handshake or a hug, went to every church supper and every spaghetti dinner. He made sure everyone knew what color he was. On November 8 he came in third by one hundred votes and secured the first seat for an African American from Cabell County.

———

Thursday, December 18, 1997, was the day Arley chose for his visit to the coalfields. The sky was brilliant blue and the temperature an unusually mild forty-five degrees. Arley set off at 9:00 a.m. from the capitol in Charleston. There were six stops scheduled for the day; the route was a 260-mile loop beginning deep in Lincoln County and moving through Blair and Rum Creek in Logan County, to Beech Creek in Mingo County, to Trish Bragg's neighbors, and back to a meeting in Logan. At each stop, people had videos cued up in the VCR or photos ready to be examined. Two groups prepared large platters of cold cuts, cheese, crackers, and cakes.

Vicky met Arley at James Weekley's house. Rows of snapshots covered the kitchen table. Weekley showed Arley pictures of the dragline and the dust coming from the mine. Vicky tried to tell Arley what it was like to live there. As he left Blair, he saw charred remains in what used to be people's yards along the sides of the road. The dragline sat on the edge of the hill.

He visited Beech Creek, across the mountain from Trish Bragg's home, and met Janice Allen, a coal-miner's widow in her seventies. She told him that she feared taking a bath because her bathtub started sinking after the blasting began. *What if that were my grandmother?* Arley thought. His last community visit was in Pie. Trish met him at Herbie and Debbie Hatfield's house. They still had no water, and their house was falling into the ground as the mine worked underneath. Debbie showed him the water buffalo in the backyard—a water tank about as big as two heat pumps. Every few days, the mine had it filled with water.

Arley mused as he drove: *What happened at Buffalo Creek was one day; this is much worse—a slow death. . . . They have no one. This time not even the UMWA is behind them; they're siding with the industry. All they have is one black legislator. Even John the Baptist had more.* He started to turn the possibilities over in his mind: *Stop mountaintop removal, control blasting and dust; try to minimize the impact and improve the mining techniques.* At each stop he made on the tour, he offered one clear message, repeating it several times: Each community must reach out to the others. They must band together and present their case as a united front.

Arley spoke of the kind of legislator he wanted to be, what he saw as his political future. He wanted to be effective, known for crafting legislation that passed, not flimsy bills cast out among the thousand rejects each year. In some ways, he felt like President Bill Clinton, who also greatly enjoyed meeting people. Someday, he dreamed, he might be governor or a U.S. senator.

At about 6:00 p.m., the tour reached its last stop. John Humphries, the brisk and efficient coordinator of WVOP—the one Trish disliked—waited at Wendy's in Logan to tell Arley about the group's plan. Members wanted to ask the legislature to pass a bill on blasting. No longer would citizens have to prove that the blasting caused damage; the mines would be required to cover damages unless they could prove blasting *wasn't* the cause. Like the premise of Joe Lovett's case, it seemed a simple solution.

"You should have one WVOP member registered as a lobbyist," Arley told Humphries, since that gives the group the authority to distribute lit-

Arley Johnson, center, looks at Arch Coal's Samples mountaintop-removal mine.

erature to legislators on the floor. "Lobbying needs to be people-driven," he continued. "The heartfelt conversations I had with people today would mean everything." At every stop, residents had emphasized they didn't want coal mining to stop, just the damages. "It's important to preface everything you say with that," he cautioned.

Charleston was an hour's drive north, and Arley's cellular phone had begun ringing with messages from home. The last leg of the journey was through a moving light show, as numerous spectacular displays of Christmas lights spun by in a blur of white, red, green, and blue. Few areas of the country can rival the colorful decorations of southern West Virginia. The best in show this night was an half-acre display, stretching from a house in a bend of Corridor G up a hillside, with Santas, sleighs, snowmen, elves, and holy figures in a gathering of wonder. There was, it seemed that night, a chance for inheritance by the meek.

————

It was the second Saturday in January 1998, a misty morning in the city of Logan. This time of year, the sun barely edged over the crest of the tall mountains by 9:00 a.m. In this dull grayness, two dozen members of WVOP gathered in the Guyandotte Room at the Logan campus of Southern West Virginia Community College. These were determined souls, ready for an important day. They were going to learn how to lobby for their blasting bill.

Trish and Vicky joined the others around the tables arranged in a U shape. On the front wall hung a blue and gold banner for the Rotary Club; this was the regular meeting room for various community organizations. WVOP coordinator John Humphries introduced their teacher: Katherine Butcher, the wife of Greg Butcher, a miner and one of the delegates from Logan County. She was also a lobbyist for an issue dear to her and her husband's hearts: they believed motorcyclists should be free to ride with their hair blowing in the wind—without helmets.

Katherine Butcher, as imposing as a Harley Davidson herself, proved to be a knowledgeable lobbyist. She explained that a bill must first be written and must have sponsors—the more the better. Then it's introduced and sent to a committee—one committee is good; two are bad because the process is slowed, sometimes on purpose.

"Would a tour of the capitol help our people?" Trish asked. "Every time you mention government to the people in West Virginia, it is very intimidating." She was speaking of the distance both physically and psychologically between the coalfields and Charleston. Katherine thought it was a good idea, even though people might be uncomfortable. Her point was, "Your legislators want to hear from you, not a paid lobbyist."

Many organizations host parties for the 134 legislators, most of whom are stranded and bored far from home. Maybe WVOP would want to join another group and organize a party. Learn how to use the media, she suggested. Every time you have an event, fax out press releases. Go in with facts and expect the other side to twist them.

Lobbying began to sound sort of seamy to Trish. "You mean there's no ethical rules and regulations? We are selling ourselves. The impression we make with this person means whether this bill gets passed."

Almost no one gets their bill passed the first year, Katherine warned. Her message sank in. A woman visiting from California sighed, "It sounds like a miracle if a bill gets passed."

John Humphries filled the flip chart with lists:

GOALS
You probably won't pass this year
You will get name recognition
You will gain knowledge of how the process works
If you get this far this year—you will gain respect

After lunch the group began role-play lobbying. Carlos Gore, from Blair, was first up. He had no trouble making blasting problems sound real, since rocks from blasts had landed in his yard several times. Playing the legislator, Katherine sat solemnly as Carlos handed her WVOP's bill. "We need to know how we can go about getting this taken care of," he said, tentatively. "It's destroying our communities, tearing our schools apart."

"Let's see here. Oh boy. If they are going to be restricted like this, how is that going to affect jobs there?" she asked. "If you put more restrictions on the coal company, we'll lose jobs down there, and I am real concerned about keeping the jobs we do have and trying to get more."

"We are just wanting to get some laws to protect the families who live so close. We are not trying to shut them down. But the people who is in the communities 600 to 800 feet to 1000 feet from the mine—they are devastated."

Carlos and Katherine bantered about jobs and damages for another minute. Then she concluded: "I didn't realize this was going on. I tell you what I'll promise, I will take a look at it. I want you to stop back in. If you can come up with some figures—I want some stuff I can sink my teeth into, I'll take a look at it."

Trish and Vicky and the others wondered if the real legislators would be so responsive.

———

The legislature begins on the second Wednesday in January and runs through the second Saturday in March, except for the year after a gubernatorial election, when it begins a month later. The WVOP members arrived at the capitol to lobby that first week, with their draft blasting bill and two-inch yellow buttons, so bright no one would forget this group. They met with Arley Johnson and Delegate Dale Manuel, whose constituents in the eastern panhandle were upset about blasting at quarries. WVOP member Ralph Preece, who had had rock from blasting land on his roof, registered as a lobbyist, and the group studied the marble maze of corridors.

In a state generally regarded as a poor cousin by the rest of the country, the design of the capitol ranks among the nation's elite. Its 293-foot-high dome, swathed in 14-karat gold-leaf paint, shone as a beacon for drivers entering the Kanawha Valley from the east—and surpassed the dome on the U.S. Capitol by a full five feet. After that building was destroyed in a fire in 1921, Cass Gilbert, one of the nation's leading architects, who had designed the U.S. Supreme Court and Woolworth buildings, was chosen to design its replacement, which stands today. Gilbert explained his intentions for the West Virginia capitol to a Charleston newspaper editor: "Public buildings, and especially the State Capitol, constitute the best evidences of the character of material, success and solidity, culture and civilization of a state." Moreover, the interior, as well as the Renaissance-style exterior, had been designed to give it a noble and distinguished simplicity. "While not extravagant or elaborate in detail or material," he wrote, "nevertheless it can properly take its place as among the best buildings in the United States."

The elegant capitol complex, with its gold-painted dome, has 333 rooms in its 535,000 square feet. Offices of the governor and the secretary of state, along with the House and Senate chambers, occupy the building that contains the rotunda. The east and west wings house executive departments, the Supreme Court of Appeals, and legislators' offices. The centerpiece is the rotunda, an opening rising 180 feet to the dome's huge chandelier, made of Czechoslovakian crystal. On the second floor—the level of the House and Senate chambers—a broad marble ledge loops around the rotunda opening. Known as "the well," this gathering place for lobbyists and visitors is a moving picture show of deal making. Between the well and the House and Senate chambers are wide legislative foyers, with ceilings high enough to dwarf the stream of people rushing through.

West Virginia is often described as the nation's natural-resources colony. Most of the mineral and timber is owned by out-of-state corporations or powerful family trusts, and these have shaped the state and county governments to serve their economic interests. To a degree, this political repression continued as Trish and WVOP made their first foray to the capitol.

In the legislature's early years, industry often stalled or weakened mining regulation. In 1897 progressive measures, such as the eight-hour day and the prohibition of company stores, died without reaching a vote. Any

The West Virginia capitol building, in Charleston.

The "well" between the House and Senate chambers at the capitol--a place where citizens, legislators, and lobbyists gather.

legislation that managed to win approval was likely to face governors who supported industry. When Governor William Alexander MacCorkle vetoed a bill in 1897 that required inspectors to have worked in the mines for six years, he explained that the bill's passage was "attended with too much risk to our greatest commercial interest. . . . Can the legislature of West Virginia afford to do anything that would impede, hamper or hinder the progress of great industry within the borders of our state?"

During the 1920s and 1930s, progressive public officials spoke of "the Invisible Government," shorthand for the influence of the coal, railroad, oil, and gas barons. According to Howard Lee, attorney general from 1925 until 1933, "Sometimes, they were subtle; at other times, bold; occasionally, brutal. As a rule they were shrewd, cunning, shadowy, shady individuals in the employ of large industrial interests. While they may have performed other duties, their main job was to prevent the enactment of any legislation that might adversely affect the financial interest of their employers." As the decades rolled by, the power of the Invisible Government waxed and waned. In 1933 Cecile Goodall wrote: "Often our Legislative Committees have been susceptible to the whims of the paid lobbyists, who backed by powerful corporations and industries, control legislation of a whole session."

During the late 1960s and early 1970s, the spirit of revolution of the Civil Rights and antiwar movements touched the legislature, which set about reforming itself. "What happened for the first time in memory," Bobby Nelson of Huntington recalled thirty years later, "was that people began to emerge in this state who had a commitment to retake the state and change the political atmosphere to make it responsive to the people who live there." In 1968 the legislature passed a groundbreaking law on black lung benefits, which became the model for a later federal law. At the same time, a citizens' commission report led to sweeping reforms, including opening committee meetings to the public.

Just as it peaked, the reformist energy began to wane, as did the energy of youthful activists across the country. By the time Jay Rockefeller was elected governor in 1976, he had become a bit more conservative. Gaston Caperton, a moderate Democrat, served two terms, beginning in 1988, and focused on education and economic development. For the first time, business leaders united with the coal industry and persuaded the legislature to weaken worker's compensation benefits, thus cutting support of disabled miners. In 1996 conservative Democrats and business and coal interests helped elect Republican Cecil Underwood, once the state's youngest governor in 1957, as its oldest. The tilt to the right increased when conservative Democrat Bob Kiss became Speaker of the House in 1997. Thus, WVOP members were entering an architectural jewel designed with high aspirations but peopled with lawmakers who often regarded reform as an unwanted intruder.

Their lobbying experience did not begin well. Arley Johnson seemed to be getting cold feet. Over several weeks, he met repeatedly with WVOP members Ralph Preece and Rebecca Hunt and staff John Humphries and Ashley Cochrane, but no bill was forthcoming. They began to get frustrated.

Arley was struggling between idealism and reality. He wanted to do something but wasn't sure what would win approval. In those first weeks, his thoughts were jumbled: *The blasting legislation isn't going to pass; it has to be toned down. Blasting is just one component of the devastation. We need to make a case for all the problems of mountaintop removal. We need to do a study, bring in the science. Most of the members don't know anything about mountaintop removal. And those who do aren't opposed to it—but they are concerned about the damage to houses. I need to concentrate on that. I have to survive politically.*

For WVOP members, the first lesson was compromise. Originally, their draft bill had two provisions. First, it shifted the burden of proof. Any damage to houses within five thousand feet of blasting would be assumed to be the coal company's responsibility. The state already had laws establishing such an assumption for well damage from blasting for oil and gas lines. And second, the vibration limit for air blasts would be lowered. As they trudged from office to office seeking cosponsors, they realized that lowering the air blast limit would have to wait for another year. They decided to rewrite the bill. One by one, legislators from the southern coalfields added their support. By February 1, Arley had finally committed. He had talked with a friend in the coal industry who didn't understand why he was taking this risk. Arley knew there would be a price to pay, but he thought it was the right thing to do.

Nine days later, the payment came due, facilitated by K.O. Damron, who presented himself with the rigid severity of his role as an officer in the National Guard and worked as a lobbyist and vice president for A.T.

Massey, the state's second-largest coal company. At one of the after-hours receptions for legislators, Damron told the son of Arley's boss at the heavy-equipment company that Arley had joined the environmentalists. Damron said he was puzzled about why Arley thought it okay to work for a prominent mining-equipment supply company while harboring deep resentment for the mining industry.

Bob Shell, Arley's boss and a grandson of the founder of Guyan International, had been extremely kind to Arley and his family. The forty-eight-thousand-dollar-a-year job came with a car and the use of a Florida condominium. Yet after Damron's comment, Shell called Arley into his office and asked if he was aware how his allegiance with radical environmentalists looked to Guyan's coal-company customers. Arley assured him that he didn't want to stop mountaintop removal, but his Buffalo Creek experience and his recent visit to the coalfields left him no choice. Shell told Arley he had to protect his business. Arley knew if he continued with the blasting bills, he would have to leave Guyan.

Any slim hope of keeping his job was blown away the next day. For a decade, environmental groups in the state had been represented at the capitol by the West Virginia Environmental Council, a small group of committed and aggressive lobbyists. These groups wanted to end, or at least severely curtail, mountaintop removal. So the Environmental Council had written a brief bill calling for a five-year moratorium and study of mountaintop removal. In the innocent confusion and behind-the-scenes attacks, word spread that Arley had supported the moratorium. Arley had already made his choice. But he kept his discussion with Shell to himself for nearly a decade. He didn't want WVOP members to try to save his job. It would be tough for his family, but he knew he had to continue because he had to protect those families and maintain his soul. He hadn't studied Martin Luther King Jr. all these years just to walk away. On Thursday, February 19, he introduced House bill number 4492.

A week later, on February 26—the anniversary of the Buffalo Creek Flood—two dozen members of WVOP picked their way down the concrete steps to the wooden benches in the gallery of the House chambers. A brass railing kept visitors from falling twenty feet to the floor of the House. Trish and Vicky gazed down at the one hundred hand-carved black walnut desks and the scarlet carpet. The walls of the House chamber are swathed in heavy scarlet drapery hung between marble columns. A gong sounded at 11:00 a.m. After the opening prayer, the delegates stood for the Pledge of Allegiance.

"For what purpose does the gentleman from the 15th seek recognition?" asked Speaker Bob Kiss, who stood at the front of the chamber.

Arley, wearing a navy suit, rose from his chair. He took the microphone in his left hand and put his right hand on the desk. "During the speech last year on Buffalo Creek, I tried to convey to this body and this state my feeling as a young child witnessing such a tragic event as a dam breaking, and 125 lives being consumed, 4,000 people being displaced and my life being changed forever. I made a pledge then and I make the same pledge now that I promised if any time that I felt any type of destruction of that magnitude potentially faced the people of West Virginia, I would try to stem that tide or try to make a difference as a member of this governing body."

Then he explained how he went to the forum on mountaintop removal and took the trip to the coalfields. "I was amazed for a couple of reasons. I was amazed at the sheer magnitude of a dragline doing the work it was doing. It reminded me as a child with Tonka toys, and we were in the sand-box and were moving all this earth. If they put their minds to it, there's probably nothing we can't do. And so says the Scripture. But there was also a downside. I was there to talk to people not just concerning mountaintop sites themselves but the human suffering inflicted on those who were around some of the sites.

"Let me say this from the outset that my personal feeling about these things is that property owners have every right to do with their property what they so desire. I am not opposed to mountaintop mining. However, in the process of mining that coal I believe it is also incumbent upon us as a delegated government body and a legislative body to ensure, as the Constitution states, the safety, the liberty and the posterity of our own citizens. Some of the sites I visited were great sites in terms of production. But in terms of the human suffering around those sites, I was not very pleased, I was not very impressed, and I was somewhat ashamed and embarrassed.

"In 1977, when the surface mining act was passed, it did not address what we see today as mountaintop removal. The kinds of things that were allowed in that act did not envision what we see today in terms of modern technology. There are a lot of rules and regulations set up and structured to handle surface mining and strip mining and deep mining and those things. But no one envisioned what we look at today. And that is a problem."

For ten minutes he discussed the blasting bill. He explained why the existing law fell short. From the papers on his desk, he read quotations from WVOP members Jack Caudill, Janice Allen, and Freda Simpkins, emphasizing that Caudill was a disabled union miner.

Now came the climax. Assuring delegates he was nearly done, he told them the story about Dr. Martin Luther King's trip from Jerusalem to Jericho. As his group traveled the winding road that drops from twelve hundred feet above sea level in Jerusalem to twenty-two hundred feet below sea level at Jericho, King told his wife he understood why Jesus used it as the setting for the parable of the Good Samaritan. The severe drop in less than twenty minutes is conducive to ambushes, and in the time of Jesus it was known as the "bloody pass." In the parable, the priests and the Levites looked over at the injured man on the ground and wondered if the robbers were still around, or whether the man was faking and would rob them if they stopped. "And so the first question that priest asked and the first question the Levite asked was if I stop to help this man what will happen to me. But then the Good Samaritan came by and he reversed the question. If I do not stop to help this man, what will happen to him? And that is the question before us today."

Arley explained what had happened because of the bill on the moratorium on mountaintop removal, declaring that he knew nothing about the moratorium and wouldn't have supported it. He was careful not to name Damron, but most recognized him from the description as a former legislator and employee of A.T. Massey. "He was wrong, it was a lie, and it has caused some concern for me on my job. I don't think any lobbyist has the right to try to cause me trouble on my job."

His voice rose. "And if that is the way things are being done around here, we need to stop it. And that individual needs to be stopped because he is out of control. The reason why I told you this story about Jesus and Martin Luther King and his wife is because the question for me when that happened was not what would happen to me or my job. The question wasn't what would happen to the Coal Association. The question wasn't what would happen to the environmentalists. But the question was what would happen to those people whose homes and lives are being destroyed by the blasting. That was the question before me."

His right index finger waved furiously. "I was not elected by the special interests, I was not elected by my party affiliation. I was elected by the people. And the people should come first. And the people are suffering. And we should ease their pain. Thank you." As he sat down, applause erupted from the galleries and fellow Delegates. One by one, his fellows members slowly rose until the standing ovation was unanimous.

After lunch, Trish and Vicky, along with Trish's daughter Kayla and Vicky's son Dustin, sat at those same desks they had looked down at in the morning. They and about seventy other WVOP members, coalfield residents, environmentalists, coal lobbyists, and legislators were there for a public hearing on the blasting bill. In a gesture of openness, any delegate can request a hearing on a bill, and it's usually granted. Delegate Harry Keith White from Mingo County had put the request in for WVOP. The Coal Association tried to get him to withdraw, but he refused.

Trish wore a pink shirt, blending with the scarlet-covered wall at her back as she stood at the wooden podium. When she started to read her speech, emotion overwhelmed her, and she could only spill out the feelings in her heart. She spoke in a trembling voice: "They're not polished speakers, but you go into their homes and you see cracks and you see wells gone dry. You are our government and you make rules that govern. If there is an unjust law on the books, it is your job to look at that law and say it no longer protects the people, and it has to be changed. In order to change that law you need to hear from your people. Today they're saying blasting is tearing up homes, it is damaging our land and it is taking our water. I don't understand a lot about technology, but I think the law on the books needs to have the dust shaken off of it, literally, and it needs to be looked at and examined and understand that technology and progress have outpaced this law. We need progress in West Virginia, but we don't need it at the cost of our people. I ask you if the law on the books is protecting our people to the fullest extent. No it is not. And it needs to be revised."

Vicky, Dustin, and Kayla spoke, too. After the hour ended, Arley hugged them, and photos were taken for the newsletter. What a day. Now they could go home and relax for the weekend. Only two more weeks remained in the session, but surely it would be less chaotic.

———

John Humphries thought good fortune had struck when the bill went to just one committee in the Senate, the Judiciary Committee. Since the

Bill Raney (left) chats with legislators before the Senate Rules Committee meeting on the blasting study resolution during the last week of the 1998 legislative session.

chairman, Bill Wooton, represented Raleigh County, he put it on the agenda on a day when he knew WVOP members from Raleigh County could attend. On March 4 John sat in the Judiciary Committee room and listened with Freda Williams, an energetic seventysomething from Whitesville whose father had been in a miners' march that preceded the 1921 battle on Blair Mountain. The staff attorney had rewritten the bill, and it drew mostly negative comments. Three senators did speak for it, but it still got shipped to a subcommittee, usually the mark of death.

Senator Jon Hunter, a supporter of environmental causes from the northern part of the state, called the subcommittee to meet at 8:15 the next morning. Trish arose at 5:00 a.m. and attended with John Humphries, Freda Simpkins, Freda Williams, Rebecca Hunt, and Jack Caudill. For forty-five minutes they sat in the blue chairs facing the committee table and the tall windows radiant with morning light. Senator Hunter arrived on time, but the other four members never appeared. The citizens sat tensely with the modern-day invisible government: coal lobbyists Bill Raney and Chris Hamilton of the Coal Association and K.O. Damron. Both men, each a presence at the capitol for nearly two decades, had proved to be extremely effective handmaidens for coal. Raney had been a surface mine inspector under Governor Jay Rockefeller, while Hamilton had headed the underground mine safety enforcement division at the same time. A television camera rolled tape for the 6:00 p.m. news. By 9:00 a.m., it became clear that the legislative leaders had used one of the oldest games to kill a bill.

Craig Shibley of WSAZ-TV asked Trish: "Have you lost faith in the system today, Patricia?"

"It has shaken my faith because I think a man is only as good as their word. And if their word to a private citizen can't be upheld, then I question what they are doing. We are living in a West Virginia atmosphere where we are told the decision-making process takes place right here in this building. We spend our time and our effort to get to know these people, and they provide us with answers, but they don't do anything. So what steps do we take to get justice in the coalfields in West Virginia?"

Shibley had some questions for K.O. Damron: "Obviously a no show today. Curious to know did you and other coal lobbyists tell these Senators not to show up today?"

DAMRON: "Absolutely not. I was surprised we didn't have a meeting this morning. It is rather early, and they were in session rather late last night. I have no idea what the situation is."
SHIBLEY: "Did you not talk to these Senate subcommittee members and express opposition to the bill?"
DAMRON: "Yes."
SHIBLEY: "What is your opposition?"
DAMRON: "I don't know if you know this or not, but the coal industry is the most regulated industry in the state. We do preblast surveys within half a mile of anyone's home that's close to where we are going to do blasting. We take films of their homes. We take water quality samples. And there are several avenues citizens have to air their concerns about blasting and coal operations, and we think there's more than adequate in the law and regulations to take care of those concerns."

Listening nearby, Trish was glad Shibley had confronted Damron—but angry at his response. When the cameras left, she and her friends confronted the absent members and lobbied friendly legislators. Trish listened to lobbyists make unflattering remarks about legislators in the hallways. Then she watched them turn around and shake hands with the delegates and senators. She wondered if they took their masks off at night, or if they lived in the grayness of half truths.

Senator Hunter tried to fashion a resolution calling for a study of blasting over the ten months before the next legislative session. He thought he had agreement from the four other subcommittee members, but one balked after the staff attorney made changes. The coal lobbyists were so busy watching the twisted machinations that they didn't pay any attention to the House for a few days.

On Monday of the last week, the House passed Concurrent Resolution 37. Arley and Delegate Manuel had quietly fashioned the resolution and hidden it in a package of innocuous resolutions that harried delegates never read. It called for a comprehensive study of blasting and contained six areas of study, including well damage, acceptable levels for the blasting noise, and how well state agencies responded to citizen concerns. Arley had beaten K.O.—though Damron certainly didn't agree. A study was just a crumb tossed out, he thought. No blasting legislation would ever impede mountaintop removal.

Now all energy had to be focused on the Senate. Trish, Freda Simpkins, and Rebecca Hunt had spent the weekend at stores and churches gathering more than five hundred signatures on a petition for the resolution. The stack of support had been presented to the Senate on Monday of the final week.

After some confusion about which committee had jurisdiction, WVOP members realized that the Rules Committee must adjudge resolutions. Chaired by Senate president Earl Ray Tomblin, from Logan County, the committee met mornings in a room barely big enough for spectators to stand along the walls. In Thursday morning's Rules Committee meeting, Senator Jack Buckalew, a Republican and one of those who missed Hunter's subcommittee meeting, tried to nullify the resolution. He failed.

WVOP members wanted to leave nothing to chance. They wanted the resolution brought up and voted on Friday, not delayed until Saturday, the last day, when it could be forgotten in the madness. Their best bet was Senate majority leader Truman Chafin, who was from Mingo County.

Ralph Preece (right) and Jack Caudill talk with Senate president Earl Ray Tomblin's secretary as they wait for the vote on the blasting study resolution.

Freda Simpkins, who was friendly with Chafin, and Rebecca Hunt, who knew Senate president Tomblin, sat in Chafin's tiny office for five hours on Thursday, waiting to ask him to bring it up the next morning.

Exhausted, they didn't return the next day to see if Chafin kept his word. Freda Simpkins asked her neighbor, Deanna Hatfield, to call her friend Truman while he was on the floor. Jack Caudill and Ralph Preece watched from the gallery. After an hour, Ralph got tired and went to lunch in the basement cafeteria. Ten minutes later, the clerk said that the Committee on Rules had recommended passage of seven resolutions calling for various studies. Then Senator Chafin rose from his chair and asked for immediate consideration of House Concurrent Resolution 37. Tomblin called for the ayes and the nays. Jack thought the nays were louder. But Tomblin declared the ayes had it. The resolution passed, an action marked forever on page 162 of the Senate Journal of the fifty-ninth day of the Regular Session of 1998. It was Friday, March 13.

At that moment, Trish was in a car with other WVOP members on the way to a meeting of SEP. They learned the news when they stopped to call the WVOP office. Cheers radiated from the car as they drove on.

A few weeks later, on a rainy April evening in the coalfields, Trish, Vicky, and two dozen other WVOP members celebrated in the cafeteria of the community college in Logan. Arley was there, along with several delegates from the coalfields. They ate dinner and played word games. The delegates got awards. Once again, WVOP members set themselves apart from the other kinds of lobbyists, even the environmentalists. They had never pushed or protested. And they said thank you. So far, their way had worked. For Trish, the legislature didn't feel so scary anymore.

———

All those weeks while Trish and Vicky and their friends were traipsing through the long corridors and up and down stairs in the capitol, Joe Lovett was traversing the halls of lawmaking as well. He had decided a stint as an attorney for the legislature would help him learn the West Virginia legal system. Along with three other attorneys, he was allotted space in a small room with four desks to one side of the House Judiciary Committee room, overlooking the Kanawha River. In the first weeks of the session, the bills came slowly, and he was assigned the easiest ones. But there was one bill that hadn't made it to the House yet that consumed his days. Week after week, he paced the halls, muttering SB 145 like a mantra.

It was just a brief bill introduced early in the session. It lingered, as bills usually do, until the deadline for passage in the Senate loomed, a week before the session ended. The bill would allow a mine to fill up to 480 acres of a watershed drainage before it had to pay fees or create a body of water somewhere else. This was known as "mitigation" for eliminating part of a stream. Under the existing policy, the mitigation requirement kicked in at 250 acres. The fee was two hundred thousand dollars per flowing stream acre filled, an area much smaller than the entire watershed. The coal lobbyists argued that Kentucky didn't impose mitigation until the 480-acre limit. The bill flew through the Senate Energy, Industry, and Mining Committee, the most pro-coal group in the legislature. After passing the Senate 29 to 5, SB 145 was fast-tracked to the House Judiciary Committee with seven days left in the session. Joe Lovett was ready.

Since he wasn't assigned SB 145, he could abandon any pretext of impartiality. Openly, he lobbied the members of the House Judiciary Committee. He even went out drinking with them if he thought it would help. He was probably the only one, besides the coal lobbyists, who understood the true import of the bill: it made into law what had just been a DEP policy. In the arcane legalities of water laws, that mattered a great deal for the case he planned to file by the end of the summer.

The environmentalists were granted a public hearing before the House Judiciary Committee on Tuesday, March 10. This hearing was the third for coal lobbyists on the proposal. "Opponents of the bill have a simple philosophy," said Dan Miller of the West Virginia Surface Mining and Reclamation Association. "If it makes things difficult for the coal industry, they are for it—if it makes things easier, they are against it."

Two days later, on Thursday, March 12, the House threw out most of the Senate's more lenient provisions, passing out a version much like the existing rules. It included a maximum fill of 250 acres before mitigation must be paid. Essentially, Judiciary Committee chairman Rick Staton had agreed to Joe Lovett's suggestions. He also added a crucial legal provision requiring that mountaintop removal comply with all federal and state laws.

Staton was nowhere to be found the next day, returning only for an evening floor session. Rumors flew that he and Speaker Bob Kiss had had a fight over the mitigation bill, as it was now known. Some thought Staton would lose his chairmanship. Kiss denied that possibility, but his reputation as a bully stuck. John Humphries of WVOP was told by a delegate from Logan County that Kiss had threatened to take away the pork-barrel items given to loyalists every year—known as the Budget Digest—if they supported the weaker bill. Staton said he had a migraine but did confirm he and Kiss had had words. They agreed to try for a resolution in a conference committee.

At 6:00 p.m. on Saturday, the five delegates appointed to confer gathered in the Senate Reception Room. Arley Johnson was one of them. This room between the Senate chamber and the roof walkway to the Senate wing held a special significance for Trish. As she had passed through the room the previous week, exhausted from the whirl of battle, she longed to rest in one of the soft upholstered chairs gathered round the marble fireplace in the cheerful yellow and blue room. She was stopped by the blue velvet ropes and the sign reading "For Official Use Only." "This is the people's building," she had said to Freda Simpkins, "And we're not allowed to sit in their chairs. All the comforts of home we can't have."

The five delegates seated themselves in the plush chairs on one side of the room. Quickly the trio of coal lobbyists, a dozen environmentalists, and Joe Lovett crowded in, spilling over the velvet rope into the other side

The chairs Trish couldn't sit in now hold delegates Arley Johnson (seated second from left) and Rick Staton (seated right). Coal lobbyist Chris Hamilton (standing left) keeps watch.

of the room. Larry Gibson, the protector of Kayford Mountain, held a three-foot-high sign listing the 1996 campaign contributions from coal companies. At 6:40 p.m., the delegates got mad and left. The five senators, who had been in floor session, appeared at 7:05. The delegates returned at 7:30. Four hours and thirty minutes now remained in the 1998 session. Quickly they decided to meet separately.

The House members were banished to the roof walkway to the west wing. It was a clear and starry night. Staton joked: "The next rumor will be I'm out on the balcony, about to jump." To which Arley responded: "And Chris [Hamilton] pushed him." Two coal lobbyists joined the roof conference, while one stayed with the senators. Staton asked them: "You can go to $300,000 an acre to preserve the 480 acres?"

"$250,000 is awful tough," Bill Raney responded.

"Why don't you write the bill?" Norm Steenstra of the Environmental Council spat at Raney. After ten minutes, Robin Godfrey of the Environmental Council shook his head in amazement. How can the coal lobbyists be allowed to dictate to the delegates?

The compromise was reached. Coal won the 480 acres. The mitigation fee was raised to a maximum of $250,000 an acre, with no minimum. If a mine chose to create a new body of water, each acre of stream would have to be replaced by two new acres of water. And Joe's clause on compliance with all laws remained, a gun with a silencer. Arley added one amendment, a requirement that DEP report what is done with the several million dollars of mitigation money. A few hours later, both the Senate and the House passed the bill—among more than one hundred others. Twenty-six delegates voted against it. Arley was not among them. The Speaker's threats were too fearsome; he had been through enough with the blasting bill.

Joe Lovett had never seen anything like these twenty-four hours. The corruption and stupidity disgusted him. He didn't know they would work in his favor.

Chapter 6

Bragg v. Robertson

With the legislative session over, Joe began putting finishing touches on the first step of the case he planned to file with Pat McGinley and Suzanne Weise. Known as a notice of intent to sue, this would let state and federal agencies know that a case was going to be filed.

Joe had heard of Trish and had followed WVOP's lobbying escapades. But they had never met. Trish knew of Joe's case and had heard he was looking to expand the scope of his case by taking on new clients. Joe was eager to have Trish as a client not only because it would allow him to challenge another mine, but also because he believed that if he took on a mine in Mingo County, he might not need to file the case in Charleston, where he would likely draw Haden as a judge. She hadn't decided whether she should join. WVOP didn't believe in lawsuits, although members were free to hire lawyers for their own cases.

On an early April evening in 1998, they finally met. The occasion was a showing of the documentary *In Memory of the Land and People*. In the early 1970s, Charleston filmmaker Robert Gates had traveled through the Appalachian coalfields, filming landslides and other devastation from the then-unregulated strip mining. The film had been shown to Congress during the debate on the surface mine law.

Joe explained his case to Trish, telling her she and the other plaintiffs wouldn't get any money. Instead, victory would bring better controls for—or even stop—mountaintop removal. Trish didn't completely understand the particulars of some terms Joe used, such as *buffer zone* (a provision to prevent mining—and disturbance—within one hundred feet of a perennial or intermittent stream), and she found Section 404 of the federal Clean Water Act (which doesn't allow waste—valley fill rubble—in streams) even more dense. But she was glad to see this man trying to help her people. She told Joe she would let him know.

Federal court procedure requires that notice of a potential lawsuit be given sixty days before the case is filed. Sometimes the parties settle after the sixty-day notice and before the legal complaint is submitted to the court. The notice was addressed to John E. Caffrey, director of DEP, who had been appointed after Governor Cecil Underwood was elected in 1996. Joe told Caffrey that he had failed in his official capacity to perform certain nondiscretionary duties and take certain actions as required by the Surface Mining Control and Reclamation Act. *Nondiscretionary* was a key term. SMCRA contains nice-sounding language about protecting "society and the environment from the adverse effects of surface coal mining operations." But these are discretionary goals. The DEP director was given *discretion* as to how and whether to limit mining and blasting in order to guard the communities.

However, Joe had searched out violations of laws and regulations that had to be enforced—no discretion allowed. His list was long: fourteen in all. The heart of his case was in Roman numerals I and II, which consumed fifteen of the pages.

These two parts dealt with filling streams. Joe believed that if streams couldn't be filled, mountains would no longer be blasted away. But court cases aren't constructed in declarative statements. Roman numeral I dealt with the Clean Water Act and contained references to four sections of the U.S. Code, one reference to federal regulations, and one to West Virginia law. They all dealt with the Clean Water Act, which was enacted in 1972 to maintain the chemical, physical, and biological integrity of the nation's waters. It is unlawful to discharge anything into navigable waters except as authorized by the Clean Water Act. One exception is Section 404, which authorizes the secretary of the Army Corps of Engineers to issue permits for the discharge of dredged or fill material into navigable waters. The secretary had issued Nationwide Permit 21, which allows such discharge from minor coal-mining activities. Permit 26 authorizes the discharge of dredged or fill material into headwaters if the discharge meets certain criteria. In bold type, Joe declared that Nationwide Permits 21 and 26 did not cover the discharge of mining waste into the waters of the United States. Now he addressed the Achilles heel he had discovered during his conversations with Dan Sweeney of EPA the previous fall. You see, he said in many legal words, valley fills are clearly waste material under the Corps's definition and therefore not permitted in streams.

Roman numeral II piled more evidence upon the first cause of action. in addition to the water laws, federal and state mining regulations prohibit mining activities that disturb land within one hundred feet of intermittent and perennial streams—the buffer zone. This area can be disturbed only if the DEP director finds that doing so will not violate state and federal water-quality standards and will not adversely affect the water quality and quantity or the environmental resources of the stream. "One egregious harm stemming from the Director's failure to make the findings is the filling and destruction of hundreds of miles of the state's streams with mining waste," Joe wrote.

At Roman numeral VI, the notice turned to the mountains themselves. SMCRA required mountains to be restored to approximately their original contour after mining. Only two narrow exceptions could be granted: mountaintop removal and mining on slopes so steep that restoration of original contour would be impossible. These two exceptions could be granted only if the land was returned to uses equal to or higher than the original uses before mining. And, Joe wrote, the director could only allow mountaintop-removal operations where an industrial, commercial, woodland, agricultural, residential, or public facility would be installed after mining. Instead, DEP had routinely granted exceptions for mountaintop removal that left the land as fish and wildlife habitat—in other words, a minimal restoration leaving waves of mined land covered in sparse weeds and a few trees.

His notice of the lawsuit was solid, Joe knew, but he was worried about his clients and their qualifications for something known as *standing*. Citizen lawsuits had been one of the bedrock principles of environmental laws. In passing those statutes, Congress had determined that regulators could get too close to the industries they oversaw. Only citizens had the aggressiveness necessary to control improprieties. Thousands of suits had been filed in the past three decades, and they had helped clean up waterways and reduce air pollution. In the beginning, courts did not care whether plaintiffs were physically harmed—a bird watcher could sue if a habitat was harmed miles away from his home. Then industries complained that environmental groups used citizen suits to tie them up endlessly over technical violations, and courts began to throw out cases if the plaintiffs were not directly harmed. The restrictions stem largely from a series of Supreme Court decisions written by Justice Antonin Scalia, which were prefaced by an article he wrote in 1983. He asserted that it would be good if federal regulators watered down the original protective intents of the environmental laws.

Joe wanted his clients' credentials to be untouchable. Only people who were directly impacted by the alleged violation could qualify. They would have standing. The number of such people was severely restricted, however. First, they had to live along a stream that was going to be filled. That would give them the standing to sue. And second, Joe would not knock on the doors of homes along the streams and ask residents to sign onto the case, because he believed it could be unethical.

Four couples, two individuals, and the West Virginia Highlands Conservancy finally met the requirements and were listed on the notice. James and Sibby Weekley, Carlos and Linda Gore, and Tommy and Vicky Moore were the clients from Blair. Cheryl Price and Jerry Methena lived in Uneeda in Boone County, on a stream that was going to be filled by an A.T. Massey mine covering about one thousand acres. Harry "Burr" Hatfield, a lawyer from Madison, lived in a stately brick house at the edge of the same mine. The final plaintiff was Patricia Bragg—she had agreed to be part of the suit.

A fourth and final member joined Joe's legal team in April 1998. He came from Washington and was a bookish attorney guided by a true moral compass. TLPJ (Trial Lawyers for Public Justice) had responded to Joe's plea for legal assistance. That group, which had helped on the Woburn, Massachusetts, case made famous in *A Civil Action,* sent Jim Hecker, who had been environmental enforcement director at TLPJ since 1990.

Like Joe, Jim Hecker had dedicated himself to public-interest law. The difference was that he had begun soon after graduating from law school at the University of Illinois in 1977. Neither as flamboyant as Pat McGinley nor as talkative as Joe, Jim had an academic bent and the ability to research the law and patiently dig into case transcripts and congressional testimony. He filled out the team perfectly.

Jim had the sad distinction of losing every case for the first five years of his legal career. The hardest loss earned a screaming headline in the *New York Post.* Despite heroic efforts by Christopher Reeve and other stars, Jim could not save the historic and architecturally splendid Helen Hayes and Morosco Theaters near New York's Times Square from the wrecking ball.

Joe Lovett (center left) and Jim Hecker (center middle) chat with an Arch Coal official during the 1998 Division of Environmental Protection mine tour.

In the late 1980s, cases under the Clean Water Act brought better success, and he pioneered in the use of citizen suits to stop discharge of pollutants into the nation's waters.

TLPJ had been founded in 1982 with the unique goal of joining trial lawyer and public interest "to create a more just society." Through creative litigation, public education, and innovative work with the broader public-interest community, TLPJ protected people and the environment and held accountable those who abused power. Just as with Joe's case, TLPJ often teamed its staff attorneys with trial lawyers across the country for cases that fit its mission.

Hecker had watched the evolution of public-interest environmental law. The large environmental groups, like Environmental Defense, Sierra Club, and Natural Resources Defense Council, have continued to bring lawsuits about the violation of environmental regulations. Otherwise, public-interest environmental law has decentralized, leaving a few large national firms and many regional ones with specialties, such as endangered species or timbering. A large portion of the firms are in the Pacific Northwest and the mountain states, with a smaller, but significant, group in the East. This is because much of the federal land and many of the national forests are in the West. Cases brought under federal environmental laws require that the government pay the lawyers, if they win. The Midwest, the South, and coal states like West Virginia don't get a lot of attention from environmental lawyers—though some law schools do offer help through environmental law clinics. Jim had been able to earn fees for TLPJ and attack polluters with his suits under the Clean Water and Clean Air acts—fees that, in turn, funded more public-interest suits. But there are few lawyers like Jim Hecker and many to defend industries. A citizen who has a problem not covered by a federal law is often out of luck.

When Jim decided to tackle mountaintop removal, he made a trip from the TLPJ offices over to the Department of the Interior. Since SMCRA had been vetoed twice before finally passing in 1977, Jim found thousands of pages of legislative history, consuming half of a shelf. For weeks, he read page after page and marveled at the bipartisan nature of the Congress of the 1970s. This was the Congress that overrode President Richard Nixon's veto of the Clean Water Act. Most of the lawmakers believed in environmental protections. A vast difference, he thought, from the present permanent gridlock, created largely by industry lobbyists and lawyers waiting to challenge every new regulation.

As he read through the speeches by various members of Congress, he was surprised to see their concern over the mountains of West Virginia and Kentucky. Representative Ken Hechler of West Virginia, fighting to abolish strip mining, had proclaimed: "Strip mining can bring us temporary profits, like taking six or eight strong drinks in a row, but when the morning after comes, the coal is gone, the land is gone, and the people are impoverished, then, we have a hangover with a mouthful of ashes. That is why I say we must shift to deep mining." Hechler told of visiting Gilbert Creek in Mingo County after a flood from a strip mine in 1972. A teacher showed him the harm strip mining had inflicted on the neighborhood. But when Hechler and some associates returned for a closer look, the teacher refused to talk because the school board had told him he would be transferred far away if he spoke against mining.

Joe's case inspired Jim. Here was a chance to recapture the crusading days of the 1970s. "This is one of those cases where the facts scream out for a legal remedy," was how he began his evaluation memo. "The remediation plans are a fig leaf to cover its [DEP's] wholesale capitulation to the coal industry. There is no way to mitigate this kind of permanent environmental destruction."

Joe had first called Jim the previous October as he began studying the issues. Though Jim had turned him down, he kept listening as Joe kept calling and calling. As Jim grew more interested, Joe grew more confident. When Joe told him about Section 404, Jim finally agreed to join. For Joe, Jim was a godsend. While Joe struggled to understand each new legal issue with the Clean Water Act, Jim had done it all a thousand times.

On May 7, 1998, the *New York Times* published its first article on mountaintop removal. Joe had to read it on the *Times* Web site, since no store in Charleston sold the daily *New York Times*. "I hope it was on the front page—with a color photo of a mine," he said. Soon his caution melted. "Great story—I was so worried." When the reporter had come for the interview, Joe had given him a hard time. The photographer kept saying they wanted to be fair and balanced and get both sides. Joe told them, "Sometimes one side is right, and you shouldn't be afraid to say it."

It was just the beginning of the national media attention. ABC's *Nightline* had already done a half-hour documentary in April starring Vicky Moore and Pat McGinley. This, coupled with the *Times* story, shook up the Clinton administration. Soon Joe and Pat were getting calls from top EPA and Office of Surface Mining, Reclamation, and Enforcement officials in Washington.

Already Senate Bill 145—the "Mitigation Bill"—had electrified Region 3 of EPA. Regional administrator W. Michael McCabe seized the opportunity to seek control of mountaintop removal. As the practice had spread across more mountains and valleys, he had become increasingly horrified. He told DEP that if the bill was enacted, EPA would take control of the state's entire water program. Under Clinton's Democratic administration, that shift could have made obtaining permits for mining and other industry much more difficult. McCabe scared Governor Underwood so much that the mitigation bill—though passed and signed—was never put into practice.

Nonetheless, McCabe had become engaged. During the SMCRA debate in 1976, he had seen surface mining in West Virginia. He had also met Carolyn Johnson of Citizens Coal Council while working for Senator Gary Hart in Colorado. Johnson had been involved in the SMCRA debate; Citizens Coal Council was an umbrella group for citizen groups in the coalfields all over the country, including WVOP. McCabe had also served as staff director of the Environmental and Energy Study Institute conference; the EESI was an ad hoc group of about three hundred members of Congress during the heyday of environmental laws.

Now McCabe realized that the federal government was operating under the out-of-date assumption that valley fills were two hundred to three hundred feet long, not one to two miles. He sent a request to Arch Coal and A.T. Massey subsidiaries, asking for extensive data on impacts of valley fills. When all he got was the same boilerplate submitted to DEP, McCabe saw that a stronger, broader approach was needed. He began to lay the groundwork for an interagency look at mountaintop removal—hopefully bringing about better and more uniform regulation.

In July McCabe brought key players to a meeting at the White House, where he showed the *Nightline* segment and handed out some of the news articles. He was encouraged that Joe Westphal, a former top official in EPA's water office, had taken over as assistant secretary of the Army Corps of Engineers. They went to dinner in New York. When Westphal flew to West Virginia to see mountaintop removal, McCabe sent along a stack of reading material. Now, McCabe thought, he could get the Corps to accept its responsibility for permitting valley fills.

Joe Lovett was astounded that day in July when he picked up the phone in his office and someone from the Army Corps of Engineers was calling him—from the White House. Quickly, though, he realized that this was serious. An attorney from the Corps told Joe Vice President Al Gore was aware of his case. The U.S. Office of Fish and Wildlife would be involved in the case too, which didn't bother Joe—they were concerned scientists. But Joe's pessimism prevailed. The Justice Department would represent EPA. He had heard that the Jackson Kelly law firm already had several lawyers working on the case, representing coal companies.

Dan Hedges, Joe's boss at Mountain State Justice, thought it was great. "It's like the 70s all over again. Amazing that so many people care about something in 1998." Soon excitement edged out trepidation for Joe, too, as he began stapling together exhibits for the case filing. Two of Pat's law students had spent the summer doing extensive research on permits, gathering hard data as support. Jim Hecker had wanted to file numerous complaints against DEP, but Joe had convinced him they should begin with

Section 404 and Nationwide Permit 21, aimed at the Army Corps of Engineers. In his heart, Joe dared to dream that the coal companies would leave southern West Virginia.

On July 16 Joe walked eight long blocks along Virginia Street and turned on the cross street to reach the front steps of the brand new federal courthouse, which reigned grandly over the entire block, an anchor for the west side of Charleston, just as the gold-domed capitol stood tall at the east end. Joe deposited the stack of papers with the clerk, unwieldy at forty-seven pages, he thought. *Bragg v. Robertson* had begun. Colonel Dana Robertson was the district engineer of the Huntington district of the U.S. Army Corps of Engineers, which oversees the coalfields. DEP was also a defendant.

By the luck of the alphabet, Trish headed the list of plaintiffs, thus becoming the "named plaintiff." She was poised on the edge of fame. There was just one problem: The districts had been realigned in June, so that cases with plaintiffs from Mingo County were assigned to the Charleston division of the federal court. The case would be before Judge Charles Haden II.

Chapter 7

Rallying Around

For Trish and Vicky, it was a season of rallies and tours and study groups.

In early summer 1998, Trish joined members of WVOP and the Ohio Valley Environmental Coalition for bird's-eye tours—flights over southern West Virginia. The plane was from South Wings, an activist group that wanted to expose environmental atrocities in the southeastern United States.

In spite of all that Trish had learned about mountaintop mining, she was shocked by seeing its effects from the air. *How could it be right to destroy mountains, communities, and the Appalachian culture,* Trish thought as she peered through tears out the window of the four-seat propeller plane. *My God, the land looks as though there is a war going on and bombs are being dropped from the skies. It is eating across our mountains like a cancer with no cure.*

The view of Blair from the plane haunted Trish for months and prompted her to write an essay, "In the Southern Coalfields Despair Has a Name: Hilltop Removal."

As I flew over the gorgeous green trees and the rolling hills, the beauty of it all took my breath away. These are not the highest mountains in the world, nor the widest mountains, oh but in the eyes and hearts of my people, they are the most beautiful mountains. Besides, they are our mountains, and we have the right, and the obligation to preserve them. We are not doing anything that the American Indians did not do to preserve their way of life. They said, "Leave us, we just want to live in peace, to be able to farm, hunt and live on our land." We haven't even asked the coal-mining giants to leave; we have just asked to live in peace and have protection of our homes and lands while they make their profits from the precious minerals under our land. To people of progress it has become a crime to state in public that our rights are being violated. Mountaineers should not allow others to make them feel ashamed of their desire to maintain what is a proud and tremendous lifestyle. A lifestyle many people across America seek after all their lives. Our way of life is a simple one or at least it was until the monsters of technology started breathing dust and rock down our mountains.

Sleep evaded me as I was lying in my bed the night I flew over Blair, W.V. I found myself having difficulty breathing. The devastation I saw in Blair will be happening right here on Pigeon Creek. The panic I felt drove me out of bed and in front of my picture window looking down the holler. I trembled inside! I questioned, "Will my neighbors, my friends and myself be driven out of our houses with the blasting destroying our homes and the dust stinging our eyes as we pack? Will we feel the frustration and despair the residents of the Blair community felt, and will all the attention that's been brought to hilltop removal also bring our community more protection than they got in Blair?"

My hope for our future still lies in the one that created these mountains. So I lifted my head and voice until the skies and I cried, "Oh God, please hold our area in your hand and let us stay here. Lord, don't let them destroy our children's heritage, but nevertheless not my will but thine be done Oh Lord. If you see fit that my friends and family must leave this place, please make us strong enough to fight for others so that some of the Appalachian way of life remains for future generations. In Jesus precious name, Amen."

I walked out on the porch and thought how peaceful it is here, how magnificent the creation called earth is. Then I wiped the tears from my eyes and remembered God helps those who help themselves. The big coal industry and government officials need to know who we are and what our views are and exactly where Mingo Co. WV is, cause our people are not going to take this anymore. We will fight with everything in us and somewhere, someone will see our need and help us. As I finally drifted off to sleep with a smile on my face, I thought of the peace and contentment I receive from this land and its great maker. This is why we want to live in the hollers and foothills of WV. I can't always tell others how I'm connected to this land, but I'm real thankful that this land can always connect me with myself and my creator. I would truly hate to be forced to live somewhere else but more important I would hate to have missed the opportunity I now have of living here and knowing the salt of the earth, "Mountaineers."

The kind of mountaintop removal sites Trish saw as she flew over southern West Virginia.

During the next months Vicky and Trish spoke or protested nearly every week—with so much scheduled they sometimes had to pick and choose which events they could take in.

On June 24 Trish, Vicky, Freda Simpkins, and other WVOP members joined representatives of the Citizens Coal Council and the Huntington-based OVEC at an OSM symposium at the Holiday Inn in Huntington featuring Kathy Karpan, the OSM director who had snubbed them six months earlier in Washington, D.C. This time, Karpan was in foreign territory—and Trish and Vicky had reinforcements. John Ailes, Joe, and Arley Johnson were there, as was James Weekley.

Early in the morning—before the conference began—a couple of dozen citizens marched around the hotel carrying yellow signs with red letters stating, "Stop Mountaintop Removal" and "Stop Longwall Mining." James Weekley, Rebecca Hunt, and Carlos Gore, Vicky's neighbor, were among them. But Trish couldn't join the sign-carriers. Throughout the legislative session, WVOP had carefully maintained that members did not want to stop mining—only to have it done correctly. In her heart, Trish wanted to hoist high one of the ban-mountaintop-mining signs. Instead, she settled for a more neutral position—marching behind WVOP members and carrying the group's banner. Her daughter Kayla, now ten, and Vicky's son Dustin, nine, followed along.

The protestors had a surprise for Director Karpan. As she was droning on about the OSM budget process, in marched the group. Kayla was second in line. "Welcome to all of you, we'll be with you in just a moment," Karpan said. The group stood silently along the walls, holding their signs. In a few minutes, Karpan spoke to them. "I think this is a perfectly appropriate presentation we are having with these people coming in. When you live in the coalfields, and what is happening impacts on the quality of your life, that is an issue that ought to be brought to the regulators. And we are here to hear those concerns and to have your suggestions on how we can do a better job. We know it won't be easy, and I'm afraid we've never acted as swiftly as we should."

Kayla spoke first. Wearing a black WVOP T-shirt, she introduced a young teenager from near Logan, who read the Coalfield Bill of Rights. Dustin then introduced several adult speakers, including Carlos Gore. Gore told the packed room how he got dust and fly rock from the blasting. "I want these rules enforced," he said. The group filed out as a woman

James Weekley (wearing Stop Mountaintop Removal T-shirt) with Sibby at a rally during the summer of 1998. Bob Gates is filming, while Mushie Bella looks on.

wearing a sign "Token" on her chest sang a coalfields protest song. The room packed with regulators and coal officials applauded loudly.

But it was James Weekley and Trish who caused the biggest commotion. During a presentation by Blair Gardner of Arch Coal on the role of OSM, they interrupted and made sure the audience heard about Blair and Pie. For the first time, they were face-to-face with a top official from Arch Coal. Gardner, who had been at the permit hearing at the Sharples school the previous December, was maintaining that valley fills did not violate the Clean Water Act and did not jeopardize water quality. Weekley, who was standing at the back of the room, interjected: "Come to Blair and I will show you some water quality effect."

"Mr. Weekley, I've been to Blair," Gardner replied.

"Come, I'll walk you around and show you," Weekley responded.

"Mr. Weekley I'll make an appointment to do that with you."

"Is that a promise?"

"Right after we're done with questions."

"Thank you Mr. Blair [Mr. Gardner]," Weekley concluded.

On the other side of the room, Trish rose, holding a map of the area around Pie. Proposed areas for mountaintop removal were shaded in pink, blue, and yellow.

"Would you like to make an appointment to stop Blair Two, over on Pigeon Creek?" she asked. "When these join the other ones, the hilltop mining will be 8,000 acres. I don't want a Blair Two." Trish paused for loud applause, then continued, her voice trembling with controlled anger.

"Now I have put a face to Arch Coal. Do you know why? Because we have a buffer; it's called DEP and OSM, they guard them, they hide them [the coal companies]. I want you to have a face to the suffering you've caused. You say you don't break the law. How many you's went without water. How many of you have been forced out of your house. Is it legal? Can I do it to your home and get away with it? No. But this man and his company can get away with it. You know why? because they got big industry. Do you know the government and big industry in West Virginia are so mixed up we don't where one stops and the other begins? The fact is we know where the people are, we're on the bottom again. And I say it's enough."

Trish paused for more applause. Then, with a television camera five feet from her face, she continued, gesturing with her left hand as she spoke. "When I don't have any water, find me water. When I got cracks, can I come live in your house—you live in Charleston? Can I move in with you?"

"If my wife would let me," Gardner responded, then waited for the laughter to subside. He laid one hand on top of the other on the lectern, outwardly unruffled but inwardly beginning to fray. "Ma'am I agree. I agree," he said and paused while several in the audience flung smart remarks. "May I respond to one thing she said. What you said—that we don't have a right to take your homes. You're right, we don't.

"I was speaking with a person from DEP. And he mentioned he had recently been in a meeting with people who live in Blair, and one of the people mentioned that over the last few months there had been a number of incidents." Looking at Carlos Gore in the audience, Gardner continued, "I am well aware, Mr. Gore, that there was an incident last summer where fly rock came from the mines and landed on your property. It is my impression that that has not happened since because, Mr. Gore, that should never happen. I am also aware there have been complaints about dust.

"I also believe we have attempted, I hope successfully, to change some blasting practices, to employ some water sprays to avoid that. And I do know there have been some changes in the management at the local operations. I do know that we have attempted to look at some of the engineering practices in an effort to address these concerns.

"But I've made a promise to Mr. Weekley to personally come down there, and I'm going to keep that promise. We will find a time that suits you."

"Any time suits me," Weekley responded loudly.

Trish was not going to be forgotten: "Are you prepared to stop us from having a Blair Two?"

"Ma'am, when you say a Blair Two," Gardner responded calmly. "I'm afraid I'm just not familiar with what you're saying. I am aware that our company has a permit 5013-97."

Trish interrupted: "I have two more on this map that are already prepared."

"We do believe those permits are lawful under existing law," Gardner responded. "And yes, Ma'am, we do intend to proceed."

After the session ended, Gardner offered to shake Trish's hand. She refused.

———

Joe was thrilled that Blair Gardner was going to visit Blair—and made sure the press would be there. However, it posed a dilemma for WVOP. The legislative study committee had chosen the same day—July 13—for a field trip to a community impacted by blasting. Legislators were eager to see Blair. It took Joe's best persuasive skills to dissuade the committee staff from going to Blair, because he wanted to focus on the Pigeonroost stream. Finally, they settled for the community of Foster in Boone County, where WVOP member Dickie Judy lived. What appeared to be heading for a disaster for WVOP actually worked out for the best.

Back in the early 1990s Dickie and his wife, Tressie, had built their dream house at the end of a bucolic hollow in Foster. Closer to Charleston than Blair or Pie, Foster was a bit more suburban. Dickie's white colonial was surrounded by more than an acre of lawn, where a bear sometimes came exploring. Although he had grown up poor in the coalfields, Dickie had made a good living as a building contractor. He traveled to construction jobs all over West Virginia and neighboring states. Because he planned to retire to this home in Foster, he built it the best he knew how—even letting the foundation settle for nearly a year before building the house. He just hadn't counted on the blasting.

Less than two months after the Judys moved in, they got a notice offering them a preblast survey, which they accepted, for the new Elk Run mountaintop-removal mine about to start on the mountain behind their house. (A preblast survey gives a written and photographic record of the condition of a house before blasting begins.) Blasting got under way quickly, and within a few months Judy filed his first of many complaints over a period of years.

Several DEP inspectors worked on the problem. Bill Cook, who had an unusual enthusiasm for enforcement, jumped right in and issued a violation: "failed to prevent damage to private property outside of the permit area. . . . Elk Run Coal Co. must provide a list of repairs that it is willing to make and a time frame for such repairs by Friday 3/24/95." On March 30 of that year, two OSM inspectors agreed with Cook's findings. The weak foundation on the Judys' older rental house next door had made it more susceptible to blasting, but their new house had definitely sustained cracks since the preblast survey—and the cracks were growing larger. Cook issued three violations, which forced DEP to issue a cessation order halting mining. Elk Run appealed to the pro-coal Surface Mine Board, which overturned the blasting violations. Cook yelled at them: "Why do you even have pre-blast surveys then?" The decision chilled inspectors. Cook decided he'd never issue enough violations to put him before that obstructionist group again.

Dickie didn't give up, though. He appealed to OSM, which issued a violation and ordered Elk Run to improve its blasting designs. However, in March 1996 the federal district court ruled in Elk Run's favor and overturned the OSM order. Blasting itself is a nearly insurmountable problem—but in addition Dickie was facing A.T. Massey, not Arch Coal. Many miners saw Massey as anti-union and as the company with more mine safety violations. To DEP inspectors, Massey played hardball, sometimes even dirty.

Cook was one of a handful of truly dedicated inspectors. Well educated, he was also a nature lover, living next to Kanawha State Forest, where he often jogged. Irresponsible surface mining offended his sensibilities—and he found many ways to force the mines to do better. He was proud that he had made Elk Run plant thousands of native hardwoods, even though regulations didn't specify the kind of tree to be replanted. The Stockton coal seam that ran through Elk Run was one of the few in southern West Virginia that were acidic—it could turn streams bright orange with the acid mine drainage prevalent in the northern part of the state. Cook had forced the mine to encapsulate any acid-causing debris.

Cook had asked DEP director Jack Caffrey to put limits on blasting near Dickie's home, but he refused "If it's a situation where the director is a coal man, your options are limited," he said. "I resent these people [coal officials and lobbyists] patrolling the halls of DEP. If I were in John Ailes's position, I would say I don't want you in this building."

There were ways to curtail the blasting problems, Cook knew, but he was powerless to implement them. Each mountaintop-removal mine had somewhat different topography. In some places, coal lies more than a hundred feet below the surface; in others, coal is much closer to the surface. In the latter case, holes to reach the coal were shallow and more likely to produce the eardrum-shattering booms of air blasts. Cook knew that putting mats over the holes would dampen the sound. But that might mean placing five hundred mats for each blast—and adding an entire day to one blast design, too much time loss for a mine.

Cook was also just beginning to deal with another problem caused by Elk Run. Dust from the preparation plant was coating Sylvester, a tidy community about five miles over the mountain from the Judys. He was helping the citizens file complaints and doing as much as he could to control the dust. Cook, who made do on about twenty-eight thousand dollars a year, resented the high pay of the mine managers. So he took particular satisfaction in what befell Elk Run when the legislators came to visit Monday, July 13.

A crowd of Dickie's neighbors, WVOP members, legislators, staff, coal lobbyists, and DEP inspectors, forty in all, were gathered at the Judys' home for the legislators' tour. Arley Johnson was there, though Speaker of the House Kiss had made sure he was excluded from membership on the study committee. So were Bill Cook and DEP official Ed Griffith. After listening to Dickie's story and examining the cracks in his house, they talked to a few other homeowners and then gathered at a small park near the mouth of the hollow. A wooden pavilion provided shade as noonday temperatures reached the midnineties.

Dickie Judy (center right) chats with Ed Griffith of DEP (center left) outside one of Judy's neighbor's homes during the legislature blasting tour.

A half dozen people from other communities explained how blasting had damaged their homes, showing legislators the extent of blasting problems. WVOP member Freda Simpkins told how blasting had ruined her well and cracked the walls of the new home she had built on Beech Creek, over the mountain from Trish. Blasting dried up the first well—then another blast caved in a second well as it was being drilled. DEP refused to blame blasting, she said, and the coal company provided no reimbursement. She had worked two jobs to pay for the home, running her cable television company after teaching every day. Peggy Parsley, of Breeden in Mingo County, blamed blasting from the mine nearby for the fire that destroyed her home in September 1997. The blasts had shaken her home, and she believed they shorted out the air conditioner, which sparked the fire.

Ralph Preece had retired after twenty-five years in the military to a tidy new house along Riffe Branch—only to find himself surrounded by surface mining. "We lobbied the legislature to try to get the burden of proof on the coal companies and extend the range out to a mile for a pre-blast survey," he told the study committee members. "We would like to see this done; we're not saying stop the mining, but we need some relief down in the southern part of the state. We're not a bunch of rednecks down here just raising Cain. There is some real problems. The problems are not going to go away; it's going to get worse. We are taxpayers, we are citizens of this state, and you people represent us, and we would like some help."

Several legislators offered proposals that sounded as if they would lessen the blasting problems. One man said he had heard that Massey met monthly with citizens near a mine in Raleigh County. This actually was about overweight coal trucks, and the meetings were ordered by a court settlement. No, the citizens replied this day, Massey had not offered to meet with people near Elk Run.

Vicky Douglas, a delegate from the northeastern corner of the state who was cochair of the study committee, asked, "Would you think it would helpful if we looked at the distance and the type of blast? It seems the rules that we follow were developed when the blasts were really much smaller." Then she had some thoughts on the complaint process. It might be reasonable to look at some earlier mediation of differences that could be handled a bit more informally.

Dickie summed up the morning's discussion. "What we are really asking, is for the mines to back down on their blasting, get a distance away from us, and take the burden of proof. . . . you have a home sitting here and there's not a thing wrong with it and they start blasting and two months down the road it is cracked all to pieces. The burden of proof saying hey we did do this, they—the mines—should come in and prove that they didn't do it. How many of you here can afford to put $200,000 to $300,000 out to collect ten to fifteen to twenty thousand worth of damage to their homes because that's what you put out when you fight the coal companies."

Some of the legislators wanted to visit the mine. Elk Run had told the legislators they couldn't because it was on the two-week miners' holiday. But Massey wasn't going to be allowed to defeat Judy, an even-tempered fellow with a good sense of humor. When the citizens finished telling their stories about blasting, WVOP organizer Ashley Cochrane pulled her slim body up to the most authoritative stance she could muster: "There's also the option of going up to the mine site. Dickie Judy will lead us to the mine site." Shock washed across the faces of coal lobbyists Bill Raney and Chris Hamilton.

They piled into Dickie's four-wheel-drive and other sturdy vehicles and set off on a narrow trail up the mountain. And when they reached the top and looked over, the mine was busily at work, giant shovels and huge dump trucks humming across the surface.

Reporters missed the excitement, though. They had sped off toward Blair. Today Blair Gardner was due at James Weekley's house on Pigeon-roost Hollow. In spite of their haste, they were all late, because one of the gigantic earthmoving machines had fallen off the trailer hauling it up Route 17 from Blair. The road was closed for hours—forcing a long detour.

With birds chirping in the background and video cameras six feet away, Blair Gardner and Mark White, manager of the Dal-Tex mine, sat on the swinging bench on the Weekleys' front porch. Gardner's glasses were perched on his nose so that he could read papers in the folder on his lap when he was not looking up to address Weekley and a friend. Weekley sat in a straight-backed chair against the front of the house.

Gardner explained that coal was in his blood. His grandfather had been a miner in Pennsylvania, taking a break only to go and fight in World War I. Blair Gardner had graduated from law school about the time SMCRA became law and then had worked for the Department of the Interior, which includes OSM, from 1983 to 1985. Gardner had testified before Congress in 1995, stating that, though jurisdictional language was imprecise, SMCRA appeared to give primacy for enforcement to the states—an issue that would play into the *Bragg* case.

Although Gardner was now dealing with Arch's Dal-Tex mine in Blair, the Catenary Coal Samples mine above Cabin Creek in Kanawha County, the highest-producing surface mine in the state, was clearly his favorite of Arch's four active surface mines in West Virginia. It was at that mine where he had developed his mining philosophy, sometimes with footnotes from mine manager Bob Bays. This mine had one of the largest draglines in West Virginia, capable of hauling 120 yards of earth and stone in its bucket and worth about $30 million. In fact, earth-moving was really what the mine did, according to Bays. Like a three-dimensional chess game, the King Kong machines moved mountains of dirt from one place to another. If the rhythm was interrupted by a broken-down bulldozer or—heaven forbid—a sick dragline, tens of thousands of dollars would be lost each day. Samples had won its share of reclamation awards by sculpting the

Participants in the Division of Environmental Protection 1998 mine tour look at reclaimed sections of the Samples Mine.

sliced mountains into gently rolling hills with a large lake. Bays was especially proud of how they had used some of the former mountaintop to cover an old coal refuse pile left from before SMCRA was passed. Runoff from a pile of old coal had leached acid water into Cabin Creek.

When asked whether the mines improved the land with reclamation, Gardner said, "I believe in God, so I am reluctant to say we are improving what the creator made. But more pertinent is, are we doing something inherently good? And I think we are." Land in the coalfields, having been mined for at least half a century, was rarely pristine, he pointed out. After mountaintop removal, not only could old scars be erased, but a new vista could emerge.

In Blair, James Weekley certainly didn't agree, and this hot July afternoon, he told Gardner so. And the world heard. Local television and newspaper reporters were joined by two documentary filmmakers and a reporter for National Public Radio who captured the gurgles of Pigeonroost Branch on her fuzzy microphone. The presence of all the media was a shock to Gardner, who had come to talk just with Weekley and his family. He felt that Joe had set him up.

Weekley and Gardner set off up the hollow that would be filled if the permit was approved. Joe went too and nervously tried to orchestrate—and keep Weekley from doing anything to damage his case. Reporters, photographers, Sibby Weekley, and a few neighbors, including Vicky, followed closely. Tree branches curved over the narrow dirt road that led to the last house in the hollow. Sunlight painted the full palette of greens from pale lime to evergreen.

"Mr. Weekley, what would you do other than just stopping the mine?" Gardner asked.

"That was the question I asked you on the porch. What would you do if you were in my situation?" Weekley replied.

"You have, I think, two options," Gardner said as they walked. "One is that if you are determined to stay here, that we try to coexist as well with you as we can. Be sure that we understand how you feel about your property and try to respect that. The other thing we can do is offer to pay for it, and if we can't pay you enough for it, obviously it is your choice to stay. If your choice is to stay we will have to do a lot better."

They walked over to the stream where water pooled about seven feet wide behind a strip of corrugated metal damming the stream. "There are trout in there," said Weekley. "They come up here. They take these trout out of here. They let 'em loose so they can come back up here. . . . Grandchildren."

"And you're saying if we continue our operations, that won't continue?"

"It won't continue because of the valley fill," Weekley answered. "The valley fill is coming to right here." Weekley pointed out the pink ribbon marking the end of the fill.

Gardner stopped and looked at Weekley, concern frowning his face. "Mr. Weekley. I've seen a lot of the fills that my company has constructed. And I know the care that we use in constructing. We are particularly concerned when we know that there are people living beneath a fill. So I am not worried about the fill failing. And number two, if you choose to remain here we have even more incentive to make sure that the water quality is as perfect as we can make it because we know you will be watching us."

"What do you all want, another Buffalo Creek?" Weekley asked.

Gardner was ready with his response, for he had heard this allegation many times. "We will not have another Buffalo Creek sir. And let me try to—"

"Are you sure?" Weekley asked.

"I am positive." Gardner gestured up and down with his left hand. "And let me explain why because this is something people confuse and shouldn't confuse. Buffalo Creek was a terrible tragedy 26 years ago in Logan County. Buffalo Creek was a result of fine refuse from a coal plant being put on a hill, and it had the effect of impounding water for acres and acres behind it. The material was never designed to be an impoundment.

"Mr. Weekley, we are not going to impound water behind the fill. What we are going to do is take the material, to take the rock on top of the coal and between the seams of coal. We're going to put it here in the valley, we are going to compact it, we are going to stabilize it. We're going to be sure when it is finished there is a trench or ditch at the edge of it so the water that comes off the top of the mountain goes down that ditch and gets resaturated. Because we wouldn't do it, and number two if we wanted to do it the government wouldn't allow us to do it."

They walked a little further up the hollow, with Dustin Moore at their heels. As Vicky looked on, Gardner assured, "What I can say we are going to do as we mine it and create the valley fills, we are going to be sure we aren't going to create an environmental problem for you or in the future because of the way we are going to mine it."

"I can't see it from what I have seen," Weekley responded as documentary filmmaker Bob Gates held his camera two feet from his face.

"But we are going to change the land, Mr. Weekley. I am not arguing with you."

"You are going to change the land all right, that's for sure," Weekley responded.

A few minutes later, the two men stopped again. Weekley began talking about the disappearance of Blair.

"How about the communities you destroy, like Blair, like Rum Creek?"

"Mr. Weekley, I don't think we are destroying the communities. I think the communities developed here in this part of West Virginia in large part because of the mining that was done 75 years ago. I think those communities are changing today for some of the same economic reasons."

———

Bang! came the sound of a shot. Trish and the Presbyterian minister turned around. At James Bailey's feet lay a dead rattlesnake. Now they understood why he had stuck a pistol in his belt when they set off to see valley fills being built behind his house at the end of a hollow in the middle of Ragland. Bailey lived about three miles over the mountain to the west of Pie, as the crow flies.

Bailey had come to the meeting at the Varney school the previous November. His house was the closest to the Ragland side of the White Flame Mine. This summer, Trish was a roving ambassador, a tour guide for newcomers to the coalfields, a spokesperson for other communities with mining problems. So when the minister wanted to see a mine in process, Trish thought of James Bailey. He was more than willing to show them what the mine had done so far. David Miller, one of Pat McGinley's law students who was gathering evidence for Joe's case, joined them.

As the group started up the hill of waste coal behind Bailey's home, Trish gazed back toward the house and saw Bailey's garden. "Look at all he's got growing. Think he's got some beans? Reminds me of Kayla planting beans. She and Dewey were planting. Dewey said she'd only planted a quarter as many as him. She was praying over every one. She had heard me say all the time 'Be fruitful and multiply.' And every one of hers came up!"

This hillside of coal bothered Bailey. He feared it might someday collapse, sliding into his home. But even more immediate was the threat of the two valley fills and their sediment ponds. Curious about the dead rattler, the security guard chatted with Bailey and then waved the group toward the valley fill. "It's muddy," he cautioned.

Through the knocked-down trees and overgrown bushes went the group, a bit like Indiana Jones in the jungle. Anyone who missed a step fell into mud up to the hips. Orange ribbons marked the site of the dam of one sediment pond. Thin wires—blue, yellow, and green like candy strings—stretching across the edge of the hill were actually blasting wires. *Hopefully none are live,* thought Trish. When they emerged from the underbrush, Trish laughed. "The *New York Times* reporter should be here for this. He showed up in a three-piece suit and wanted to go to people's homes right away."

The minister was invigorated. "I went to King's Island amusement park in Ohio this week. But this is more exciting."

———

It was déjà vu all over again. Another DEP director had been appointed—the fourth so far in Trish's experience—and it was time for WVOP to host another get-to-know you meeting and another tour of problems in the coalfields. Jack Caffrey had been in the post not more than a year. His replacement was Michael Miano. Miano rhymes with piano, as he told people upon first meeting them.

"What we are going to do today is visit two, possibly three communities," Ashley Cochrane, the young WVOP organizer, told Miano and the group of DEP inspectors, WVOP members, and citizens this late July morning in Rawl. John Ailes was there. "Hi, Patricia," he said, as she held the video camera today. Ed Griffith was there, too, as were Freda Simpkins and Larry Wilson, of nearby Lick Creek, which also had water and blasting problems.

Rawl is a few miles southeast of Williamson, "Heart of the Billion-Dollar Coalfields," as the sign says, and county seat of Mingo. Massey's Rawl Sales mine lay above Rawl. Rawl was created by the relocation of people left homeless in the horrific floods of 1977 around Williamson. It is one of the few communities in the coalfields with its own sewer system—but it has no public water.

James Scott, a heavyset man in his late forties, spoke about a mine blast that had damaged the community of Rawl. "On February the 27th," he said, "they came up after the blast and said they knowed they were out of compliance. Sixty-seven homes which we could find out were damaged in this area here structural wise, water damage was done also." Scott had been a union leader and deep miner for Rawl Sales until a mineshaft roof collapsed and nearly killed him.

He walked over to the side of his blue prefab house and continued explaining about the impact of the overlimit blast on Rawl. "The air blast came off this side mountain and got between this hollow. Once it gets in this hollow it had no way of getting out." Pointing to the side door, he said, "The force of the shot this way blowed the hinges on the inside off the door, shoved the house."

The adjuster for Massey's insurance company had decided that the mine was not responsible—even though it had exceeded the 133-decibel limit for the air blast. "They knowed they were going to be out of compliance because they had hit what they call a void. It's an air pocket. When you drill a hole if you can't get your charges in the ground, you are supposed to, by law, reset, drill again. They could not do that. They had to put off what they had," Scott said. "They went ahead and let that shot go off knowing all this damage probably would occur. That should never have happened that day."

Scott believed regulations required blasters to redrill the hole properly before blasting. But Ed Griffith and Jim Miller of DEP disagreed. As the inspectors and citizens debated the regulations, it became clear to Trish—for the first time—why blasting problems were out of control.

"A lot of times if a void or fraction is encountered," explained DEP inspector Harold Ward, who also dealt with Trish's problems, "it's not reported by the driller to the loader. That's a common mistake that happens. Anytime you have that, you can have a blowout. Energy can escape from the blast site. When energy escapes, then levels can be higher than anticipated. There's no way to forecast that."

After listening for awhile, Miano finally spoke. He had been standing to the side, a businesslike man in his forties. "Let me say the point here is that there are blasting concerns that you have that are apparently not covered by the current regulations. We don't know all the answers. That's obvious. It's a very difficult job that these folks do on a daily basis trying to make sure they're properly interpreting regulations and issue a paper that will stand up in court.

"The company has no market over being right either. They have a plan they developed using the best engineering practices. When things go wrong as you described, then we need to jump on that and come up with ways to see it doesn't happen again. It would be nice in a perfect world that, first of all, these folks [at the mines] would know when they put off a shot, something is going to happen. And so they say, 'No we aren't going to put off the shot.' Then when something would happen, they would come down and say we're going to fix it and plus we're ashamed we did it and we'll give you something extra to make you happy. But unfortunately that's just not something we as an agency have control over." A whistle from a nearby coal train nearly drowned out Miano as he concluded.

John Ailes, typically, summed up in plain speech: "You always pray when you go out to these things that it's clear-cut. That's a sad thing to have to say. You say, boy, I hope when I drive up it's very obviously blasting damage."

"You hope there's a 400-pound rock that went through the roof of the front porch and didn't hurt anybody," Griffith added.

Blasting wasn't Rawl's only problem. For years their water wells, most supplied by water-filled deep mines, had run orange or black. "This lady down the hollow, she's been buying water for 19 years, that's how long she's been buying water," Scott said. "My understanding the cold water is red, the hot water is black, that's how bad it is. If you've not got too good a clothes on, I will show you when you turn on down here the color is completely red water."

The group trooped down the steep hill to see the community water supply as Scott unlocked the pump house. Orange water ran out when he opened the faucet.

"How can people use this water?" one man asked as startling colored water ran out on the floor of the pump house.

"Well, you know, you can wash your hands in it, water your flowers," responded a woman who lived nearby.

Living near mines, though never easy, as Trish learned that summer, had become a compromise. Mines, both deep and mountaintop, now gobbled so much buried coal that it was becoming nearly impossible to have life's necessities of clean water and peaceful quiet.

Chapter 8

The Moores' Case

Even before the visit of James Weekley to Joe Lovett—which prompted the launch of *Bragg v. Robertson*—Vicky and Tommy Moore had initiated their own suit. They had hired Robert Shostak from Athens, Ohio, to sue Arch Coal over the nuisance of dust and blasting. Then early in 1998 Pat McGinley and Suzanne Weise had joined the case, and soon they would take the lead. Vicky did not just sit back and wait, though. Every morning in the spring and early summer of 1998, she arose with one thought on her mind: What can I do today to help my case?

Pat and Suzanne came to the coalfields with great compassion for those who were forced to live next to—and on top of—the monstrous mines. In the late 1990s, lawyers would rarely take nuisance cases against the mines. Expensive investigations by experts had to be done just to prove damage from blasting and dust. Even if the case was airtight, judges and juries in the coalfield counties might favor coal companies. But Pat had lived in West Virginia most of his life, and though he made a good living as a law professor at West Virginia University, he never shied away from a chance to help those less fortunate. Since the husband-and-wife team financed their cases on a shoestring budget—and operated without a secretary—Vicky was of great help in gathering records on complaints and fires.

Many lawyers hated depositions. Not Pat. He relished them, loved to lead a witness step by step, pulling out each delicious piece of evidence. The process usually took hours, and perhaps that was a key to Pat's success: the witnesses grew so tired that they finally relinquished the most juicy information—just to get out of the room.

Terrence Irons was the first witness Pat deposed in the Moores' case. Irons was in charge of buying the homes in Blair for the coal company's land-owning affiliate. Pat and Suzanne surmised that no major corporation would go about property acquisition without a profit-and-loss plan.

Still, Pat was amazed at what the man revealed. Irons had first visited Blair in 1992 or 1993, as Ashland Coal was acquiring the Dal-Tex mine in Blair. Because the company expected complaints from those residents—problems with blasting, dust, and flooding—Irons prepared an estimate of the cost of buying the homes.

As several other Ashland representatives would say in later depositions, Irons acknowledged that the blasting did shake windows and bother residents. And Irons said that coal companies knew cloud cover often made blasts feel harder, increasing vibration in houses. "Might rattle," he answered Pat. "Depends on how close to the operation it is and atmospheric conditions . . . whether it is a clear day, an overcast day. It has something to do with the way the air is compressed." This was one of the continuing revelations about why blasting is troublesome.

Oddly, Ashland did not create a plan to help those who lived in these houses close to the future mining. Nor did it warn them or offer protection. The company did not even plan to approach the homeowners and offer them fair market value. No, Ashland waited for each resident to call the coal company when conditions became intolerable.

Ashland's original intention was to keep the houses vacant, after Irons had purchased them from the owners, and resell them when mining was complete. But local arsonists voided that plan. What did Ashland do to protect its property investment? Pat asked. They called the state police twice and the county sheriff once. Did Ashland consider sending the twenty-four-hour mine security guards through the community at night, or using motion detectors to deter arsonists? No, it would not be cost effective.

Irons provided the clue that led Pat and Suzanne to the most damning piece of evidence, a document they would finally see three months later. Pat spent some time asking Irons how Ashland determined which properties it should buy. Irons explained that the Dal-Tex mine had mapped out areas of future mining when Ashland bought it. He identified all homes within three hundred feet of present or future mining. Why? Because no mining is allowed within three hundred feet of a homeowner's property without a variance.

PAT: "Would you get written information that would indicate what the latest version of mining plans were?"

121

IRONS: "The written information that we would get would usually be in the form of maps showing those proposed operations."

PAT: "What other form might they take other than the usual form of maps?"

IRONS: "That's pretty much the way we planned our operation. We would sit down at a table just like this with maps and go over it."

Pat immediately requested all maps on property acquisition.

Thrilled about these revelations, Pat expected to depose more Ashland and Arch representatives in short order. But the companies' lawyers said they needed more time. The law requires both sides to try to mediate a settlement. That took at least a month—with no settlement. Meanwhile, Pat had written the Jackson Kelly firm naming about twenty people to be deposed—at the coal company's convenience. By June, he and Suzanne realized they had been sandbagged. Jackson Kelly attorneys had denied them the usual courtesies of time extensions. Such discourtesy was surprising, coming from the largest corporate law firm in the state, known nationally for its coal expertise and filled with top law students and former federal prosecutors.

Jackson Kelly lawyers had taken advantage of Pat's easygoing nature. Pat realized later that he and Suzanne should have sent notices of depositions, with set dates. Jackson Kelly finally supplied, in a letter dated June 12, a list of witnesses whom Pat had requested and dates for depositions. When Pat and Suzanne got the letter, they panicked, realizing that the court-ordered deadline for requesting documents under discovery was looming on June 17. Shostak and Pat spoke to Jackson Kelly attorneys about extending the deadline, but to no avail.

Discovery is a crucial part of litigation. Lawyers usually ask for every imaginable document, not knowing what might be revealed. Often a "copy to" at the end of a letter can be a key. Pat had hoped depositions would help him refine his request for documents. He and Suzanne were disappointed, but the deposition schedule didn't give them much time for self-pity. With a court-ordered deadline for depositions impending as well, the couple rushed into a swirl of depositions coming so fast that they didn't have time to digest one before starting the next. Because they couldn't afford to fly, Pat and Suzanne even spent the Fourth of July weekend driving to St. Louis for depositions of Arch Coal executives.

Despite Jackson Kelly attorneys' attempt to block documents, Pat still got the big prize—the target acquisition map. It showed all eleven communities around Blair that Arch expected to be eliminated as the mine expanded. All who sold their homes were barred for the rest of their lives from relocating to any of these places circled on the map.

The man hired by Arch to set a value for the Moores' home had had a surprising reaction when Pat asked him about the Option to Purchase agreement. On this form, sellers agreed not to protest against the mine again and to withdraw previous protests. They also agreed not to live in the eleven adjacent communities and hollows.

"I have seen some funky deed provisions at times, but never something in a contract like that," Donald Mueller testified. "I don't think you can take that right away from someone. It's like putting in a deed restriction that if you are black, you can't live in this property or whatever."

The frenzy was worth it. *The company is even worse than I expected,* Pat thought—*and that's saying something*—as he wrapped up a half dozen nonstop inquiries. Actually, the sandbagging made Pat and Suzanne just try harder. And with the depositions back-to-back, company officials didn't have time to compare notes between them.

When Pat deposed Tarah Burdette, the "dust expert" hired by the company, he discovered that she had no training or experience in dust monitoring. Pat learned that Ashland didn't know how to calibrate the monitors or interpret the data. Pat had hired his own expert. When he examined the readouts from Arch's dust monitors, he found they had classified the air as pure as atop the federal Dolly Sods Wilderness Area in West Virginia's highlands. Surely the monitors were malfunctioning.

On July 15 Pat and Suzanne got the chance to drag Jackson Kelly attorneys up to Pittsburgh to depose Pat's dust expert. During a break, Pat wandered over to the lead attorney, Warren Upton. "You know we've got a powerful case," Pat told him. "There's no telling what a jury would do. You might want to see if your company is interested in settling before an expenditure of a significant amount of money to prepare for a trial."

The attorneys weren't ready to agree; the $250,000 proposed during mediation seemed a little high. Still, they told Pat they'd put the offer before Arch officials. Later Pat would wonder if he should have asked for more. But his area was really public-interest and regulatory law. Settling a nuisance case was something new.

Finally the Arch officials agreed, and on Sunday, August 1, Vicky and Tommy were in their modest second-floor apartment at Tommy's grandmother's small farm, considering the settlement offer. They had to make their decision the next day. Wearing a WVOP T-shirt and blue shorts, Vicky sat at the kitchen table amid the comfortable disarray left by two active young boys. Vicky had been with Pat and Suzanne at most of the local depositions. She loved them and Shostak, too. Pat was so tender-hearted, Shostak worked really hard, and Suzanne was so sweet. But were they giving her the right advice?

Not only were Vicky and Tommy up against one of the nation's most powerful coal companies, but they also faced the sometimes real, sometimes perceived, political corruption in Logan County, which could have swayed the court against them. Logan's legacy of vote-buying and control of elections has a storied history, centering around Raymond Chafin, now in his eighties, whose role in "buying" the 1960 primary for John F. Kennedy has been told in books by F. Keith Davis and by Raymond Chafin and Topper Sherwood.

———

In the 1940s and 1950s, Logan County was a well-greased political machine, like Mayor Daley's Chicago. Everything was political before Civil Service; supporting the machine's candidate got a voter a well-paying job in county government. Raymond Chafin's seat of power was Omar, ten miles south of Logan on Route 44, which ended at Horsepen Mountain, above Trish's house. Born in a blizzard in 1917, the eldest of eight children of a miner, the smart and personable Chafin quickly rose in politics and mining. Logan was a rough place, with stills, gambling halls, brothels, and frequent murders. Two events of his late teens set Chafin's course. He got a job in road-building, essential in the mud and dust of the coalfields, and he was paid to work the polls on election day, palming an envelope of dollar bills to voters who supported the slate of correct candidates. So tough were politics then that Louise Chambers, whom Chafin later married, lost her own father, a deputy sheriff, in an election-day scuffle along Rum Creek.

Though "one-hand-washes-the-other" politics sounds corrupt today, at the time Chafin was actually doing whatever he could to help advance the community around Omar and Cow Creek. In fact, Topper Sherwood, a former Associated Press reporter, began his project dubious. "People like me, in the more urban parts of West Virginia, often look down their noses at Logan County, much in the same way that cosmopolitan America often appraises West Virginia itself," he wrote in his preface, concluding, "West Virginia's traditional political culture may have something to teach us, even as it disappears with progress and the passage of time."

In the 1950s, Chafin's proudest accomplishment was road building. "I was able to get many, many county roads put into the system," he told F. Keith Davis. "There's nothing that will make ya feel any better than when you can take an ol' muddy path or abandoned logging road—maybe the only way to several mountain homes—and have it put into the roadway system. Then we could grate, gravel, and start pouring the blacktop to it. That makes people happy—and very thankful, ya know."

A few years later, Chafin switched from road-building to mining; he worked for the A. T. Massey coal company, which had gone into mining in 1949. At this point, when he was head of the county Democratic Committee, he faced a choice between Hubert Humphrey and that handsome young Massachusetts senator John F. Kennedy. Humphrey had promised support for a new courthouse, but Kennedy and his family had captivated Logan. Even Chafin's wife and daughter were smitten. On the business side, Morgan Massey pressured Chafin, sensing a winner in Kennedy.

The deal was brokered by a coal buyer for Massey, Chafin said. When asked how much money he needed, Chafin did the math in his head and asked for thirty-five, thinking $3,500 was a little better than what Humphrey had given. A few days before the election, Chafin and a friend went to the tiny airport near Logan. Rain was pouring down when the pilot jumped out and handed two sealed bags to Chafin and his friend. They returned to Room 220 at the Aracoma Hotel, the seat of the campaign, where they met Elvie Curry. They dumped the bags on the bed and saw—both were filled with bills—$35,000. Chafin called Massey's coal buyer, who told him, "You have a job to do. We know you'll be able to take care of things with those two bags of . . . uh . . . literature, right?" The rest is history.

Chafin said years later that the money wasn't really what made him switch to JFK. When he met with him at the Aracoma Hotel before the election, he genuinely liked the young man—and believed he would help the coalfields. Kennedy led Chafin to the window, two stories above the street. "These are your people," he told Chafin. "If you'll be for me, you'll never regret it. I'll help these people—I can help them greatly." Kennedy didn't take long to make good on the promise, calling Chafin to the White House a few weeks after the election. Logan County was in desperate straits, coal prices plummeting, thousands of miners unable to find work. However, Chafin told Kennedy, people didn't like the commodity food program with its bland flour, cornmeal, and "thick-tastin'" cheese. "I know how relief folk think," Chafin told the president. "I've been there. They want dignity most of all." Food vouchers would be much better, Chafin said. On April 26, 1961, in Welch in McDowell County, an out-of-work miner was the first person in the nation to sign up for Kennedy's food-stamp program.

————

In that summer of 1998, as Vicky contemplated the settlement, Chafin was still a power broker, but he had a more visible younger helpmate. Nearly every morning at 7:00 a.m., the phone in Rick Abraham's house in Chapmanville would ring. "What do you know?" asked Chafin. So the senior and junior political bosses began their day. Chafin had been best friends with Rick's late dad, Bill. Both of Rick Abraham's grandfathers, of Arabic descent, had found their way in the 1930s to the booming coal-fields, where they set up grocery and clothing stores in adjacent buildings. A brick building in Omar still proudly displays "Shaheen 1938," the name of his maternal grandfather's store. In those days, the two grandfathers had competed with coal-company stores—and thrived. They passed their enterprising skill on to their grandson Rick, who had run several coal companies and helped shape grand schemes for economic progress in Logan County.

Although vote-buying had been curtailed in the 1980s after former congressman Ken Hechler was elected secretary of state, federal convictions of five leading Logan politicians in 1971 had already quieted the practice. But Abraham was still a powerful presence, and he tended to grandiose gestures. Just as Raymond Chafin was proud of paving up a hollow, Abraham had expansive plans to bring jobs and new industry to the area. Some coalfield residents praised his altruism; others saw only self-interest. Now Abraham was leading the battle against "those environmentalists," seeing them as an enemy to Logan County.

Because Abraham was organizing miners and bringing them to hearings on mountaintop removal, Pat and Suzanne told the Moores they were concerned about trying a case before a Logan County jury. Citizens had rarely won cases against mines in coalfield courts. In Logan County's small world of politics and business, Tommy had been laid off from a heavy-equipment job at one of Abraham's companies and had just gone back to work for Alvis Porter, one of Abraham's political allies. Porter had already told Tommy they should settle. Vicky was afraid Abraham would find a way to hurt her if they did go to court. Nevertheless, she had her heart set on court.

"I kept thinking I want vengeance on them [the coal companies]," Vicky said. "I think of everything I've been through. Me and Tommy been married 10 years, and we never bought one piece of furniture. We were going to build a house at Blair, and now we're not going to do that."

"The mountaintop removal issue hurt us," Tommy said.

The previous week, Arch had proposed a settlement that barred Vicky and Tommy from protesting any mines within seventy-five miles. Vicky told Pat to tell Arch to go to hell.

That Sunday afternoon, Vicky thought about the case she had imagined: Jurors spellbound as she told them about the dragline, and the blasting, and the fires, and dust so thick it made you choke. At the end, the jury foreman would open the folded verdict and pronounce Ashland/Arch guilty. The money didn't matter—just GUILTY in front of television cameras. Later she commented, "I don't know if I believed in what I saw on TV and then when it didn't happen that way it upset me. I didn't know that only 5 percent went to court."

Pat and Suzanne had more than a hundred conversations with Vicky, weighing the pros and cons of settling. Following their policy of "client-centered" lawyering, they reminded her that if her case went to trial and the jury found against her, the message to the world would be that the coal company had done nothing wrong. Though Pat and Suzanne never urged the Moores to settle, Vicky had begun to feel that she should think about the two boys, who would get ten thousand dollars each under the settlement, to help them move on with their lives.

I don't see this as a victory, she thought. *Did I sell out—or did I not? I will always think what would have happened if I went to court. I would risk everything to walk away with nothing—I couldn't even sell the place. A lot of people are waiting on my case, waiting to see if they should go to court. I think I let a lot of people down.*

Then her mind's seesaw tipped up and she found comfort. *If I live to be 90, I will still remember this time and what I had to do. The only thing I feel good about is that my kids will know what went on . . . that their mother went to Washington because this happened where they lived.*

The next day, Vicky and Tommy agreed to settle. They were able to keep the mobile home, though it had little value. Vicky had to agree not to protest permits—but was not barred, like the others, from living in any of the communities on the target acquisition map. Actually, Pat told her to go ahead and speak out—he would represent her for free if coal companies tried to shut down her First Amendment rights. The amount of money given to Dustin and Levi was supposed to remain secret. The full amount to the Moores was close to what Pat had requested. In November Ken Ward of the *Charleston Gazette* found the case unsealed in the Logan County Courthouse. He reported that Arch had settled for $225,000. Some would go to lawyers' fees and expenses, but Pat and Suzanne kept those to a minimum, even personally paying more than $19,000 for court reporters and expert witnesses.

Despite her immediate despair, no one could stop Vicky from talking. And now she knew about the map and had a copy of the contract people had to sign agreeing not to protest or live in the acquisition area. So when she spoke to supportive citizens or before government officials, she could tell them just how bad things had been in Blair.

Chapter 9

Internal Wrangling

As the summer of 1998 waned, Trish found herself in the unusual position of peacemaker at WVOP. John Humphries had resigned after the legislative session in March. Arley had been sad to see him go, because he had relied on John's quick grasp of issues.

Toward the end of John's tenure, he and Trish had been increasingly at odds. John was an engineer by training and tended to approach organizing with a slide rule, rather than a handkerchief. Trish, who spent hours on the phone with whoever needed help, resented John when he limited her phone calls to him to fifteen minutes in the evening.

By midsummer, young Ashley Cochrane had decided to resign as well. Trish liked her better, even though she had grown up on the Virginia coast, not the coalfields. In fact, the WVOP board was hoping Ashley would stay on when a new coordinator was hired. But Ashley, an earnest young woman fresh out of college, felt tensions among board members and thought WVOP would be better off with new staff.

WVOP had about 120 members in the summer of 1998. Most were from mining families in southern West Virginia. But a few were from outside the coalfields. They wanted to help the coalfield residents, but their good intentions were a source of friction. At the beginning, WVOP had grown out of the idealism of two attorneys from Charleston and Beckley. Paul Sheridan, now an attorney in Charleston, had been young when horrible floods washed along the Tug River and removed much of the Mingo County seat of Williamson. These were the same floods that inspired Jay Rockefeller to call for a ban on strip mining. After helping flood victims, Paul continued in public-interest law. Another founding member was John McFerrin, a public-interest attorney who now worked for the state.

Though John and Paul never spoke publicly for WVOP, they attended annual meetings and were in touch with the staff. Trish had criticized Ashley Cochrane for not doing enough organizing. "That's what an organizing project does: raise money and organize," she told Ashley. "You can call people for five minutes, just to chat." At a rally against mountaintop removal shortly afterward, John McFerrin chastised Trish for telling Ashley what to do. "That's real classicism," Trish said later, feeling like she had been put down.

Within the members from the coalfields, there was a split in interests. WVOP was becoming known for its fight for better-run mines, but a smaller group of members wanted improvement in schools. Community elementary schools had been built in coal camps when coal was booming. As machines took over miners' jobs, the population in Mingo and Logan Counties had dropped 25 percent between 1980 and 2000. Still the communities tried to hang onto the small schools, partly because the twisty roads up and down and around the mountains made for hour-long bus rides to consolidated schools. In the spring of 1998, test scores and administrative bungling were so bad that the state board of education had taken over Mingo County schools.

That move gave WVOP's education group an opening to present concerns to top education officials. Members had "high expectations and hopes to see improvements that will solely concentrate on our children's needs and not on politics as usually has been the case," Phyllis McCoy wrote in WVOP's newsletter. After coal, local government—especially schools—was the biggest employer in the coalfields. These were good jobs, with benefits, and were much sought-after. Political connections helped immensely. WVOP education members also joined Challenge West Virginia, a statewide activist group, trying to stop the rush to consolidate schools. Although all WVOP members wanted better schools, staff members were pressed, trying to answer the needs of both parts of WVOP.

For several months Trish and Vicky were on the phone with other WVOP members, in an attempt to mend hard feelings. They were both on the personnel committee, which met for hours trying to figure out where WVOP should be going. One night some of the committee members turned against Pearl Short, the part-time secretary for WVOP. At the moment, Pearl was the sole support for her family of three children, since her husband was laid off. Trish felt terrible when Pearl was put on the spot. *They don't realize what would happen if she left,* Trish thought. She jumped in and tried to find a solution. Later she told June Rostan, her mentor at SEP, "I'm supposed to be the loud mouth. I was the peacemaker. Maybe I've grown up."

The stress was showing up at home for Trish. Dewey told her she might as well put her bed at the office, she spent so much time there. Fed up, Trish marched into the bedroom and slammed the door. WVOP or her family? How could she choose? She couldn't sacrifice her family for the cause, she realized. Twenty-two years she had been with this man; what could she do without him? And what about college? She was the first one in her family trying for a college degree. Was the struggle worth losing everything she had worked for? *I'm going to have to cut back,* Trish thought.

During the months of reorganization, it seemed as if the only way for members to vent their frustrations at the mines and the schools was to lash out at each other. Again and again they had hit roadblocks when asking the government for improvements. So their anger turned inward, fellow members being easier targets. Their experience was not unusual: community organizations often dissolve into internal bickering. Some disappear; others grow stronger.

Save Our Cumberland Mountains (SOCM) in eastern Tennessee and Kentuckians for the Commonwealth (KFTC), both philosophical older siblings to WVOP, have survived and often prospered for more than two decades. Both held lessons for groups like WVOP facing growing pains amid fierce battles for social justice. SOCM and KFTC were among the groups examined in the 1993 anthology *Fighting Back in Appalachia,* edited by Stephen L. Fisher. The two groups represented the most successful kind of organizing because they dealt with a variety of issues and encouraged members to participate in government.

With its shoulder-squaring acronym, SOCM (pronounced "sock 'em") has waged battles on everything from surface mining to underpaid temporary workers. In the late 1960s, Tennessee coalfield residents worked with Vanderbilt University to bring health care to their poor communities. The students discovered that the owners of mineral-rich lands paid next to no property taxes. Citizen outrage led to SOCM's formation. Soon SOCM jumped into the debate in Congress over surface mining, standing firm with the abolitionists. Their eventual defeat was a devastating blow that might have rendered any other citizen group defunct.

"One of the real differences between SOCM and other organizations is how we look at our work and what it is we are trying to do," Connie White, a past SOCM president told writer Bill Allen in 1991. "We don't just care about winning issues; we care more about helping people get stronger. In the long run, that is how you win issues and make real changes. . . . Back in the old days, we thought that getting a strip mine permit denied or getting a tougher reclamation bill passed in Nashville was why we existed. Now we understand that our real success is measured more by how many members participated in protesting the permit or lobbying their legislator and whether they feel empowered by their participation."

Surface mining also jettisoned Kentuckians for the Commonwealth. Born in 1981, KFTC from the start had leaders who realized they must build a statewide group that could withstand the enemies that had felled many an Appalachian group. Writing in Stephen Fisher's *Fighting Back in Appalachia,* Joe Szakos, longtime KFTC staff coordinator, listed those obstacles, which sounded much like the ones facing WVOP:

> Appalachia's long dependence on coal makes residents fear losing jobs if they speak out.
> The long distance and poor roads between communities prevent residents from linking arms.
> Local government officials are widely regarded as corrupt—so what's the use of trying for better laws.
> Fundamentalist churches value redemption in the afterlife rather than attempts to make the current world a better place.

From the start, KFTC defined itself as a "citizens social justice group," defining its image as that of a fighter for fundamental and long-lasting change. Two decades later, WVOP was still struggling to teach the press that it stood for social justice and wasn't an "environmental" group. Social justice also helped KFTC gain support across the state. Early on it had learned that only grassroots activists from Kentucky—not out-of-state groups—would win it respect in the state legislature. Joe Szakos believes the organization has thrived because it achieved five goals basic to successful social justice groups:

> —Empower people: Instead of only acting on issues, KFTC tries to develop members into leaders in their communities.

—Build the organization: Individuals are important, but groups get things done.

—Win issues: Tackle issues that can be won. Victories build momentum. People don't want to be involved with a group that can't accomplish anything.

—Foster democratic values: Everyone is created equal; everyone deserves to be heard.

—Change societal institutions: Unjust institutions include corrupt political machines and corporations that place profits before people.

WVOP embraced the same five goals. But in the late summer of 1998, Trish and her fellow members were swept up in a battle over mountaintop removal so far-reaching that it pushed aside other matters. Trish watched and worried. The organizing project had been her Pygmalion, bringing her a new life. She wanted new lives for the other residents of the coalfields.

In September Trish and other board members sorted through six resumes. They chose a stranger from nearby Mercer County as coordinator—and an old friend as organizer. Elaine Purkey was coming back. Trish felt hope. *If we get through this growing spell, we'll be one heck of a project, she thought.*

Chapter 10

The Governor's Task Force

Elaine Purkey felt overwhelmed. Although she had been reading newspapers and watching television news, she faced a cram course on lawsuits, blasting legislation, and now something called the Governor's Task Force on Mountaintop Mining and Related Mining Methods.

Governor Underwood had set up the Task Force in May and had chosen J. Wade Gilley, president of Marshall University in Huntington, as chairman. The Task Force split into three committees, one to study environmental impact, one for economic stimulus, and a third on mining's impact on communities. Among the seventeen members were several legislators, coal lobbyists, and former and current EPA, OSM, and DEP officials, but citizens and environmentalists had only one representative—John McFerrin, cofounder of WVOP and president of the West Virginia Highlands Conservancy. Environmentalists like Cindy Rank quickly called the Task Force a whitewash. Trish was more willing to wait and see. And a few years later in hindsight it could be seen that this dismissed group produced remarkably prescient comments and recommendations.

The Task Force soon surprised critics with unexpected sharp criticism of SB 145, the recently approved mitigation bill, at its first meeting in July. That was the bill that had increased from 250 acres to 480 acres the size of watershed a mine could fill without "mitigating" the impacts. Among those calling for repeal were former heads of the state environmental agency David Callaghan, Larry George, and Ben Greene, who now headed the West Virginia Surface Mining and Reclamation Association. Callaghan, who had served under governors Rockefeller and Caperton, pointed out that most valley fills take up less than 480 acres of drainage area. So coal companies would be doing very little mitigation. Federal law allows streams to be filled only if the water loss is compensated—either by building another waterway, or monetarily. Most coal companies paid into a reclamation fund—the fund Arley Johnson had asked to be investigated in the final version of SB 145, passed in that raucous final night of the legislature.

Despite the promising start, two weeks later the Task Force lived up to critics' words. As typical Charleston heat and humidity hovered over the parking lot at Marshall University's proud new Graduate College building, a tour bus disgorged nearly fifty miners from the southern coalfields, making Trish, Vicky, Freda Simpkins, and their friends wonder if there would be violence. Armed state troopers guarded the building entrance. Signs pointed to two places where people should line up to enter the Task Force hearing room: For Mountaintop Removal and Against Mountaintop Removal. Why do we have to choose? Vicky and Trish asked. Then guards told them that Kayla and Dustin couldn't come into the hearing room unless they chose. Vicky told the Task Force she found it offensive that nine-year-old Dustin had to choose whether he was for or against mountaintop removal. Even coal operator Rick Abraham was stumped. "I don't find the issue that simple," he told the *Charleston Gazette*. "Against what? For what? The mitigation bill or mining in general."

The *Charleston Gazette* chose Trish for the front-page photo the next day. Wearing a white V-neck button-front shirt, she read from a prepared statement addressing the three study areas: environment, economics, and communities. West Virginia has a law to protect the waters, she noted, and then she read from the regulation, moving on to the failures of reclamation. Because topsoil isn't replaced, even the Hobet 21 mine has difficulty regrowing hardwoods. When the closing bell sounded, she wasn't willing to be cut off: "If you are going to study this, think about the physical and psychological damage of dragging people from their homes to a place they do not wish to live in," she demanded. "What is that going to do for the Appalachian culture?"

Rick Abraham was one of the last to testify. "I may have the distinction to be the only coal operator here from Logan County," he said. "I didn't plan to respond to who hired the buses. There were approximately 35 people on the bus. I think three are in this room and the rest are downstairs. I did get a call from the press today asking was I bringing a demonstration. I was at Marshall University during the Vietnam War. I didn't demonstrate against that, and I'm not here to demonstrate today."

Abraham made several salient points. "One of the things we're not doing real good at is post-mine land use. Neither me as the coal company nor you control the land, it is the land owner. I would suggest as part of the permit process that we change the law to cause this permit to go to the governor's office of economic development and on a county level to let the permit go through these folks. If they know of any possible economic use, they have the opportunity to condemn the land and purchase it at its pre-mining value when it is steep unusable hillside. When it is somewhat level, value tends to go up and it's tough to get hold of it."

After testifying, Vicky, Trish, Freda, and Rebecca Hunt gathered as late-afternoon rays of sun dribbled across the parking lot. Nearby was the charter bus. Despite the heat, Trish shivered. She knew the battle had begun.

Over the next two months, the three subcommittees did the bulk of the Task Force's work. The economic committee was headed by Larry George, a person Trish had never met; his career uniquely illustrated the complex influence of coal.

As a young attorney, George, like many who first encounter the un-usual separation of mineral-rights ownership and home ownership, had thought he would be the one to bring economic justice to descendants of those people who sold mineral rights to out-of-state corporations in the late 1800s. He took on a case in Lincoln County with so many plaintiffs that an auditorium was required for the eight hundred people who showed up. When they claimed that their ancestors never agreed to sell the mineral rights, George had the court retrieve court records from the sale a century earlier. But no proof was found, and he lost the case.

What George got out of the case was a thorough education in why most longtime residents lost their mineral rights. Now he was an attorney for owners of mineral rights. It was not land corporations that he served; rather, he represented wealthy family trusts. Such entities own nearly as many mineral rights as the land corporations. As an attorney, he also dis-covered dangerous gaps in mining procedures. Once a land company leased the same seam of coal to both a deep mine belonging to a client of his and a surface mine. The surface mine sent shock waves through the deep mine every morning when it blasted. Another client's deep mine filled up with water because the land company had neglected to warn it about an adjacent old mine filled with water.

Before going into private practice, George had served briefly, but sen-sationally, as head of the state environmental agency under Democratic

Some members of the Gibson family. On the right is Larry Gibson, who has battled to protect his family cemetery and home place atop Kayford Mountain in Kanawha County.

governor Gaston Caperton in 1990 and 1991. George had taken the job with what he later called an erroneous assumption that he would enforce the rules. When he wanted to shut down a mine in Wyoming County that had failed to carry out nearly $4 million in reclamation, he was fired.

So it was not surprising that George's economic committee recommendations were predominantly about DEP and mining regulations. The committee report stated: "A zealous commitment must be made to post-mining land uses, which provide economic and social benefits to the citizens of the coalfields. Regulatory agencies, landowners, coal producers and economic development agencies must establish a new partnership to achieve these goals which require unprecedented cooperation and regulatory innovation."

As for specifics, the report wanted fish and wildlife habitat outlawed as a post-mining land use, since it was never authorized by law. Instead, as SMCRA required, commercial forests should be restored on land mined by mountaintop removal, and public recreation should be allowed on the land.

The chairman of the committee on the impact on the people also proved a surprise to those who considered the entire Task Force a white-wash of the coal industry. State senator Lloyd Jackson had been born to privilege in Lincoln County but earned his way in business and politics with Phi Beta Kappa at West Virginia University, followed by a law degree there. His days were busy, with law, service as chairman of the Senate Education Committee, and the family business of natural gas.

Elaine Purkey was never one to offer trust easily, especially not to strangers in power. But now, as she spoke to Jackson on the phone, he was saying, "You choose the place. We'll show up." Jackson's open-ended approach to the tour of the coalfields brought immediate rapport between the miner's wife and the businesslike senator, who looked as if he belonged more in the nation's capitol than in Lincoln County. As Elaine grew to know him better over the next couple of years, she would marvel at his haberdashery—the neatly pressed navy suits, the crisp white shirts, and those silver cufflinks. "Did you see, they are watches?" she exclaimed to a friend.

On October 22, the committee went on the tour set up by Elaine. She took them to Scarlet Hollow, a little south of Logan. It was a community Elaine had worked with during her previous time as a WVOP staff member. Now only a bleak skeleton remained. After numerous complaints about blasting, the coal company had bought out some of the residents. Those who wanted to stay had to live among empty shells of houses. Compared to numerous other tours of coalfield communities over the several years of intense public sentiment, this one was short and to the point—features much appreciated by the committee members who motored back to Charleston to put together their report.

Bill Raney had come along, ever present to monitor coal's interest. After seeing Scarlet Hollow, he said to a companion on the bus: "We've got to stop shaking the neighbors."

It appeared that Jackson's committee agreed. "The effects of blasting sometimes are very detrimental to the lives of those living near mining operations," stated the report. "The noise, vibration, dust and air shock not only damage property but sometimes significantly impair the quality of life of those impacted. Second, the elimination of a community through the process of property acquisitions serves to diminish the value of property and the quality of life for those who remain during and after the mining operations."

To ease the mining blues, the committee made three proposals. First, a separate office should be established within DEP to deal with the impact on individuals and communities. Second, another office at DEP would handle blasting complaints and develop better ways to blast. Interestingly, the committee recommended that blasting would be assumed at fault if the quality and quantity of a person's well water diminished. And third, the permitting process should be expanded to assess the potential impact on individuals and the community, including the extent of property acquisitions and the future of the community when mining finishes.

"History teaches us that some communities exist only because of mining," the report continued. "Long before mountaintop removal mining ever was conducted, the hills of West Virginia sheltered many communities which simply vanished when mining stopped. It would be less than fair to the community and its residents if the community impact process did not bring about an honest discussion of the future of a community when coal mining ceases."

While alleviating impacts, coal companies should also improve lives and communities in the coalfields. "To whom much is given, much will be required," the committee recalled. "If the coal industry, and those benefiting from the extraction of mineral resources are allowed the short-term privilege of exploiting our state's wealth through mining practices . . . then with that privilege must come the responsibility of helping address the long-term needs of the people impacted by the activity."

The committee proposed ways to ensure a new future. For example, land companies and coal companies should work together to identify land near multilane highways and commercial districts—and then donate that land to land trusts as compensation for the negative impact of the removal of mountains and filling of valleys.

At the conclusion of the eighteen pages of well-considered recommendations, the committee acknowledged that it had sought to balance interests of seven groups, including the coal industry, employees, citizens of the state who wanted to limit the removal of mountains, residents of the committees, and environmentalists: "The balancing of these and other interests resulted in the committee recommendations. They are sure to be controversial, but in the face of so controversial a topic as mountaintop removal mining, nothing less should be expected.

"One other principle guided our deliberations," said the committee at the very end of its report: "Whatsoever you would have others do unto you, do likewise unto them." Jackson had tried to call Elaine before this meeting to announce his task force recommendations—to be sure she was okay with the findings. But WVOP's phone had been disconnected; the office had relocated.

Trish was pleasantly surprised, as was Dan Radmacher, editorial-page editor of the *Charleston Gazette*. "I would say the Gazette and other critics owe the task force an apology for assuming it would be a tool of the coal industry," Radmacher wrote on November 13, 1998.

Trish had initially dismissed Jackson as a "Bill Clinton clone." She still wasn't convinced that any changes would come; but, more hopeful, she told the *Daily Mail* that she was surprised at how much time and thought went into the committee's work. "These are recommendations," she told the newspaper. "We're still holding out to see what the outcome is. There is still mining going on when they're deciding what to do."

Trish's instincts would prove all too true—but not because of committee allegiances.

Chapter 11

Settling for Less or More

"This is the last hearing I'm going to," Joe Lovett commented as the car sped down Corridor G to Logan on October 24, 1998. Joe was headed for the EPA hearing on mountaintop removal to be held at Southern West Virginia Community College.

He was prepared for the worst, knowing that Arch and Massey had both put notices requesting attendance in miners' paycheck envelopes. Arch had written that water quality was improved and claimed that the environmental extremists had no scientific proof otherwise. W. Michael McCabe, the EPA regional director who had been so enraged by SB 145's valley-fill expansion and had held the summit at the White House in July, had actually told Joe to request the hearing to slow down the court proceedings on the *Bragg* case and provide breathing room to attempt to negotiate a settlement. It was the first the EPA had held in the coalfields since the one seventeen years earlier that dealt with the mine near Cindy Rank's home in the central part of the state.

The past few months since filing the *Bragg v. Robertson* case had been a whirlwind. In the first weeks of September—just a year after James Weekley had walked into his office—Joe was spending sixteen hours a day in that room. He had never been so busy in his life. In a self-deprecating way, he would say he really was a lazy person, preferring to lie around and read novels. Now he felt responsible for all the people and mountains and streams of the coalfields. This do-gooder life was not for him. He couldn't sleep, and he worried all the time. He wished he could be more like Jim Hecker. "Do you ever get depressed?" Joe asked Jim. "No," Jim replied. Perhaps, Joe thought, he'd feel like that too after two decades as lawyer.

As the *Bragg* case files began to fill with briefs from both sides, Joe was being pressured by the officials from the EPA and the Justice Department. They wanted him to settle their portion of the case, the Section 404 part.

It was not because Joe had a weak case; rather, it was too good. The feds knew he could win the Section 404 argument: the Clean Water Act allowed filling streams only if the resulting dry land was used for development. Valley fills were not considered development. EPA officials warned Joe that if he won, the rules would quickly be rewritten, allowing valley fills under Section 404. Victory soon would become complete defeat.

Why not take a compromise, federal officials told him. It would only settle the case against the federal agencies—allowing Joe to continue with the case against DEP. For much of September and October Joe debated with himself. *Was it realistic to think he could stop multiseam mining that took off the tops of mountains, or would better control be the best anyone could wish for?*

In his heart, Joe wanted to make mountaintop removal cease forever. He knew his case was strong, but he worried about the strength of the army of lawyers and lobbyists on the other side. Coal-industry representatives had even gone to the Justice Department in Washington, D.C., to proclaim that mountaintop removal was an essential part of the nation's energy supply.

Yet, momentum was on his side. Amazed, he and Jim had just won a minor motion in front of Judge Haden. Ken Ward had already done several exposés on mountaintop removal, including one that uncovered how DEP had somehow forgotten that the Approximate Original Contour rule did not permit lowering a mountain more than fifty feet. *And,* Joe thought, *couldn't the rest of the nation be more like him and do a better job at saving energy: turn off lights, turn down the air conditioner?* Then his darker side would win out. After winning that first motion, he said to Cindy Rank, "We won the battle; we'll lose the war."

So he decided to put the compromise before Trish and the other plaintiffs. That was why he was on Corridor G that October morning, dreading what he would find in Logan. This would be a public hearing on Arch Coal's Spruce Fork mine behind James Weekley's house and on the Massey mine planned behind the Madison home of attorney Burr Hatfield, a plaintiff in Joe's case and a prominent lawyer in Madison, the seat of Boone County.

He started seeing pro-coal signs as he drove down the street leading to the college. The parking lot had been divided into two factions. In the corner down by the street, a huge television screen and speakers and a Winnebago anchored the pro-coal side. A Logan County Coal Vendors Association sign covered one front window, with a table of coal-company material and free food out front. A young boy and girl carried bright pink and green placards pronouncing: "I Love Coal." Later the West Virginia University football game would beam from the huge screen.

Environmentalists had claimed the tiered bank on one side of the college entrance. There artist Carol Jackson unveiled her traveling stream graveyard. Names of streams and nearby locations already buried under valley fills were written in black on several dozen white cardboard stones. Blair Mountain was memorialized, as was the tomb of two hundred unnamed streams.

By the time the hearing began, the auditorium was filled with more than one hundred people who had signed up to speak, the majority coal supporters. For many of the miners, this was their first appearance in the spotlight. Among the environmentalists and citizens, the event was old hat. Most had been to at least one hearing of the various study groups in the past year. Trish, Elaine, Vicky, and Cindy Rank were all there.

Michael McCabe hobbled onstage, supported by hand crutches, the legacy of multiple sclerosis. Slim and in his late forties, he sat down and quickly made it clear that EPA would not stop mountaintop removal. "If that is what you are hoping for, you will be disappointed," he said. "We are, however, determined to ensure it is done in the most environmentally responsible manner. EPA's job is to follow the law and balance environmental protection with economic growth.

"The problem is that the gargantuan size of these mountaintop mines has grown at such a fast pace that we don't have enough scientific data to determine the local or cumulative environmental impact. The mountaintop mining of 10 years ago dealt mostly with valley fills several hundred yards long and a few hundred acres. Today's permits encompass thousands of acres of land and the valley fills several miles long.

"We've seen this type of mining grow bigger and bigger," McCabe began. The Hobet permit [Blair/Spruce Fork] is the largest ever in West Virginia history. It is five square miles and would include four valley fills a mile long. But Hobet is not alone, he explained. In 1994 less than one thousand acres were permitted for mountaintop mining; three years later, in 1997, twelve thousand acres were permitted. "These are matters that will leave their mark on West Virginia for as far into the future as we can imagine." What kind of mark, no one seemed to know, McCabe stressed. "We need a more complete understanding of what the ultimate legacy of these mines will be before we launch into another round of mega mine permitting."

Trish was dizzy when she walked up the stage steps. So much pressure those last few months—from miners, from internal WVOP problems, from neighbors with problems caused by blasting and water loss, even from Dewey. Her health was failing. But she willed herself forward to the microphone. "I came here expecting a lot of things," she said, pointing at the audience with her left index finger as an exclamation point. "But I didn't expect to see miners against their own people and private citizens against miners." Her voice grew louder and angrier as she felt stronger. "This is not about whether miners are right or private citizens are right. This is about whether it is okay to destroy our water and our private property."

Finished, she walked unsteadily to the edge of the stage. Hoping she didn't stumble, she finally made it back to her seat. *How was she going to keep up with everything—school, the case, her family?*

Outside the entrance door, two miners who worked with Bob Schultz at the Dal-Tex mine wondered about their future, too. They weren't paid to be there; they were there because they could lose their jobs.

———

Gretchen, Joe's wife, was fixing dinner at a quarter of six a week before Christmas. Ben, an active two-year-old, dashed underfoot. "Stop," Joe yelled harshly.

"If you're going to do that, don't bother coming home for dinner," snapped the normally kindly young woman. Joe reached down and hugged the sandy-haired little boy who looked so much like him. Then he helped the little fingers light the Menorah. "Toss the salad, Joe," Gretchen asked.

"Don't have time," Joe said as he rushed toward the door, all nervous energy.

Everything was going wrong. Once he met Cindy Rank, at least five minutes late, he couldn't find Pat and Suzanne. Turned out they had confused the meeting place. So the group was twenty-five minutes late leaving for Madison. Tonight they would present the settlement terms for the Section 404 portion of *Bragg v. Robertson* to their plaintiffs.

They had gone to Washington, D.C., twice in the past month to hammer out the terms. Four agencies had drawn up the proposal. The Corps of Engineers and OSM didn't seem to care much, but EPA and Fish and Wildlife kept pushing. Agency representatives and Justice attorneys met with Joe, Pat, Cindy, Suzanne, and Jim Hecker in a small, windowless conference room at the Justice Department building. Joe rocked in his chair and glowered. Pat was effusive, while Jim remained calmly silent, only occasionally interjecting a salient comment. Cindy had found it strange to be asked to show a photo ID upon entrance (9/11 hadn't happened yet). *How are the people in this building going to understand the people in the hollows,* she wondered. *How can we translate between these worlds—unless you have an all-out revolution of a million people?*

After the second meeting, Cindy was visibly shaken, and they gathered at the Au Bon Pain across the street from the Justice Department. She hadn't wanted to give up the case over Section 404. But the others thought they had to. What they were offered sounded pretty good: a thorough examination of the environmental and social consequences of mountaintop removal in what is called an Environmental Impact Statement, or EIS, as it quickly became known. The plaintiffs would choose several experts to do the study, paid for by the federal government. They had a real champion on their side—Mike McCabe. There were two more years of the Clinton administration—with Al Gore expected to win easily and carry on the Democratic, pro-environment administration.

The most important part of the settlement was known only to the lawyers and top Clinton officials. The administration had assured Joe that a settlement would result in a two-year moratorium on issuing permits for mountaintop removal, but for political reasons it had asked Joe to keep mum. During that time, the buffer-zone rule would be reworked so that it clearly applied to mountaintop removal and limited valley fills to the small ephemeral streams at the top of hollows, where water ran only after rain and snow.

But how would the clients feel? Joe had already spoken with most of them. Trish had quickly accepted his advice. About James Weekley, he wasn't so sure.

As they neared Madison, the nearly mile-long coal tipple of Arch Coal's Hobet 21 operation sat close to the road, lit up against the night sky. "A coal amusement park," Pat mused.

When they got to Burr Hatfield's law office, they couldn't find their clients. Eventually, they saw them in the parking lot, and everyone came inside. The interior of the stalwart brick building looked more like something out of *Architectural Digest* than a law office in the coalfields: wide moldings, Colonial shades of paint, wing chairs, plush carpet, a brass chandelier.

Most of the plaintiffs were there, gathered in the conference room. Jim Hecker called in from Washington, D.C., on the speaker phone. Trish had brought Kayla. James Weekley leaned back in his chair with his hand on his chin. Carlos Gore, who lived up a hollow at the opposite end of Blair from Vicky, was the most talkative of the plaintiffs.

Joe wanted to take the plaintiffs through the steps that had brought them to the settlement proposal. The complaint filed in the case had thirteen separate legal claims, ten against DEP and three against the Army Corps of Engineers and EPA. Besides Section 404, claims centered on violation of the buffer zone within one hundred feet of a stream, the failure to use mountaintop mines for industrial development, and tardy reclamation of the mined areas. What had caused the urgency for settlement was Arch's threat to lay off miners if it couldn't proceed with expanding the Blair mine behind Weekley's home.

"I don't think we should give the state of West Virginia our hollow," Weekley said.

"None of us want to," Joe replied.

"We are history," Gore said.

"I don't think Pigeonroost is history," Joe tried to assure him.

"I mean us," Gore said, referring to what remained of the people in Blair.

Shrugging off what he feared might be true, Joe explained the Environmental Impact Statement that would be a part of settlement. Pat joined in, trying to put the regulatory concept in terms that the plaintiffs could relate to. "The good thing about the EIS statement," Pat said, "Is that we can develop very specific information that people in communities can use to fight this later on. They have to look at the impacts of valley fills, if they have impact on communities like Blair."

Joe was encouraged by the three experts for their side: John Morgan, a British-born mining engineer who lived in Kentucky, was well-respected, but he hadn't sold out to coal. Besides, his accent made him sound so authoritative. J. Bruce Wallace, a professor at the University of Georgia, was one of the country's preeminent stream scientists. Steven Handel was a professor of plant ecology at Rutgers University. The EIS also had a mandatory completion date of December 2000, before the next president took office.

"We negotiated a lot of citizen participation," Joe said. "They will send us documents once a month or so."

"Do you have a volunteer to read them?" Trish asked.

Joe pointed at Cindy.

There was another victory. Joe told them that every valley fill over 250 acres would get intensive individual review by the Army Corps of Engineers. Of the thirty-nine pending valley fills, thirty were large enough for the review—another way to slow down the steady creep of mountaintop removal, Joe told them. Joe also believed that this deal would allow him to stop the Spruce mine because its valley fills great exceeded the 250-acre threshold. Then he explained how the case would proceed against DEP— that part of the case was not up for settlement.

Pat had big plans. "It will give us time to get out information about DEP," he said. "Ken Ward can do articles and expose stuff. We can concentrate on who should have been regulating this in the first place." It was time to seize a moment that might never come again. "I have been suing coal companies for 30 years," Pat explained. "The whole climate has changed in the last year. There never has been this kind of public attention on the impact of this kind of mining on communities and the environment in a hundred years. Look in the *Charleston Gazette*. There are letters every day. We never had anyone like Joe and Jim to help. We never had the money to litigate. I have never seen a situation where there was more opportunity to take a sledge hammer to King Coal and whack him on the head."

Nonetheless, the momentum could hit a wall. Pat told a story about lawyer friends that helped the group understand the real danger of too big a win. His friends had won a case in the Pacific Northwest, halting logging of a virgin forest in order to protect the spotted owl. Quickly, Congress had passed riders to appropriations bills barring citizens from suing to stop timbering in ancient forests. "There's a very good chance that could happen here," he said. "Congress would sneak changes into the law."

The discussion turned to the mine at Blair.

"What they are saying," Joe explained, "Is this is our deal with the devil. If we want to get this long-term policy, they want us to allow a slightly smaller permit in Blair. But we still have a lot of ammunition to use against the state and federal government to stop it—but that's very difficult to do."

Cindy unrolled the map of the southern coalfields showing surface mining. She showed Weekley that the valley fill would probably be farther from his house than originally planned.

"They aren't giving up on your case," Trish told Weekley, who was becoming agitated.

"I'm not giving up, period," Weekley said.

"Unfortunately, you are sitting in front of the most valuable coal around," Joe said. "And you've got the biggest company against you."

Weekley shot out of his chair and headed toward the door. "Go to hell, this mine is a no."

"Please stay, we've put a lot of work into this," Joe yelled, turning and rushing out the door.

"That's nothing to him," Gore said, "only pushing it back a mile."

"We are not explaining all these options fully to Mr. Weekley," Trish said. "We need to have these steps written out where this man can see them." She thought a minute. "We've got to let him crash—emotionally. I crashed when Joe told me on the phone. He's going to feel that way."

Joe came back in the room with Weekley.

Trish wanted to turn the conversation back to the question at hand. "What we have to decide tonight is are we going to go ahead and try. We have to be willing to trust our lawyers."

Gore looked at Weekley, "We go with you. Tell Joe yea or nay."

"Yes," Weekley said.

The whole evening, Trish had kept her feelings bottled up. When she got to the parking lot, she began to sob. Kayla put her arms around her mother and asked, "Why can't we win for Mr. Weekley?"

———

The calls started a couple of days later. Two from Philadelphia, one from North Carolina. They had heard Weekley had walked out of the meeting, that he was upset with the settlement. "You still have a good case," one lawyer told Trish, urging her not to settle. *Who were these lawyers? Why were they calling?* Trish wondered. Dewey was upset. He didn't want her to go to the press conference in Charleston on Wednesday, when they would announce the settlement. In the end, as Trish would put it, God, not Dewey, kept her away.

The press conference was scheduled for 2:00 p.m. Wednesday, December 23. But Joe's morning had been anything but smooth. He was on the phone with James and Sibby Weekley for a long time. She wasn't going to agree, wasn't going to come to the press conference. Neither was James. "I know it's difficult for you," he said to Sibby. "I wish you could have come to the meeting. I hope you put in your mind that the settlement will help and I will fight like the devil against your permit. . . . No, the judge won't talk to Arch."

"No, James," Joe said. "I don't know who told that you walked out. I thought everyone would keep the meeting secret. . . . The whole reason for the press conference is to say we will keep fighting your mine. Please come."

Joe hung up, praying that he'd adverted disaster.

He had an idea who was behind those calls from lawyers to the plaintiffs: Harvard Ayers of Appalachian Voices, an organization that brings people together to solve environmental problems in the southern and central Appalachians. Ayers had discovered mountaintop-removal mining in the early 1990s as he worked on *An Appalachian Tragedy*, a coffee-table book about air pollution. Perhaps having come to the issue before Joe did made Ayers feel possessive of the outcome. Neither Joe, nor Jim, nor Pat was pleased with the interference.

The press conference was in the conference room at Secretary of State Ken Hechler's office. Hechler affectionately called it the People's Room for all the activist groups that met there. When Joe arrived, Shireen Parsons, of Appalachian Voices, was already in the room talking with plaintiffs and their friends. Ken Hechler gathered up Joe, Shireen, and a few other key players and shepherded them to the cafeteria in the basement. There, Joe and Cindy tried to explain the settlement.

"You know toothless, environmental impact statements don't stop the rape of the earth," countered Parsons, a wiry woman.

"If this buys us two years without mountaintop removal, it's two years we didn't have before," Cindy said, inadvertently referring to Joe's unwritten agreement with the Clinton administration.

"What do you suggest we do?" Joe asked. "We have the same goals. Nobody's making money, no one's doing it for glory." If he had been able to tell them about the two-year moratorium and explain that fills would be forever shorter, perhaps the acrimonious exchanges would have vanished.

"Demand what you want," Parsons countered. "Demand: Build that pond back 200 feet. In the meantime, we owe it to these people that they understand."

"I won't do anything against the people," Joe said.

"Jimmy feels like he was coerced," Parsons said. It was a belief she would maintain throughout the case.

After a few more minutes, truce seemed to be reached. Everyone headed back up to the Peoples Room. James and Sibby Weekley walked in a few minutes later—and were quickly surrounded. Sibby was crying. Parsons hugged them, then held James's hand as she murmured, "You'll be all right."

Joe wanted to talk with the Weekleys. They left what was now a large gathering in the People's Room. There were members of the Ohio Valley Environmental Coalition and members of West Virginia Citizen Action. Larry Gibson, the diminutive man who starred in the documentary the citizens had attempted to show at OSM in January, held a sign:

Save Our Homes
Save Our Jobs
Stop Mountaintop Removal.

Reporters from the two Charleston newspapers, Channel 8, and West Virginia Public Radio were awaiting the 2:00 p.m. press conference. Around 2:30, the Public Radio reporter asked, "Not sure what the story is. You almost have a settlement?" Soon the press left, and Joe, who had been waiting outside the door, came back in with the Weekleys.

"Look at Sibby, look at Jimmy, do they look happy?" Parsons asked. "Jimmy is agreeing to this because he has been pressured."

"A lot of people who weren't privileged to all the information," Larry Gibson said, "want to know what this will do to help Jimmy and his people."

Trying to be conciliatory, Joe said perhaps he hadn't explained all the details clearly. The experts he had chosen would show how much mountaintop removal damages streams and forests and wildlife. Extensive citizen participation was guaranteed. Valley fills would, in effect, be limited to 250 acres; they would be much smaller than those proposed for the Spruce mine.

Janet Keating, one of the leaders of OVEC, explained that lawsuits can be excellent ways to stall permits and change public opinion. OVEC's lawsuit over plans for a huge pulp mill actually stopped the mill.

Parsons wasn't satisfied. "The EIS is a red herring. What we want is a moratorium on mountaintop removal until it is studied. We are organizing people of the state to oppose mountaintop removal. We can't organize on capitulation."

Frank Young, president of the West Virginia Highlands Conservancy, interjected the reality of fighting coal in the state. He was a person who, like Pat McGinley and Cindy Rank, had long memories. "Ma'am, I think that is unfair of you. Some of us have been involved in this for years."

Finally, Weekley spoke. He had been sitting next to Sibby, holding her hand. "This is what the coal company is wanting—us to start arguing among ourselves. I'm here to stop mountaintop removal. I was under a lot of pressure this morning. It will take people to stop this. I am speaking to you out of my heart and to the best of my knowledge. I don't want to give up my hollow. I don't want to give my community up. But let's consider what we might want to do for others. Let's go forward and try. Joe's still going to fight. Let's not let this one permit stop us."

Joe had to hurry to get the settlement to the courthouse. "Get me out of here before they change their minds," he said as he pulled on his overcoat and speed walked down the capitol steps. In the car, he called the Justice Department attorney. "Yes, we have an agreement—unless we crash on the way to the courthouse and James changes his mind while I'm in the hospital."

An ice storm had already descended on the coalfields, catching Trish and Kayla unaware as they tried to get to Charleston. When a woman pulled in front of her, Trish hit the brakes and the brake line on her ancient car broke. Kayla turned white and threw up in Trish's lap. God didn't want her in Charleston, Trish decided.

If she'd been there, she thought, after Joe told her what had happened, she would have told them all to get out. They didn't belong there. Trish worried about the split between the environmentalists and WVOP. She understood what the miners meant when they hollered "outside environmentalists." She resented it when the miners said it like a dirty word. She didn't think environmentalists were all fanatics; they were often caring people who wanted the best for the land. But she was willing to tolerate some damage because mines were such a big part of life.

Trish thought about what had happened at the capitol. Joe, he'd done a great job to hold his temper. She'd say an extra prayer for him that night.

Chapter 12

Before the Judge

M aybe it was the prayer that Trish said. Joe awoke at four o'clock one morning not long after the settlement turmoil and realized they hadn't given up everything when they settled Section 404. They still had the buffer-zone argument, as well as Approximate Original Contour (AOC) and several other claims. They would attack DEP on those. It was the agency's responsibility to prevent disturbance within one hundred feet of all but the tiniest "ephemeral" streams.

Joe spent January 1999 in a swirl of motions and discussions with Jim Hecker and Pat and Suzanne. Outside Joe's office, turmoil escalated. The legislative session had begun. Elaine, and sometimes Trish and Vicky, had to focus on their blasting bill. Shireen Parsons and Harvard Ayers were still helping Weekley, and he held a rally at the school near Blair in mid-January. The miners at the Dal-Tex mine were getting agitated. They had received notices of layoffs. Bob Schultz's sister, Debbie Thompson, picketed Weekley's rally with a sign: "I'm For! Mountain Removal."

Judge Haden had called all the lawyers on the *Bragg* case to a status conference during the second week of January. Jim Hecker and Joe had felt overwhelmed in the room filled with two dozen coal executives; lawyers for DEP and the Justice Department; and lawyers from Jackson Kelly and other firms representing Arch Coal, the UMWA, the Coal Association, and landowners who had joined the case. Joe watched and worried that Haden was against him. He could see it in his eyes. *Haden has never made a good environmental ruling,* Joe thought as the hearing ended. *His father and brother were in the coal business.*

Joe and Jim did have a plan. As soon as the Spruce Fork permit for the mine near Weekley's house was granted, they were going to ask Haden for a temporary restraining order that would halt work on the Spruce mine

Debbie Thompson pickets James Weekley anti-mountaintop-removal rally in January 1999.

until the judge could hear arguments for a preliminary injunction, the next step, which would, if the injunction was granted, stop mining for several months while attorneys on both sides presented arguments and the judge ruled. They spent the last weekend in January preparing for the TRO hearing. Not knowing exactly what to expect, they tossed around legal concepts and juggled ever-changing developments as the permit neared approval. Joe, wearing his usual blue shirt and greenish khakis, leaned back in his chair, feet on the desk, as he talked on the phone with an OSM official "Four hundred and fifty trees an acre!" he exclaimed. Jim grabbed the calculator. "That's 1,350,000 trees they have to plant on the 3,100-acre permit." "Ultimately," Jim said, "we can't stop mining until we get the preliminary injunction issued." They knew that in order to obtain a preliminary injunction, they'd have to prove to Haden that there was imminent harm and no hardship for the other side.

As their days of deliberation stretched to include nights, a blown-up poster of a well-known photo hovered on the wall. In the 1960s, Widow Combs had been carried away by police when she refused to move for bulldozers taking her home for a strip mine in Kentucky. Joe was equally resolute.

––––––

The clock on the wall of Judge Haden's courtroom stood at 3:55 p.m. on February 3, 1999, as a full house of lawyers and spectators awaited the judge. The Spruce Fork mine permit had been approved, and they were here for the TRO hearing.

At the plaintiffs table on the right side, Joe rocked in his chair as Jim read legal briefs. Joe wore the light gray suit that normally hung on the back of his office door. Pat greeted well-wishers. Suzanne had been unable to attend since her grandmother had died. Pat's mother, Patricia McGinley, who had received her law degree in her sixties, watched from the gallery. Later Pat's son, Sean, and daughter, Molly, also lawyers, would join her.

The trio was dwarfed by the army of opposition. Three tables were required on the left side of the room for the thirteen lawyers. Closest to Joe were the Justice Department and DEP attorneys. Roger Wolfe of Jackson Kelly claimed the next table. To one side was a table for other Jackson Kelly attorneys and those representing the land companies.

Arch Coal officials and coal lobbyists Bill Raney, Chris Hamilton, and Ben Greene sat on the left side. Several OSM and EPA officials sat toward the middle, including Dan Sweeney, who had revealed the Section 404 issue to Joe. On the right were Cindy Rank, Jimmy and Sibby Weekley, and more than a dozen members of OVEC. Two of the environmentalists wore hooded sweatshirts proclaiming, "Save Our Mountains. Help Stop Mountaintop Removal."

Trish couldn't come. She had college. And she had been sick again; terrible stomach pains had sent her to the hospital early in January, with a bill for five hundred dollars she couldn't afford to pay.

Judge Haden's courtroom had carpeting the color of spring grass. An avid bird-watcher, he loved the outdoors. While each judge had chosen the decor of his or her own courtroom, Haden, an art lover, had shaped the design of the $80-million building. Tall stained-glass windows by West Virginia artisans radiated orange, black, and grey in a quilt pattern over the public gathering area on the fifth floor. Haden had wanted the building to be used as a gathering place for local groups. A person with the many facets of a Renaissance man, Haden had now met an issue as complex as he was.

The Judge appeared at 4:10 p.m., coffee mug in hand. With his white hair, clipped white beard, and eyes that could twinkle a bit behind wire-rimmed glasses, he could have been Kris Kringle's double. Immediately, he jump-started the case. "I now have the opportunity between now and Friday morning at 11 o'clock to hear the preliminary injunction," Haden told the lawyers.

Flustered, Joe quickly conferred with Jim and sought to clarify: "May it please the Court, Your Honor, we are just seeking here a TRO and not a preliminary injunction."

Haden peered at Joe: "And I am told there is a great deal of immediacy, so as far as I am concerned when I have to approach it, I would rather approach it when I can hear the evidence, work my way through it, and make the appropriate ruling. So if I would grant you a TRO today, I might put you to your proof as early as tomorrow and certainly by some time early next week and, again, we all have time constraints.

"Okay, Mr. Wolfe?"

"If I may, Roger Wolfe on behalf of the intervenors. We, too, came prepared today to address issues related to a TRO application. But I should say that we are anxious to have the issues determined as quickly as possible and so if you do have available dates this week or early next week for a preliminary injunction hearing, the sooner the better as far as we are concerned."

"Okay," Haden replied. "9 o'clock or 9:30, tomorrow morning?"

"Whenever you like," Joe replied.

"Well 9 o'clock, as long you can have your witness here," Haden decided.

"Your Honor," Wolfe said. "I can represent there will be no mining activity occurring pursuant to these permits before tomorrow morning."

"Well," Haden responded dryly, "I would feel more comfortable if you would say 'before this matter is resolved by preliminary injunction.'"

Haden's next comments made it clear that the temporary restraining order and the preliminary injunction could have sweeping ramifications for all surface mining. Haden seemed to have already concluded that this case affected more than the one Arch permit in Blair. Suddenly, the swirling muddle of the past two months calmed to crystal clear. Despite the settlement, Joe could attempt to stop mountaintop removal.

"When we talk about the preliminary injunction request being heard beginning tomorrow," Wolfe asked, "are we talking about the injunction request as it relates to the whole industry practice sake or are we talking about this Spruce Fork permit?"

"I would say probably either one or both but I'll leave that to the parties to fashion the relief they want to ask for," Haden responded.

Joe squared himself at the podium and began. It was now 4:30 p.m. He explained that he would address three of the issues: irreparable harm, the buffer zone, and the relationship between Approximate Original Contour and valley fills. Hecker would address two issues involving the Army Corps of Engineers. The rest of their argument would rely on written material filed with the court.

"No," Haden lectured his former clerk; "I don't mean to be facetious about this at all, but all of you want a reasoned decision from this Court and you do have to recognize that you filed an immense amount of written material with the Court in a short period of time and so to say that one relies upon his brief is not really giving a fair opportunity to the Court to address the matters that are of immediate concern."

Chagrined, Joe began again, holding on to the edge of the podium to steady his nerves. Eloquently, he described the imminent danger to the streams and mountains in Blair. "If the TRO does not issue, Hobet [the Arch subsidiary overseeing the Blair mine] will immediately begin destroying a five-square-mile forest, filling some of the highest quality streams in the region and blasting the mountains into oblivion. The damage to the valleys in preparation for a valley fill is irreparable. First trees will be pushed over by the bulldozers so trees and their roots are laid bare. Here the killing of the forest and stream ecosystem will be total, swift and irreparable. If the TRO is not issued this process will begin tomorrow."

Joe, Jim, and Pat spent the rest of their allotted twenty minutes laying out the key arguments that would frame the *Bragg* case over years to come. In the months of depositions and Joe's endless questions of officials, they had built what they hoped was an airtight case that DEP had allowed mines to blatantly break the federal and state surface mine laws and the Clean Water Act.

First Joe spoke about the buffer zone. Larry Alt, the permit supervisor who had run the permit hearings in Blair and Varney, had admitted in his deposition that he did not make the detailed assessments required before granting the variance to the buffer zone. "The reason the DEP did not attempt to make the buffer zone findings is because it comes to the process with the preconception that valley fills of any size and in any quality stream are approvable." Joe noted that there is an escape clause. Weakening water quality standards is allowed when the state's long-range planning process determines that important economic development will follow. But no such determination had been made for the Blair mine.

Joe's next point would be made again and again in future debates on just how big a valley fill should be: "Intervenors and DEP argue that following the water quality rules would set up a conflict with Section 404 of the Clean Water Act. That is not true. The water quality rules do not prevent all fills. They only prevent fills in high quality waters."

Then Joe moved on to the complex question of Approximate Original Contour. He maintained that valley-fill areas, as well as mined areas, must be returned to AOC—unless DEP had approved industrial or commercial use for the land, as state and federal law required. He pointed out that 1,700 of the 3,100 acres involved in the disputed permit would be valley fills. Much of the mountainous mined area would become a plateau. The spirit of the Surface Mining Control and Reclamation Act intended that the material taken off the peak would first go to restore the original contour. Only then could the rest be placed in valley fills.

Pat had just one issue, a simple one, he told Haden: the cumulative hydrologic plan. This plan provided that mines should prevent disturbance to the hydrologic balance between mined and adjacent unmined areas. Preventing disturbance would include preventing increased runoff caused by altering the topography of the land—a requirement whose true importance was not revealed until a few years later. Pat had subjected DEP permit supervisor Larry Alt to his usual withering and wearisome deposition style. Pat told Haden, "Mr. Larry Alt, the permit supervisor for DEP's southern region in Logan County, who has passed upon 8,000 permits during his career as permit supervisor and passed upon the Spruce Fork [Blair] permit, testified at deposition that he did not have any idea what a hydrologic reclamation plan must include."

When Pat concluded, Haden stared at the battalion of lawyers on the other side of the courtroom and asked, "Who wishes to be heard?" Russ Hunter of DEP rose first.

"I'm here trying to determine who they are trying to get the TRO issued against, and I'm still not any more enlightened than I was, but I'll speak first."

"Well," Haden said, "They were talking about your agency.

"Pardon?"

Haden repeated, "They were talking about your agency."

"I will work on the agency, then," replied Hunter, expressing the legal confusion that had engulfed just about everyone except Haden. He began by painting a portrait of an agency overwhelmed with past as well as present mining problems. "And you only have to go back in history several years and look at the large number of bond forfeitures in West Virginia and see where there were [coal] companies that were in poor cash flow situations that walked away from their environmental responsibilities and the state is still trying to retire the backlog of those unreclaimed permits." If the TRO were issued, Hunter believed, the agency would get even more bogged down.

For environmental attorneys, like Jim, Joe, and Pat, the fact that there were several federal and state acts controlling mining, or other environmental issues, presented a wealth of opportunities for lawsuits—and delaying tactics. But for regulators, enforcement could become a quagmire.

"Now, the Surface Mining Act was enacted after the National Environmental Policy Act," Hunter said. "It was enacted after the Federal Water Pollution Control Act, which is known as the Clean Water Act. The scheme was approved as part—as acceptable under those two regulatory functions. So the purpose is, again, protection of the environment through the regulatory programs and enforcement of the performance standards, not the absolute prevention of disturbance. And the only way to prevent the harm of cutting the trees that has been alleged is to prevent the disturbance, and that is not what the Act envisioned, I would suggest."

Hunter then tried to respond to the *Bragg* case plaintiffs' charges about the buffer zone and hydrologic reclamation. Fairly simply, he said, once a mine proves it needs a place for excess spoil, the valley fill is assumed. And DEP then assumes the Corps will grant the 404 permit for the fill. This nullified the need for a buffer zone determination.

Finally, Haden turned to Roger Wolfe, who was Arch Coal's attorney. Wolfe was not Jackson Kelly's usual environmental attorney. That role fell to Robert McLusky, a wiry man in his late forties, who represented Arch and Massey in the multitude of hearings before the Surface Mine Board and circuit court. Wolfe was one of the firm's star trial lawyers. A partner in Jackson Kelly since 1980, his specialty was labor law, but he had quite a bit of experience with injunctions and in federal court. He frequently represented coal companies in labor disputes. A musician, Wolfe considered trials largely performance art, a challenge to bring someone to your position, a matter of knowing whom to communicate with and what will persuade the person.

This late afternoon, Wolfe sought to persuade Haden that Arch could keep on mining in Blair. First, he said, the court should look at the plaintiffs' true motives: "No matter what the plaintiffs' protestations to the contrary or they may have said earlier in this proceeding, what they really want to do is abolish large area surface mining in this state. I have heard them say at one time or another they would like simply to reasonably limit valley fills. But given the circumstances that we are now in, given the review process and the scrutiny that was afforded this Hobet permit application, it's clear that that is not the case."

As for this court proceeding, the arguments, Wolfe said, belonged more before the Surface Mine Board. The plaintiffs hadn't proved imminent danger. "They didn't address a single solitary thing that is going to happen to them in the next ten days that will result in harm to them. There won't be seven square miles of deforestation or anything else like that occur within the next ten days or until tomorrow or the end of the week or when the Court might have a reasonable chance to rule on the preliminary injunction request."

Haden was curious about just how much land would be disturbed.

Only enough for a sedimentation-control pond, Wolfe said. McLusky, the mining expert, jumped in and added specifics: five to seven acres. However, Arch faced huge repercussions. "We have obligations to the 300 plus employees who face the prospect of layoff," Wolfe said. "We have obligations to stockholders, a board of directors, and all of that. But the point is, we are no longer to the point of speculating about harm. Significant harm is occurring now. This company is losing a million dollars a month. This company has a 70 million-dollar capital investment in this project which is at risk. Each day it's delayed is another day that these folks are laid off and have—and will continue to be laid off and increases the likelihood of further layoff."

Wolfe then deferred to McLuskey to respond to the alleged violations of environmental laws. He immediately boiled the case down to an essential point: this case is about a pattern of many years of violation of basic mining regulations by DEP. Those included the buffer zone, the size of valley fills, restoration of the mountains, and hydrologic reclamation. All of these issues belonged before the Surface Mine Board, not federal district court, McLuskey said.

As for the individual issues, "Mr. Lovett and Mr. McGinley have professionally asserted what are very novel claims," McLuskey continued. "Unfortunately, they are supported neither by law nor the facts which they have cited in their motion." He focused on the plaintiffs' charge that the mine had not requested a mountaintop-removal variance. "The appropriate test for determining whether an operation will be restored to AOC is to look at the overall operation before and after mining, not to try and pinpoint specific areas within that operation and say, aha, there was a bump here before and there is not a bump here now." Then he rebutted the plaintiffs' argument that valley fills should be minimized and fit to the original mountain shape. In 1998 OSM had written: "Valley fills themselves are not subject to a requirement to achieve approximate original contour."

When McLuskey addressed the cornerstone of the plaintiffs' case, he actually clarified the swirl of legalese. "With respect to the buffer zone regulation, it is a surface mining regulation that prohibits land disturbance within a hundred feet of intermittent or perennial streams unless DEP makes four findings.

"First, that it will not adversely affect normal flow and stream gradient. Second, it won't adversely affect fish migration or related values. Third, it won't materially damage water quality or quantity of the stream. Or, fourth, cause violation of applicable water quality standards.

"Plaintiffs have a two-fold argument. First, they claim that DEP does not make independent findings in order to allow disturbance within that hundred-foot buffer zone. More importantly and secondly, they argue that DEP can't make those findings. As matter of law, they contend, valley fills violate the buffer zone regulation and DEP can never, never approve a valley fill under the buffer zone regulation, which on its face applies only to intermittent and perennial streams."

The bottom line, McLuskey said, was that the buffer zone is a SMCRA rule and does not prohibit or modify the use of Clean Water Act permits. In fact, when a coal industry representative asked whether the buffer zone would prevent valley fills, OSM said the rule was flexible enough to allow fills.

Joe was given a few minutes for a brief rebuttal. Then Haden looked across the courtroom. Joe was sure he was defeated.

"It is abundantly clear that there are serious legal questions raised," Haden began. Joe started to hope. "What the Court must look at, after finding, as I have, that there are serious legal questions here, is the harms analysis and to balance the harms that might accrue to the plaintiffs if the Court does not grant the TRO with the harms that would accrue to the defendants if the Court does grant." Now Joe wasn't so sure what Haden would say next.

For those in the audience befuddled by the back and forth over arcane, yet vital, clean water regulations, what Haden did say made them feel not so dumb after all. "While economic considerations are a consideration, the paramount considerations have to do with environmental matters such as water quality. There is a great deal of uncertainty as to whether regulations and statute conflict or not, and there is a great deal of uncertainty as to which statutes have primacy over other statutes. It, as I hear each agency argue, is pretty clear to a particular agency as to who ought to be in charge and usually that has to do with its agency, but it is not clear to the Court at this point. To complete my assessment of the matter of whether an agency would be hurt, I think that as much daylight and analysis as we can put on these issues where they can be resolved appropriately in this Court, the better off the agencies are and, thus, the better off the public is.

"We all understand, despite our levels of sophistication or lack of sophistication, that in environmental areas where streams are diverted, trees are cut, aquatic life is disturbed, human residents of the area and animal residents of the area are involved, that this is an area where you cannot unring the bell."

As Haden declared the TRO granted, Joe was able to exhale. Afterward, Steve Rusak, the Justice Department attorney, walked over and shook his hand. "Guess I'll have to buy a toothbrush," he joked—he had planned to fly back to Washington that night.

———

"I'm going to run out of clean shirts," Joe said as he hung his suit jacket behind his office door and grabbed brown slacks and a sweater off his chair.

"The first rule," Jim said, "is no one criticizes anyone else's clothes. None of us planned to stay."

"I can't believe that judge is making us be there at 9 a.m." Joe said. "I should have said 9:30—and did you see his face when he said it? This is a fatherly thing he is doing—baptism by fire."

After a few minutes of enjoying the shock of victory, the three lawyers and Cindy Rank began planning strategy for their 9:00 a.m. court appearance on the preliminary injunction. Pat took out a yellow legal pad. John Morgan, their mining expert, was on the speaker phone. Witnesses? Four or five from DEP, including Larry Alt, the permit supervisor. Cindy. James and Sibby Weekley.

Joe wanted Morgan's opinion on the crux of his case. "What would happen if the plaintiffs were right and no one could put anything in ephemeral streams?"

"There would be very small valley fills," Morgan replied. "It would tend to preclude large draglines. However, there are certain occasions where one large fill is better than disturbing several valleys."

Suddenly, Joe remembered that the door to the building was locked — automatically locked at 5:00 p.m. Their delivery of Chinese food couldn't get in. Someone ran downstairs to await the delivery person.

Preparations continued for several hours amid empty food containers and piles of depositions and permit documents. Pat called his lawyer son for advice on a legal procedure. Cutting through confusion, Jim pulled out typed notes on highlights of DEP depositions. After midnight, they decided they'd prepared the best they could.

The first item on the agenda the next morning was not testimony but a debate over where to take Judge Haden to see mountaintop removal. Roger Wolfe had filed a motion asking Haden to view Blair Gardner's favorite mine of Samples and then go to the area to be mined in Blair, including Weekley's hollow. Joe said he wouldn't oppose the motion if the army would fly the judge over mountaintop-removal mines. Haden said he would like a tour, perhaps both on the ground and in the air. If the defendants wanted him to see the best mines, he asked the plaintiffs to show him the worst. The tours would come within the next two weeks, after testimony ended.

That testimony took five days, far longer than Haden had expected, and the transcript went to more than twelve hundred pages. Several witnesses took a half day or more, with much tedious debate over the minutiae of Sections 401, 402, and 404 of the Clean Water Act. Many in the audience were somewhat confused, as were thousands of miners, coalfield residents, and people throughout the state following the case in the media. Yet, this was the public's only opportunity to hear first-person accounts of how mountaintop mining is done—and how it is regulated. Legal questions argued here formed the basis of attacks against mountaintop removal for years to come.

Although questioning frequently seemed disjointed, the plaintiffs and the defendants had clear goals. Joe, Pat, and Jim tried to establish DEP's pattern and practice of failure to enforce laws having to do with the buffer zone, AOC, hydrologic reclamation, and contemporaneous reclamation. DEP attorneys brought personnel who calmly showed how thoroughly they had examined Arch's permit. For Arch, attorneys tried to show how carefully the company protected the environment, how much the company contributed to the economy of the state, and how much harm would come from halting the mine.

Pat's first witness was Larry Alt, the DEP permit supervisor. Pat was hoping he could get Alt to reenact his unusual description of AOC. Pat needn't have worried. Alt bumbled through his time on the stand so badly that Trish could only say afterward, "Poor Larry."

Pat quickly established that Alt had a two-year degree in forest technology, received in 1978, but had taken no courses in mining, engineering, hydrology, or geology. Then he moved on to AOC.

> PAT: "How do you explain to those new permit review team members how to determine whether a permit applicant's proposal to mine or reclaim will result in approximate original contour of a post-mining land surface?"
>
> ALT: "In most cases we work with the chalkboard and do drawings. But I also use my hand as a mountain, these being the peaks, and then this would be flat with an AOC variance. And then if it comes back close to that, you know, close to approximate original contour would be like simply an open fist. But the mountain itself would be a fist."
>
> PAT: "In your deposition you drew circles around your knuckles?"
>
> ALT: "Using the circles would be contour lines. My pen don't work as well

today, and these circles would equal the contour lines. And some of the contour lines would be just a little bit flatter in an AOC back stack and then everything would be flat and spread out further then if it wasn't approximate original contour."

PAT: "I'm sorry?"

ALT: "It would be flat and spread out more."

PAT: "Why do you draw circles to represent contour lines?"

ALT: "Because these would be points, like on your topo maps. They are the same like the contour lines on your topo mine."

PAT: "Contour lines indicate elevation, among other things."

ALT: "Right."

PAT: "But you don't consider elevation when you determine whether post-mining land surface has been restored to approximate original contour, do you?"

ALT: "No, sir."

Since Pat was building a record for appeal, he tended to pile four sentences into one. Haden interrupted, "You want to break that question down a little bit."

"Yes, sir," Pat responded. "It sounds like some of the questions in my class."

"That's right," Haden quipped. "The kind you give at the end of the semester."

Pat moved on to his specialty—contemporaneous reclamation. This obfuscating term can be understood by thinking of new planned communities around major cities, like Ashburn in northern Virginia. Vacant farm fields transform into dusty or muddy bare earth, which is soon crisscrossed with streets. Tantalizing new houses and townhomes spring up, followed by drainage ponds, green sod, and leafy trees. All the development is done according to plans approved by local government officials. If developers stick to regulations, the sequence of ground disturbance will minimize dust and flooding and other environmental harm. So, Pat argued, it should be with the vast land disturbances in the coalfields.

Through a series of questions, Pat had Alt confirm that a coal company must submit written reasons and alternate plans for postmining development if it requests a variance from contemporaneous reclamation. Then Alt confirmed what Pat already knew: Arch had requested a variance for the Blair mine.

Now show us the written engineering data that justified granting the variance, Pat said to Alt.

ALT: "I don't see it contained in the request."
PAT: "Is it contained anywhere in the permit?"
ALT: "I'm not sure. I didn't look."

Pat pressed Alt. The permit had sections lettered alphabetically for each section of the regulations. Contemporaneous Reclamation was in section O. Alt began thumbing through the hundreds of pages. For two long minutes, he fumbled. Perhaps, Haden interrupted, the court should recess while Pat helped him search. The ten-minute recess stretched to forty-five minutes as six lawyers, including three from DEP, gathered around the witness stand. Every few minutes, Haden's clerk came to check the progress. Finally, court came back in session, and Pat continued.

PAT: "Mr. Alt, before we adjourned, I was asking you a question about section 14.15.f.2 of the DEP regulations with regard to a written statement as to the technological or economic infeasibility of the applicant complying with contemporaneous reclamation requirements; do you recall that?"
ALT: "Yes, sir."
PAT: "And you said you didn't see anything in the writing in the permit file relating to technological or economic infeasibility. Have you had a chance to further review the file to determine if there is anything in writing that is responsive to that particular requirement of the regulations?"
ALT: "I didn't see anything, sir."

Spectators were in for more long hours with the next witness, mining expert John Morgan. He was the first witness Joe had ever questioned in court. They spent hours delineating deficiencies in the permit for the Blair mine. Early on, Morgan put numbers to the huge amount of earth being moved. When coal was uncovered, 826 million cubic yards of earth and rock would be removed. Of that, 676 million cubic yards would be put back on the mountaintop. The remaining 150 million would go into valley fills.

EPA had reversed its reservations about harms to the streams, because

Arch had said the valley fills would be smaller. However, Morgan calculated, that was impossible given the amount of excess earth and rock needing a disposal site. In addition, the sequence of mining appeared to create more land disturbance than in the original permit.

At 7:00 p.m., Haden decided he'd heard quite a bit of testimony. It was time to adjourn until the next day.

Joe, Pat, and Jim went back to Joe's office. Dusk had settled, but Joe didn't turn on the lights.

"Well," Pat said, "My fellow lawyers, anyone who walked into that courtroom today would have thought you had been doing it for years."

Actually, Pat and Suzanne were the only ones who had previously had cases before judges and juries. They had been astounded when Jim told them his two decades of practice had been appeals briefs—he never had even taken a deposition.

"I'm surprised we dodged so many bullets," Jim said.

"Did Larry look so stupid to you today?" Joe asked Jim.

"It was great," Jim replied. "Reminded me of a guy on the Ed Sullivan show. We made DEP look bad."

"Mr. Understatement," Pat said.

John Morgan was on the stand all the next day, Friday, February 5. Judge Haden had other matters on Monday, so he reconvened the case for Tuesday afternoon, February 9, when Morgan's testimony finally concluded.

When McLuskey cross-examined Morgan, he spent the first half of his questioning establishing that Morgan had worked on mines in Russia, Indonesia, and other foreign countries but had little experience with mountaintop-removal mines in West Virginia.

Joe didn't think McLuskey did any damage to Morgan's credibility. But Joe didn't think he'd done the best job with his own questions. Everything took too long to make the points. His next expert witness was much different, one both Joe and Judge Haden enjoyed hearing.

Ben Stout was as boyishly appealing as John Morgan was Britishly authoritative. An associate professor of biology at Wheeling Jesuit University and director of the environmental studies program, Stout brought to life what had become tedious recitations of water regulations. He bubbled with enthusiasm for the tiny benthic macroinvertebrates—crayfish, worms, and flies—demarking life in streams.

In the language of a biologist, Stout explained that Pigeonroost is a third-order stream, formed by the convergence of two second-order streams, themselves formed closer to the headwaters by the joining of several small, first-order streams. Pigeonroost is a perennial stream, meaning it runs year round. Stout had examined more than one thousand streams in West Virginia and had studied many in the coalfields while living in Mingo County for three years and teaching at Southern West Virginia Community College. Pigeonroost ranked among the top 10 percent in quality. Joe asked him why.

STOUT: "Well, I base my judgment on the strength of the macroinvertebrate community, the organisms that live there. Macroinvertebrates play an important role between primary producers and top level predators such as fish and salamanders. And I found diverse, abundant, and vibrant macroinvertebrate communities in all the streams that I examined in Pigeonroost."

JOE: "Does the forest canopy influence the quality of the stream?"

STOUT: "These streams are intimately tied with the forest, and the forest canopy provides the bulk of the energy nutrients that enter into these streams."

JOE: "Would the character of the stream be significantly changed if the canopy were not there?"

STOUT: "It certainly would. In all the research that I have seen, when you remove the forest canopy, the stream daytime temperatures go up dramatically and nighttime temperatures plummet."

JOE: "In what other ways does the forest support the stream?"

STOUT: "Well, the forest—the stream side forest, called riparian—riparian vegetation or riparian forest, is very important to the stream. It provides some structure in root masses and logs that—well, even in limbs that fall into the water forming debris dams. These debris dams are critical in the productivity of these streams. They capture the leaves, the leaves that come off the trees in the fall, and hold them long enough for the macroinvertebrates to consume them and the macroinvertebrates convert that leaf material into fine particles. These fine particles are eventually then washed downstream and become food resource for the larger communities."

JOE: "Would it be beneficial to the environment to have a hundred foot buffer zone around the stream during mining for instance?"

STOUT: "It's always beneficial during any human disturbance to be able to protect the stream from that disturbance."

Testimony continued another three days over the next ten days, interrupted by criminal cases that Haden had to hear. Ruth Ann Storey, the other Justice Department attorney, commented that she'd never had a hearing for a preliminary injunction last more than a day or two. "I've eaten in every restaurant in Charleston," she sniffed.

When court reconvened Wednesday, February 17, yellow crocuses had popped up outside the courthouse. Warren Upton of Jackson Kelly, who had defended Arch in Vicky and Tommy Moore's case, made a motion on behalf of the Coal Association and the Surface Mining and Reclamation Association. He pointed out that in the middle of Joe's original motion, he asked that DEP director Michael Miano not approve any valley fills in intermittent or perennial streams for any permit because they violated the buffer-zone rule. All thirty-seven pending permits could be halted if Haden ruled in Joe's favor.

Joe explained that he was focusing just on the Blair mine for the injunction. However, he had not given up his claim against other mountaintop removal. "We think this Spruce Mine is part of a larger pattern and practice," he told Haden. "And we will establish the pattern and practice and that the other mines will eventually fall under it."

Upton seemed satisfied. Interestingly, he seemed to have accepted that the preliminary injunction would be granted and the case against all mountaintop removal would be argued later in the year. Haden denied Upton's motion to halt the across-the-board injunction.

On this day Arch Coal and the agencies began their defense—actually before Joe and the plaintiffs had finished. Judge Haden had allowed this first witness, Pete Lawson, general manager of Arch's Samples mine, to be questioned out of order because he would be out of town later. Roger Wolfe started with a lesson in how Arch plans a mountaintop mine. Lawson was going to present a slide show. But before doing so, he portrayed Arch's importance to the state: Arch mined 30 million tons of coal a year (17% of the total) and had 2,500 employees, $450 million in investments, and 1 billion tons of coal in reserve.

The first step in planning a mountaintop mine is to examine the geology of the area to be mined, Lawson said. Then the locations of the multiple coal seams are located on the computerized drawing, and the amount of coal and amount of earth and rock (called spoil) covering the coal are calculated. The less spoil for each ton of coal, the more profitable the mine.

Lawson explained the sequence of taking off the mountain tops. Smaller shovels begin reducing the mountain, assisted by blasting for loosening the spoil. Some of this spoil is placed in valley fills. This preparation could take as long as a year. At that point, the dragline comes in. Blasting occurs ahead of the dragline to loosen the earth. The dragline then shovels the rubble off the coal, placing the earth back into pits where coal has already been removed.

Lawson spent the entire morning describing mountaintop removal, first for the defense attorneys and then for Pat McGinley, who scrambled to pull together an intelligible cross-examination for this unannounced testimony. As he tried to concentrate and formulate questions, Suzanne handed him Lawson's first slide: a black bear, standing like Smokey the Bear. The next slide showed phases of mountaintop removal, with a seaport and an oceangoing vessel in the distance. "What the hell are they going to do with the bear," he muttered to Suzanne. Then he went back to monitoring the testimony, emboldened by the odd tactical error that Charleston's powerhouse trial firm had made.

Haden wished the case would move faster. "I'll point out," he told Wolfe, "We are using one entire morning for a witness who is only to set the stage for the defense."

DEP's first witness, Ken Stollings, came next. He explained why the steep slopes make it physically impossible to maximize mountain restoration. Stollings had bachelor's degrees in mining and industrial engineering from West Virginia University and had worked for Island Creek and other coal companies for two decades before starting his own engineering business. In 1994 he became a DEP permit review engineer.

"You can't stack the material steeper than its natural angle of repose, which is the angle that it naturally stacks itself in when it's piled up," Stollings explained. "It's very similar to the angle that, say, sand would pour down into an hourglass or salt out of a salt shaker. It automatically assumes an angle, and you can't stack material steeper than that angle, and different materials normally have around a 37-degree angle of repose.

Normally in Southern West Virginia, you encounter a lot of steep slopes that are much steeper than this. They are not solid rock, but they are layers of rock that were sort of chiseled or eroded out, and they are very steep, sometimes as much as 60 degrees."

Stollings had spent at least six hundred hours on the Blair permit in the past year and a half. "I personally think it is one of the best permits that I have ever looked at," he said. "One thing that made it one of the best was the extent that they had provided in their mine plan, they accounted for all the spoil in very specific ways. They accounted for areas to be mined, they accounted for each tabular layer of strata that would be between each coal seam, and it was broken down. From an industrial engineering standpoint, they just did an outstanding job of laying it out."

Stollings emphatically refuted Joe's charges on AOC, contemporaneous reclamation, cumulative hydrologic impact, and the buffer zone. This Blair permit complied with the laws on each, he said. One by one, he read relevant sections of the law and explained how the permit met the requirements. Where Larry Alt had faltered on contemporaneous reclamation, Stollings was able to show that Arch had, in great detail, explained why it needed a variance.

Watching from the plaintiffs' attorney table, Pat was exhausted. Nearby on the table was his copy of the laws, marked with a blizzard of red and yellow tabs. As the hours dragged on, he had to listen to every word as testimony twisted and turned. Cindy Rank sat in the audience and thought, *No wonder no one understands the laws.*

Joe was on firmer ground when DEP brought up Ken Politan, assistant chief in charge of certification of compliance with Sections 401 and 402 of the Clean Water Act. Clean-water laws were Joe's strength. Politan's tell-it-like-it-is approach yielded revealing testimony under Joe's persistent questioning.

Section 401 required that a valley fill not degrade the state's streams and rivers if it was granted a Section 404 permit for filling the stream. Section 402, known as the National Pollutant Discharge Elimination System (NPDES) prevented harmful discharges into state waters.

JOE: "When EPA withdrew its objections, the specific objections to the permit on December 23rd, 1998, did the NPDES permit application look the same as the original application?"

171

POLITAN: "No."

JOE:"Were the valley fills smaller?"

POLITAN: "Yes. And some were eliminated."

JOE:"Two were eliminated. So weren't there practicable alternatives originally?"

POLITAN: "Yes, with the understanding they confined or limited the amount of mining that could occur during the first five-year period."

JOE: "Does that mean to lessen environmental impacts?"

POLITAN: "For the short term, Joe, yes, I would say it would. But, again, if the end result is if they can get the 404 permit and the programmatic EIS is conducted and done, I mean the end result may be the same. The fills may look the way that they were originally proposed and the ponds at the original locations. So the end result may be the same. At this time we don't know."

Suddenly, Haden jumped in. Did he hear what he thought he had heard? He asked, "Mr. Politan, I think you probably pretty much said this, but I want to see if I have the same understanding you do. You suggest that the permit as revised is smaller and will have less of an immediate or short-term impact on the environment than the permit as originally filed. Is that a fair statement or would you put it another way?"

"Can I put it another way, Judge?" Politan asked.

"Yes," said Haden.

"I would like to say that the fills were reduced, not necessarily the size of the operation." Politan said.

"The fills, the two valley fills were eliminated and the size of the operation changed; didn't it? Downward?" Haden asked.

"Well, two valley fills were eliminated and two valley fills got reduced. Wait a minute, I need to look at the map. Yeah, two valley fills got reduced and two valley fills got eliminated," Politan said.

"Okay," Haden continued. "But as I take it, the second part of your conclusion you said you can't predict the impact, but the impact in the long return, in other words when additional mining inevitably occurs, would be about the same as projected on the first application."

"Correct," Politan said. "If you, it's spelled out in EPA's conditional withdrawal of their objection that in order for them to extend the fills down to the original locations, they would have to seek a 404 permit and have this programmatic EIS study done."

"All right," Haden said. "So what it comes down to is if I deny the preliminary injunction at this point, then we will down the line, within five years, be at the same extent of mining as was contemplated in the original permit."

"As I understand your question, yes," Politan replied.

After that revelation, McLuskey put Eugene Kitts, a consulting engineer, on the stand. He explained that valley fills are necessary for deep mining as well. "The primary use of a valley fill in support of deep mining, though, is in refuse disposal," Kitts said. "Most underground mined coal in this state must be processed or washed to remove impurities before it is a marketable product. The rock that is removed from the coal has to be put somewhere. And that typically is a form of valley fill, whether it's a coarse refuse embankment which is placed just as a conventional valley fill or it could be a refuse impoundment where a dam or an impounding structure is built out of the coarse refuse material and fine refuse is pumped in slurry form behind that. But it is critical that deep mining must have the ability to construct valley fills of some sort."

McLuskey then had Kitts respond to the crux of the plaintiffs' case— the buffer zone. What percentage of the mountaintop-removal mines in southern West Virginia could operate if valley fills were only allowed in ephemeral streams?

"The prohibition against placing fill in intermittent or perennial streams would end the practice of mountaintop mining," Kitts responded.

That afternoon, Joe, Jim, Pat, and Suzanne left the court depressed for the first time. They had to counter Kitts, who had sounded so authoritative. Late into the night they worked. Joe asked for an e-mail of the transcript, and they practiced how Pat would question Kitts the next day.

By the time he began questioning, Pat was prepared: In his usual drawn-out style, he established legal definitions of ephemeral streams that would be debated repeatedly during future studies of mountaintop removal.

> PAT: "Mr. Kitts, the definition of ephemeral stream that you suggested to the Court would provide the basis for your opinion that valley fills could not be used anywhere in Southern West Virginia in connection with mountaintop mining was based on the DEP definition relating to mitigation under the Clean Water Act?"
>
> KITTS: "The definition of it being a stream that flows only in direct re-

sponse to runoff is an uncontested definition of ephemeral stream to my knowledge."

PAT: "But the definition of intermittent stream where certain types of Benthic and aquatic life is present is not the definition utilized under the Surface Mining Act in the enforcement of the buffer zone requirement; isn't that true?"

KITTS: "That is correct. There are different definitions for intermittent streams."

Now, Pat knew he had Kitts.

PAT: "Mr. Kitts, I have handed you a copy of the final rule-making by the Office of Surface Mining, Volume 48, Federal Register, No. 127, dated Thursday, June 30, 1983. I direct your attention, sir, to the second page of that document."

KITTS: "Okay. How much did you ask me to read?"

PAT: "The paragraph."

KITTS: "OSM has rejected the suggestion that it continue to require protection for any stream with a biological community. . . . It is impossible to conduct surface mining without disturbing a number of minor natural streams, including some which contain biota. For this reason, surface coal mining operations will be permissible as long as environmental protection will be afforded to those streams with more significant environmental-resource value."

Pat had nullified Kitts's scare tactic: smaller fills would still be allowed under OSM standards.

Testimony concluded after 5:00 p.m. Friday, February 19. Haden told the attorneys he had the following Thursday and Friday open for visiting and flying over the mines.

———

Rain had turned to wet snow by the time Judge Haden and the lawyers, the expert consultants, and the media gathered at McDonald's parking lot at the shopping center south of Charleston early Thursday morning, February 25. Mark White, Arch's mine manager, had the seating chart. Judge Haden would be in the front seat.

The first stop was Arch's Samples mine east of Charleston. After an introduction in the Samples office, the group put on white hard hats laid

News media surround Judge Haden (facing the camera) as he tours Arch Coal mines in a snowstorm.

out a table and set off for the mine. High above a valley fill in progress, they crowded under a white tent. As fat snowflakes swirled outside, Pete Lawson kept Haden engaged with a running commentary on the mining sequence. Haden had numerous questions. Coal-industry attorneys rushed to answer them, violating the agreement made not to have ex parte (one-sided, partisan) discussions with the judge. Ruth Storey, an assistant U.S. attorney, joined in. Suzanne attempted to shut down the dialogue, but then gave up and urged Ben Stout, the plaintiffs' stream expert, to present his arguments to the judge.

The last stop would be Pigeonroost. As the van drove past Weekley's house, attorneys Warren Upton and Bob McLuskey talked loudly about the trash in the stream. They peered out the van window at the straight pipe that dumped sink and toilet waste into the creek. "I have a picture of sewage running into the creek," McLuskey said.

The vans parked in the flat area beyond Weekley's house. Ben Stout wanted to show Haden where he had found tiny macroinvertebrates indicative of the health of Pigeonroost. TV cameras, reporters, and the

Ben Stout searches out bugs in Pigeonroost as Judge Haden and news media watch.

couple of dozen others on the tour followed closely as they climbed to a bend in the creek.

Stout, wearing wader boots, jumped into the stream, pulled up a fistful of leaves, and began picking out tiny critters. "Mayflies, caddis flies," he exclaimed. Haden was rapt, peering over Stout's hands each time Stout pulled a bug out. The judge had known Stout when he was a boy and was friends with his parents.

Stout held his hand flat and picked out a bug. "This is a caddis fly." Grabbing another fistful of wet leaves from the stream, he said, "Here's another one. This guy's only a year old." The dark-colored insect, about the size of a sesame seed, was crawling on Stout's thumb "Oh, yeah," Haden said with obvious interest.

Early the next morning, Haden, two of his law clerks, and Ed Griffith of DEP climbed aboard a helicopter for the judge's bird's-eye view under a clear blue sky. It was Friday, February 26, the twenty-seventh anniversary of the Buffalo Creek flood.

Haden had asked Joe to chart the route. At Joe's request, Cindy Rank, with help from an OSM official, chose a route that stretched from Nicholas County, north of Beckley, down through Mingo, and back up through

Logan and Boone. The flight lasted a bit more than two hours, and they were almost never out of sight of a mine. Haden was astonished. "What were they [the defense attorneys] ever thinking to take me up there?" he said to his clerks after they got off the plane.

That afternoon he heard closing arguments. He had many questions and seemed to speak nearly as much as the lawyers. Even Joe, the perpetual pessimist, sensed how Haden was going to rule—though it would take another week to find out.

Joe's closing argument closely adhered to his arguments on the four regulations he had hammered over the past three and a half weeks: buffer zone, AOC, contemporaneous reclamation, hydrologic reclamation. "Congress knew how to exempt surface mining requirements from the AOC requirements," he told Haden. "It created specific exemptions for steep slope and mountaintop removal operations with very strict and detailed provisions for such variances. It did not exempt valley fills from AOC. As Hobet's Mark White testified, however, because Arch owns a dragline currently operating on the Dal-Tex site, it summarily rejected any alternatives that could have reduced the size of the valley fills.

"Hobet, DEP and the Corps of Engineers must not be allowed to twist the law to accommodate the coal industry's move to larger machines and larger mines with deeper cuts. Rather the industry must be required to conform its technology to the law.

"In a deposition taken in this case, Rodney Woods of the Corps of Engineers testified that the Corps just sort of 'oozed' into allowing this kind of mining. Mountaintop removal practices have increasingly come to dominate surface mining in West Virginia. As the number and size of these operations has quickly grown, DEP has likewise sort of just 'oozed' into approving these operations without considering the law. That is why its post hoc rationalizations which bend and distort the law are so strained."

Russ Hunter, the DEP attorney, punctuated his closing with sweeping generalities. "Mountaintop removal mining is regulated by both the Surface Mining Act and the Clean Water Act programs," he told Haden. "And environmental positives associated with this type of mining process is the fact that there is a one time large scale disturbance by one responsible permit holder that optimizes resource recovery rather than a multiple smaller scale approach which results in spread out and less—or more people creating environmental disturbances as opposed to one permittee."

Haden interrupted: "Was there a 50-foot rule?" referring to the rule that supposedly had required any mine planning to lower a mountain more than fifty feet to get a mountaintop removal variance, which Arch hadn't done.

"There was at one time a 50-foot rule of thumb that had been applied," Hunter said. "I am unaware of it being an official Office of Surface Mining directive, which is sometimes a policy document. There is a history in the records of exchanges back and forth probably in the early '80s in the agency relative to the 50-foot rule."

"And the 50-foot rule," Haden asked, "if I understand it correctly, is that not only was the replacing of the overburden to be done on the approximate configuration or contour, but also that the site, when finished, could not be more than 50 feet higher or lower than it once was. Is that overstating it?"

"Well, it's always been my understanding," Hunter replied. "And I'd have to go back and look at the particulars, that a 50-foot rule dealt with the elevation of the backstacked area rather than the valley fill area itself. But that I can't represent."

Roger Wolfe made the final closing argument. "We all know what the standard is," Wolfe declared. "Balance the harms, consider the merits, and consider the public interest. We submit, Your Honor, in this case we need go no further than the inquiry with respect to the balancing of harms.

"On the one hand you have the harm that will result to Hobet from the continuation of this injunction. And although the Court has acknowledged the seriousness of the harm to the company previously in issuing the temporary restraining orders, I don't think it's really possible to talk in six minutes about the impact of the potential loss of a 70 million dollar investment, over 500 jobs, both directly and indirectly, 20 million dollars in lost revenue to various sources, at least 1.6 million dollars in lost tax revenue.

"But the evidence was clear. Layoffs will begin soon. These are not idle speculations. You heard Mr. White's testimony. The impact to Arch is obvious and catastrophic if this injunction continues. But the impact, Your Honor, I submit to you goes even beyond Arch. There are issues here that affect the coal industry in this state and, in fact, the United States. An unfavorable ruling on some of these legal rulings will be a mortal blow to coal production in this state. I don't think there is any doubt about it.

Love it or hate it, coal is West Virginia in many ways. Wipe it out and we better be prepared to face the consequences." At this point, Wolfe was pointing his finger, staccato, at Judge Haden. Pat and Suzanne got chills, thinking Wolfe was threatening Haden: "You rule against us, and you will destroy the coal industry and the economy of West Virginia. "On the other hand, plaintiffs have offered no evidence of specific harm. When a tree is cut, there is a change to the physical environment. Now, if you want to call that harm, I'll accept that term for purposes of our argument. But we must acknowledge that harm then exists when a house is built or a highway is built, or there is any kind of construction. And certainly a surface mining complex is a construction project."

Haden disagreed. "Well," he told Wolfe. "I think it's conceded all the way around that the extent or magnitude of this particular permit application is significant. It would be the largest in the state's history. And while I agree with you that if you take the environmental argument to the extreme, if one tree is cut that that is environmental harm. But from the standpoint of scale that we are talking here, many square miles of complete—a rather complete change of the water, the topography, the wildlife, we aren't talking about the same thing as losing a particular tree. And the reason I take it that this litigation is so important to so many people is that, one, it does, if granted, allow a significant economic savings to the Hobet organization and others who would mine this way by full utilization of men and equipment and complete recovery. And then, on the other hand, of course, it will change, if not degrade, a significant portion of the environment.

"I suppose the real question is, here again, are the standards set down in the Acts being met when decisions like this are being made?"

"Indeed that is the question, Your Honor," Wolfe replied. "But perhaps more to the point, Your Honor, all of those issues were considered by the people who should have considered them, OSM, EPA, Corps of Engineers, DEP, the people whose responsibility it is to consider whether we have gotten too big with valley fills.

"Additionally on the issue of harm, Your Honor, heaven knows, as well as the rest of us, that Pigeonroost is not a pristine stream. I didn't see any 18-inch trout floating around the stream when Mr. Stout was vainly looking for his bug as the rest of us stood by that rusty refrigerator."

Haden jumped in to disagree. "He found his bug."

"Did he find his bug?" Wolfe challenged.

"Indeed," Haden replied.

"I don't believe he did," Wolfe countered. "Not the one bug he was looking for."

"All right." Haden wasn't going to argue anymore.

"He found several others," Wolfe said, determined to have the last word. "It might have qualified as a segment for Saturday Night Live, but I don't think he found his bug, Your Honor."

Joe smiled to himself. He knew Haden didn't like being argued with.

———

Now the wait. Haden was going to write the opinion, not make a pronouncement that afternoon. All Joe and his colleagues could do was wait.

But the following days were not free from mining controversy. In that last week of February, EPA had held public hearings to gather information for the programmatic Environmental Impact Statement. The third and last was in Logan.

Just hours after Judge Haden's tour ended at Pigeonroost Branch, tension between miners and environmentalists was reaching flash point as more than one hundred residents, miners, coal officials, and environmentalists crowded into the restaurant at Chief Logan State Park. "I wasn't going to come," an older man told the group. "But I was at the Chevron station, and one of these environmentalists said they would take my job. It reminds me of when I came home from the war, and they were burning their draft cards."

"I am not much a speaker but I am a proud employee of Hobet Mining," said another man. "I live in Mingo County under a surface mine in the reclaiming phase. I think the water will be cleaner and there'll be less run off. This place here was built on coal. I wish you wouldn't do this study and issue these permits."

Trish walked to the microphone, hoping she could spread some reason. She had a prepared statement to read. "There is a problem, and it needs to be addressed," she began. "The true impacts to the communities and to the natural resources are very understated in a lot of these permits. This issue has become an advertisement for the coal industry, and I resent that. I resent that because there are common citizens who have problems and there are people who need jobs. I don't think they are different. Mining has been important to West Virginia. But I also feel mining has taken a lot and will take a lot."

———

Judge Haden paid attention to the news. Just like tens of thousands of other West Virginians, he read the papers and listened to quotes from the EPA hearings. He knew how he would rule. But how, he asked his two clerks, could he get there?

Haden, age sixty-one when the case began, had had an impressive career in law. Marrying right after high school, he had planned a career in retail, following his grandfather, who had founded the Morgantown Glass Company. His father persuaded him to commence a legal career instead. His first elected position, on the Monongalia County school board, was also his most challenging, he said years later. He was one of the few persons ever to serve in all three branches of government: he served as a state legislature delegate, as state tax commissioner, and, beginning in 1975, as chief justice in the state Supreme Court of Appeals. When President Gerald Ford appointed him federal district judge for the northern and southern districts of the state, he was the youngest federal judge. He became chief judge for the southern district in 1982, was elected to the federal Judicial Council by his Fourth Circuit colleagues, and was appointed to the Executive Committee of the Judicial Council by Chief Justice William Rehnquist. He was the first West Virginian ever to chair the Executive Committee. Over the course of his career, he received enough awards to fill an entire page.

Among friends—who called him Chuck—he was as affable as the kindly Santa Claus face he presented in court. But in his judge's robes, he required respect for the law and the court. His harsh penalties for trespasses of manners were legendary; once he fined a former state Supreme Court judge one thousand dollars for unacceptable behavior in his courtroom. In several previous cases on coal, he had come down on both sides. Miners recalled that he had ruled that coal companies were still responsible for retirement benefits even after they quit mining.

———

Rulings in federal cases often make themselves known on cats' feet, spilling silently out of fax machines in law offices. On the afternoon of March 3, a reporter told Joe there had been a ruling.

Joe had to skim through twenty-three of the forty-seven pages before he found the decision: "The Court finds the balance 'tips decidedly' in favor of the plaintiffs." Haden had weighed the protections of both the environment and the nation's energy needs offered by SMCRA—and decided that "against a backdrop of prior mining with little environmental protection, it is clear the law's primary protections extend to the citizenry and environment."

Haden spent the remaining twenty pages explaining his reasoning: "The Court's helicopter flyover of all mountaintop removal sites in southern West Virginia revealed the extent and permanence of environmental degradation this type of mining produces. On February 26, the ground was covered with light snow, and mined sites were visible from miles away. The sites stood out among the natural wooded ridges as huge white plateaus, and the valley fills appeared as massive, artificially landscaped stair steps. Some mine sites were twenty years old, yet tree growth was stunted or non-existent. Compared to the thick hardwoods of surrounding undisturbed hills, the mine sites appeared stark and barren and enormously different from the original topography.

"If the forest canopy of Pigeonroost Hollow is leveled, exposing the stream to extreme temperatures, and aquatic life is destroyed, these harms cannot be undone. If the forest wildlife are driven away by the blasting, the noise, and the lack of safe nesting and sleeping areas, they cannot be coaxed back. If the mountaintop is removed, even Hobet's engineers will affirm that it cannot be reclaimed to its exact original contour. Destruction of the unique topography of southern West Virginia, and of Pigeonroost Hollow in particular, cannot be regarded as anything but permanent and irreversible."

Joe sat in his office, thumbing the pages. *This is amazing,* he thought. *He didn't address many of the issues. But that's what judges do, just the tip of the iceberg.*

The full trial for the *Bragg* case, Haden ruled, would come later in the year.

Chapter 13

Back at the Legislature

Tossed on a chair near the well of the capitol building, the *Logan Banner's* March 9 headline read: "Commission: This Is War." Logan County Commission president Art Kirkendoll was declaring the second Battle of Blair Mountain—this time against out-of-state environmentalists. More than one hundred miners and local government officials from Logan and Mingo counties were milling around the well, periodically surrounding a friendly legislator who came scurrying through. Rick Abraham was there, as were top officials from Arch Coal.

How different from two months earlier. Afternoon sun had shone through the tall windows of the House Government Organization Committee room as Arley Johnson awaited the outcome of the blasting bill on January 11. Bill Raney and Chris Hamilton were on the other side of the aisle. Trish and Elaine rushed in halfway through. Elaine's car had died and they had to rent one.

Like late Christmas packages, eight proposals tumbled out: most importantly, well-water loss or contamination would be assumed to be the fault of the coal companies if there had been blasting. Amazingly, surface mining would be prohibited within one thousand feet of a home—more than three times as far away as the current three hundred feet. Blasting over limits would draw stiff fines, starting at five thousand to ten thousand dollars for the first offense. Preblast surveys would be given for all structures within seven-tenths of a mile of the mine. DEP's environmental advocate would help residents learn whom to call with problems. Finally, the bills would repeal last year's SB 145—the mitigation bill that had prompted such wrath from Michael McCabe.

"I want to go home, lock myself in a closet, read the bills, and scream when I find something I don't like," Trish said when the group had returned to Arley's office for a strategy session.

"This is much more than I anticipated," Arley began. Especially since the proposals floated a month earlier would have done little to cure blasting problems. The chairman of the House Government Organization Committee had merely proposed a separate office on blasting at DEP. She didn't even tell Senator Jeffrey Kessler, cochairman of the blasting study. Arley had spent an hour and a half with Kessler. "He was pissed," Arley said.

Still there were two long months until midnight on the final Saturday. Who knew what was to come? "If we get 75 percent this year, I'll be happy," Arley said. "We can try to get the other 25 percent next year." The lawsuit, he cautioned, could make passing the blasting bill more difficult.

"My concern," Arley continued, "Has always been the people in those homes, the water they drink, the disruption of their lives. Just because they [coal corporations] control the mineral rights, they don't have the right to disturb the communities. That's why groups like WVOP are so important. Without press and public uproar, there would be none of this. Grass roots make government work. Bureaucrats just worry about their salaries. Grass roots bring emotion." As the group got ready to leave, Arley warned them: "You need to follow your bills every day."

We know, Trish thought, remembering last year's skullduggery. A veteran of the legislature, who had joined them, commented, "It's worse than a soap opera. By the end you know who is sleeping with whom, who is mad at whom."

Indeed, most Americans give little thought to their state legislatures. Many meet only a couple of months per year; some every other year; and a few larger states, like New York, have seemingly endless legislature sessions, stretching months past their appointed conclusion. But lobbyists and people like Trish and the other WVOP members, when they want a new law, must spend weeks in an odd closed society. Unfounded rumors spread like wildfire. Victories can bring adrenaline rushes much like those climbers experience on reaching the summit of a mountain. Important bills often take unpredictable paths. In this case, no one could have dreamed up the journey of the blasting bill.

A few days later behind-the-scenes maneuvering began. At an evening reception a week into the session, Bill Raney took Arley aside and asked him to hold off on working the blasting bills until the two of them could sit down with the governor and some of the WVOP people. *Amazing,* Arley thought. *Now everyone wants to talk to me.*

Amazed—in a different sense—was how Vicky felt about what happened next. A couple of days after Raney's conversation with Arley, Governor Underwood formed a task force to write mountaintop-removal legislation. The only WVOP member invited was Ralph Preece. Arley was very angry. He confronted Raney, backing him up to a wall. "If you don't put me on that task force, I will introduce 10 bills and talk for three hours." Faced with threats by the *Charleston Gazette* under the open-meetings law, the governor disbanded the task force.

Elaine and WVOP members decided to take the initiative and set up meetings with legislative leaders. During the week of February 1, the head of the Senate Judiciary Committee told them Jackson was planning a bill. On February 10, while Joe was questioning DEP officials in court, Elaine and Freda Williams spent forty minutes with Senator Jackson. He took off his coat and sat on the couch with them. Elaine was dying to ask how much he spent on his clothes—he always looked like a million dollars. His shirt was soft as butter; the ever-present suspenders, though, she wasn't sure she liked so much. After a few minutes of casual conversation, he got up and sat behind his desk. Business now.

"You won't like everything in the bill," he told them, with the honesty Elaine had come to respect. He and the other members of the Governor's Task Force on Mountaintop Mining and Related Mining Methods had decided they wouldn't let their summer's work go for naught. Elaine was confident Jackson's bill would be as strong as circumstances would permit. He would catch hell from the coal guys, he told them. But he didn't need their money with his family's natural gas business. His father, who had been president of the Senate, had told him, just do the best while you're there in the Senate. WVOP had helped him stand firm on principle. You don't know what impact you had on this place, Jackson told them. Your group is the only one looking at both sides.

Halfway through the meeting, his secretary rang. "Tell them I'm in a meeting," Jackson replied. "They can wait if they want." When Elaine and Freda left, Chris Hamilton, Bill Raney, and K.O. Damron were in the waiting room. "How do I get so lucky twice in one day?" Jackson joked. Freda smiled at the trio. Elaine felt a little smug.

Arley was feeling a bit smug, too. Halfway through the session, and the press was crediting him for the blasting bill. The coal guys were coming to him to broker deals. Along with Kessler, he had cochaired the study—and now a bill—on family law. His hometown newspaper in Huntington had featured him in a Sunday profile. Arley was having fun. *Got to be careful,* he thought. *Too much publicity and they get jealous up here.*

Another week went by, tense with expectations, dampened by the reality that nothing big happens until the final week of the session. Legislators and coal lobbyists kept one eye on the federal courthouse. Arley wasn't optimistic. *Haden's toying with them,* he thought. *He's more Republican than any federal judge I know.* Anytime there was a coal strike and the coal industry wanted a judge to shut down the union, they went to Haden. *But maybe . . . in his old age . . . he's developed a heart.*

Trish hadn't come to the legislature very often. She had been sick and also needed to concentrate on school. But Friday, February 19, was Kayla's big day—serving as a page for Trish's delegate, Harry Keith White. They set off early and met Elaine along Corridor G. A few miles later, a tire blew out on Elaine's car, bringing Kayla close to tears. She said a little prayer. A car stopped. A Department of Labor official offered them a ride, talking nonstop with stories about how he worked in the mines when he was young, and saying they had to stop that blasting damage.

Kayla wasn't there the following Monday, February 22, though, when a group of students witnessed history. The students took up most of the first four rows in the committee room when the Energy, Industry, and Mining Committee members filed in. The room quickly filled to standing room only. "This is a very important meeting," Senator Kessler said, looking at the high school students. "We will move to originate and initiate in this committee a bill to regulate surface mining in general."

Kessler had been appointed to fill a vacant Senate seat, then won the two remaining years in the 1998 election. Slim and tall, this dark-haired lawyer from the northern panhandle might narrowly best Jackson in a most-handsome-senator contest. He was never sure how he became cochair of the blasting study. Maybe, he joked, someone was out to get him—or maybe, living far from mountaintop removal, it was thought that he could be objective. Like Arley and Jackson, he had been moved by meeting coalfield residents and seeing damages firsthand. This wasn't a few isolated people—like the coal lobbyists had tried to tell him. Although his concern was genuine, not political, his involvement with blasting, as well as cochairing the family law bill with Arley, had caused the press to tag him as a rising star.

Kessler and Jackson had combined the Task Force proposals with the blasting bills. The previous Friday had actually been the last day for introducing Senate bills, but Jackson didn't want to give the coal industry a whole weekend to pick apart 681. Legislature rules allowed a bill to initiate in committee after the cut-off day.

According to Senate Bill 681, there would be two new offices: one for blasting, the other to oversee the effect of mines on communities—and the use of completed mountaintop mines for economic development. Importantly, loss of well water would be considered the fault of blasting, and replacement water would have to be provided within seventy-two hours— a provision similar to one in the law on deep mining. Residents with damages to their houses could go to free mediation with coal companies, rather than paying a lawyer to go to court. Blasting would be prohibited within five hundred feet of occupied dwellings; all structures within seven-tenths of a mile of larger mines would be offered preblast surveys. Blasting within one thousand feet of a structure would require a site-specific plan that took into account unique topography and house structure. Fines for violations would start at five thousand dollars. Senate Bill 681 would come to represent the 1999 session—just as SB 145 represented the 1998.

Yes, John Ailes, listening from the audience, thought. *We can get some good stuff out of this.*

Hundreds of miners and coalfield politicians, who rode up from Logan on three buses, swarmed though the capitol Wednesday, February 24. "Senate bill 681 is the best thing for Wyoming Coal," Arch Coal spokesman David Todd told them from the microphone at one side of the well. "I never saw so many restrictions."

Chris Hamilton joined Todd. "In 20 years up here, I've never seen such anti-coal sentiment." Then he sent the legions of coal off to lobby against SB 681. Legislators were given chunks of coal, which some set proudly on their desks on the House and Senate floors.

Industry supporters from Logan were clearly worried. An employee of Walker Machinery, which supplies bulldozers and other heavy equipment to the mines, sat in the gallery above the House floor. He predicted that his firm's Logan office could shrink from eighty-six workers to about a dozen. "It's really hard to understand why all of a sudden mountaintop removal." He wanted EPA out of the coalfields. "If some offense is committed at the local level," he said. "Amends should be made at the local level."

Jackson's office was overwhelmed with calls from miners. The secretary patiently told each one that SB 681 would not take their jobs. Jackson hoped to write and tell all those callers that SB 681 would actually help bring other industries to the coalfields. On Friday, as Haden was flying over snow-frosted mines, Jackson predicted that the judge wouldn't halt the Dal-Tex mine.

Five days later he was proved wrong. Haden ruled, and coal lobbyists and coalfield officials descended on Jackson and Kessler. A staff attorney rushed out of a meeting with Kessler and coal lobbyists muttering about that "frickin mitigation bill." Kessler stood strong.

Late in the afternoon, SB 681 passed the Senate Finance Committee. The only loss on blasting was that the distance between the mine and private property reverted to the three hundred feet of existing law. But the provisions for site-specific blasting—taking into account type of house structure—were strengthened, and prevention of dust was added. Importantly, the presumption of water loss by blasting was still in the bill. In Jackson's part, the name of the office was changed from "Office of Community Impact" to "Office of Coalfield Community Development" and moved from DEP to the state development office. SB 681 passed the Senate that evening—even though most senators had barely skimmed the dozens of pages.

Now the fate of SB 681 was up to the House—though it was obviously greased and few doubted its passage. Nonetheless, WVOP members were not pleased. "I feel like they've thrown us a bunch of bones," Vicky Moore told fellow members. "I don't see the things we asked for." Vicky and Trish and other members decided to try to amend 681. They drew up a list of seven changes, including reducing ground vibration from one inch per second to half an inch—hopefully reducing damage. They also wanted the limit for air blasts lowered from 133 decibels to 110 decibels—most of the complaints were for blasts between 120 and 129 decibels.

Trish spent the weekend of March 6 and 7 planning strategy for the last week of the legislature. The legislators have to realize, she thought, that the miners are worried about their jobs. That doesn't have anything to do with the blasting problems. Busily she called neighbors and asked them to write letters to the newspapers and legislators.

On Tuesday, March 9, the House Judiciary Committee held a public hearing on SB 681. Trish was one of the first of three dozen speakers. After thanking the legislature for putting so much time into the bill, she began, "This is not just about returning mountains to approximate original contour. It is about the people below hills, about their water and their homes. Mining will continue. We want relief; we don't want to be relocated. It is our lives, too." Then she handed the members the list of amendments. "You go down to the coalfields and tell residents all the reasons why you don't amend this bill."

At 5:38 p.m., the Judiciary Committee began considering the bill. Despite his frenzied schedule, Arley had prepared for discussion of SB 681, reading Haden's ruling and formulating his line of questioning—hoping to put into the record facts that could aid a court challenge of the blasting law. "So you have this preblast survey in hand," he asked the staff attorney, "and blasting starts, and the well goes dry. Then the presumption is that blasting caused the damage?"

"Yes," responded the attorney.

"Conversely," Arley continued. "You have damage to the foundation when the well is damaged, and you have no rebuttable presumption that blasting caused that damage as well."

"Do you want me to answer that?" the attorney asked. "Or is it rhetorical?"

"If I live within the required range of the blast," Arley continued. "And the well goes dry, and foundation is cracked and my home is worth $35,000 to $45,000. My well is replaced, but I have to hire a lawyer to fix my house."

"You don't have to hire a lawyer," the attorney said.

Many in the audience laughed, including Trish and Elaine, doubting that the mediation process of SB 681 would ever bring compensation for house damages—which is the point Arley was trying to make. What came next made Trish chuckle even more.

"Are we aware of the efficiency of the DEP office handling these blasting complaints?" Arley asked.

"Yes," the attorney responded.

Arley read the section of Haden's ruling describing how Larry Alt drew contour lines on his knuckles. "He then shows a closed fist as the original mountain and a semi-open fist as the restored mine site," Arley quoted. "Is this science?"

"I am not familiar with approximate original contour," the attorney responded.

"Is there a knuckle clause in the law?" Arley quipped. Then he continued more seriously. "DEP does not use science on these very important issues. What science will DEP use to set up the blasting office? Should citizens be concerned with the expertise? DEP seems to me lacking in effectiveness." Point made for the record, though Arley knew he couldn't change SB 681 now. The Judiciary Committee passed the bill with a few noncontroversial amendments. Once the House passed it, the Senate would have to approve the amendments.

After the meeting, an environmental lobbyist asked Trish if there was any delegate brave enough to offer WVOP's seven amendments when SB 681 came up for vote the next day. Another environmental lobbyist jumped in. "If they stand up, their county won't get money for fairs from the Budget Digest." The legislature's dirty little secret. Every year, some $35 million is left over from budget allocation. The Senate splits the money evenly among the senatorial districts. But in the House, the leadership rewarded those delegates who voted the way Kiss and other leaders wanted by allotting far more money to hand out at home—thus garnering votes for reelection.

This long day for Trish and Elaine got even longer when Elaine remembered she'd forgotten to take her car out of the free parking area by the 5:00 p.m. closing. The two climbed under the wire fence and got a few belongings out of the car. Then they found a room at the Days Inn—even getting a discount and a free bag of toiletries for being stranded. At dinner, Elaine prayed for their enemies—coal lobbyists.

The next day, Wednesday, March 10, WVOP and the environmental groups made a last-ditch effort to improve the blasting bill. At 2:00 p.m., they held a press conference in the now-familiar People's Room in Ken Hechler's office. Freda Williams had asked Kessler to amend the bill. He told her that he was afraid they'd lose the entire bill at this point. It was the first time, he said, that the coal industry had ever agreed to presumptive liability. Still WVOP members were not convinced. "This legislative session has not produced the desired laws, despite our good faith efforts," Freda Williams told the press.

Trish and other WVOP members were mad at Arley, for he had only agreed to support two of the seven amendments. Arley did make a speech the next day, Thursday, March 11, when the bill passed the House. This bill is not enough, he pronounced. More must be done next year. Then he warned: DEP has been in the pocket of the coal industry for years.

That evening, Trish and Elaine made sure they got to talk to Jackson. One waited at each of the doors when the Senate adjourned its evening session.

"Ladies," Jackson exclaimed. "So you finally made it. Come walk with me." Noticing that Trish looked tired, he opened the door of the elevator usually restricted to legislators and took them up to his office, where they spent twenty minutes. "You've got coal on one side," Jackson told them, "And you've got the environmentalists on the other side who want to stop mountaintop removal at any cost. You and the miners are in the middle. The other groups aren't considered with the respect you are.

"Haden's decision changed everything," he continued. "People started to run scared. You've got to walk away and declare victory. On a scale of 1 to 10, this is a 7. This is a beginning. The way the Organizing Project handles itself after the session will make all the difference. If you run away screaming, you won't be listened to."

"If it doesn't work," Elaine asked. "Can we come back?"

"I will do everything in my power," Jackson assured them.

Jackson left for an AFL-CIO reception, and Trish and Elaine wandered out of the now silent capitol building. Trish wasn't satisfied—Jackson had let them down, too. Elaine looked at her, not ready to give up on Jackson: "What of what he said is a lie?"

All that remained was for the Senate to consider changes and approve the bill. Slight changes would force it back to the House for a vote on the final night. However, SB 681 was in for one more slam attack—one startling even in a legislature that always managed to shock.

———

Two thousand strong, miners, supporters, and coalfield politicians came marching up Kanawha Boulevard to the capitol Friday morning, March 12. Placards stated: "Haden's Decision Reflects What He Protects—No Vertebrae—I <heart> Coal," "My Kids and Grandkids Mean More to Me Than Crawdads." "Protect The Species at Top of the Food Chain." Bob Schultz was among the marchers. His wife, Debra, helped open the ceremony, singing "Amazing Grace."

Nearly all the state's top officials stood on the capitol steps above the crowd filling the plaza. Terry Vance, the UMWA leader for the Dal-Tex mine, joined UMWA president Cecil Roberts, as did Bill Raney and Chris Hamilton. Miners carried a coffin up the steep steps and set it in front of the podium. A handwritten sign on the side stated: "All Strip Mines."

A minister spoke. "If Mr. Haden don't change his ruling, we may just as well bury this state. God let there be light. And in the beginning, as light began to shine, he made a substance called coal. He put coal in West Virginia so we may sustain our lives."

Bill Raney introduced Terry Vance as the voice of the miners. "This is the guy who put this day together," Raney added. Wearing a black shirt and tie under a grey suit coat, Vance was greeted by loud applause. "Because of the halt of this permit, families are suffering temporary economic harm, as Judge Haden put it. There ain't no thing temporary about it." Vance paused for breath as cheers interrupted. "It's really unbelievable that a few environmental extremists—and that's what they is—extremists could accomplish derailing the whole coal industry. They place microorganisms, mosquitoes and lizards above human needs. You got to rate that as the number one dumbest argument ever made.

"I would like to say to Judge Haden, and I'm going to quote another Biblical verse: 'You shall do no unrighteousness in judgment.' I've never begged for nothing for myself. But I'm going to beg him to look at this." Vance pointed to his wife, his son, and his daughter sitting near the podium. "Here's my family. When you hurt my baby girl and my baby boy, you've made me madder than hell, and I'm going to fight and do anything I can." The crowd applauded madly. Vance walked back to his seat and pulled his young daughter close.

In the crowd, Bob Schultz looked at his friends and neighbors and worried.

———

Senators Jackson and Kessler both wore navy suits the morning of the last day. When SB 681 came up for vote, Kessler explained that he had added a requirement that DEP study ground vibration. The vote was perfunctory: Unanimous yeas.

Kessler looked over at Jackson, who smiled back. Together, they gave a thumbs up.

———

At the end of March, the governor's office held a bill-signing at the Logan

Airport, where Elaine's daughter worked. Elaine, Ralph Preece, and WVOP secretary Pearl Short drove up to the small landing strip on an old strip mine. In the public speeches, Jackson spent two minutes heaping praise on WVOP. But when it came time for the signing, no one had a copy of the bill. Elaine dug her dog-eared copy out of her satchel and handed it to them. When the ceremony concluded, Elaine tucked the only signed copy of SB 681 back in her satchel and drove back to the WVOP office.

Chapter 14

Frenzied Negotiations

Sun warmed the narrow streets of Logan Saturday afternoon, March 27, but the mood in the shops was gray. A poster that hung in the window of Nu-Era Bakery, a Logan landmark, verbalized the pervading concern:

> Southern West Virginia
> Coal Field
> Worship Service
> 3/28 2 p.m.
> We ask all Southern West Virginia [words obliterated]
> Church special meeting. Let us come together
> One mind and one accord and pray for God
> To perform a miracle by saving our jobs.
> Our very livelihoods and the State of West Virginia
> Is endangered by the mountaintop removal catastrophe
> Gene Phillips 369-3276
> Bob Schultz 369-4961

Arch had already begun taking heavy equipment off the Dal-Tex mine, and miners had been told they would be laid off by the end of the year.

"People are afraid to buy anything," said the proprietor of a pawn shop, "because they are afraid they will lose their job tomorrow. It's not just the miners. It backs up all the way down the line to automobile dealers. Where 300 people aren't going to be working, that's 300 pairs of boots, 300 tanks of gas, 300 lunches. It hurts everything."

Indeed, Logan was built on coal. Now about three-quarters of that coal came from mountaintop mines in the county. The assessor estimated that at least half of the county's $16 million budget came from taxes on coal. The 5 percent severance tax on the sale of coal made up about 5 percent of the state's general revenue. Of that, 80 percent went back to the fifty-five counties, and those with a lot of mining, such as Logan and Mingo, received the most.

Most county residents have a relationship to coal, a tie that those who live elsewhere can't presume to understand. Like members of a dysfunctional family, they cling to the security of this shadowy brother—for better or worse. "We grew up in coal camps, and we didn't turn out so bad," said Jerri Hamaker in a gift shop on Stratton Street.

Jim Hutchinson, who owned the shop, had lost his father and his grandfather in mine accidents but still saw coal as the only economy for Logan. "You take a miner five years before his UMWA pension," he said. "It's a kick in the pants. Retrain for the furniture market—that's an insult. I have no idea what else you would do here.

"I lost my classmates and classmates before me to Michigan, Ohio, Florida, industrialized areas. They went into the steel industry. In places like Cleveland, Ohio, you could step out into a mall and holler 'West Virginia,' and half the parking lot would come to you.

"If you poll the environmentalists raising hell," Hutchinson continued, "not a one from West Virginia. They don't have any business shutting down our mines. I think what started this is they want to fill in a few little streams, dry 10–11 months out of the year. That would eliminate some old memories. You can't eat memories."

Those who grew up in the coalfields were accustomed to mistreatment by mines. They recalled when the Guyandotte River through Logan was black with coal waste. Nowadays, mountaintop removal—governed by dozens of regulations—seemed far better than the old, unregulated strip mining. Besides, many local residents liked having flat land on the mountains—after a lifetime crowded up in hollows or perched precariously at the edge of a river that tended to overflow in storms. The view from inside the coalfields was far different from that of East Coast environmentalists, who would settle for no less than a pristine environment. For years, this clash of perspectives would color the mountaintop-removal debate.

Bob Schultz couldn't understand the big deal about the streams—or Approximate Original Contour—either. "The water isn't bad—and we've been stripping here since the 1970s. I can guarantee you will catch bass in Spruce Fork. If you stay down here by my house, you will catch trout because they stock trout."

After his many years of watching mountaintop mining, he agreed with Arch's experts that there's only so much mountain that can be put back. You can't pile dirt that high—anyone who has reclaimed a strip job knows that. What he, and many in the coalfields, wanted was flat land. Farmers, he believed, could grow trees and make pastureland up there—as long as the topsoil had been put back after mining.

In the weeks after Haden's ruling, anger at Weekley scorched through Blair and Sharples. Most everyone knew the Weekley family. They thought the world of his father. But they'd seen Jimmy take short-lived jobs at the mines or logging, finally settling into welfare and disability. The miners knew he had been convicted of a small drug charge. When Jimmy's son Jackie began drinking, Bob and his friends feared Jackie had beaten his wife. Then his wife killed Jackie and was now serving her sentence. "That's why we're so mad," Schultz said. "We know these people."

Now the situation in Blair—that was different. They were done wrong—dust, blasting. Bob knew that. "Instead of being a good neighbor, Arch rode roughshod over everybody. Now everyone and their mother hates the miners' guts."

Most of all he worried about where he'd find work. A truck-driving job started at $8 with no insurance. Crane rental paid $10 an hour. That was about all there was. Bob figured he needed at least $13 to take care of his family. If necessary, he'd go to North Carolina like other Dal-Tex miners. At least his diesel-mechanic skills were transferable.

————

A delegation of about forty-five coalfield officials and coal representatives went to Washington, D.C., in April. They told their senators and their representatives in the House that OSM had to speed up approval of mountaintop-removal permits—and find a way to keep Arch mining around Blair. Soon staff for Senators Jay Rockefeller and Robert C. Byrd were calling Joe Lovett. No elected official wanted to be responsible for miners being out of work. *Don't they realize,* Joe thought, *that the coal will be all mined off the mountains in a decade anyway—then there won't be anymore mining jobs.* Nonetheless, he agreed to try negotiating a settlement of the issues of the *Bragg* case, as the senators wanted.

The first meeting at the Jackson Kelly law office was mass mediation. Jackson Kelly attorneys Roger Wolfe and Warren Upton were there, as was coal lobbyist Bill Raney. Blair Gardner and Bob Bays participated for

Arch. Blair Gardner kept asking Joe to tell them how Arch could improve the Dal-Tex permit and satisfy the plaintiffs. But again and again, the coal folks said they could only do so much and afford to mine coal at the current low prices. In thirty years of environmental law, Pat had seen this argument proved wrong again and again. The reason was technology. Yet coal always seemed to be the last industry to innovate. Pat told them they probably wouldn't be able to mine every ton—but they would mine enough to make a profit.

In April Governor Underwood wanted to meet with all sides and hammer out a solution. Pat and Suzanne, the only ones who had to drive 160 miles, came in a bit late. Four state troopers surrounded the entry to the Robert C. Kelly room at the Jackson Kelly office tower—which Vicky had dubbed the Darth Vader building for its dark glass exterior. Photos of the firm's African safari covered the walls—the one familiar link for Pat and Suzanne, who had spent part of their honeymoon on safari. Just two seats remained when Pat and Suzanne opened the door. Pat gently nudged Suzanne into the one next to the governor. The discussions stretched for hours, with Roger Wolfe trying to calmly take steps toward settlement. Moving for a summary judgment—for quick resolution—was considered. But in the end, nothing was resolved—a wasted trip down from Morgantown, Pat thought.

What made quick resolution so difficult was that action was occurring on numerous fronts. It was kind of like fighting a war instead of a battle. Meetings had begun on the design of the Environmental Impact Statement, an outcome of the partial settlement of *Bragg v. Robertson*. Joe was meeting with the Corps of Engineers about the Section 404 permits for the larger valley fills. What he needed was a team of engineers to monitor all the fills in the pipeline. All he had was John Morgan, who was very expensive. Already, Trial Lawyers for Public Justice had spent more than one hundred thousand dollars on the case. Joe was fielding calls from various national media. Several documentaries were in the works. And he had just learned Gretchen was pregnant with their second child. Some days, he just wished the case would settle.

———

Trish spent the weeks after Judge Haden's ruling—and the passage of SB 681—finishing up the semester and going to out-of-town conferences. Early in April, she, Kayla, and Elaine attended a meeting on headwater

197

streams at the Breaks park on the Kentucky-Virginia border. Kayla wrote her speech on the way down. She told the crowd she didn't think she could live on the property her mommy was going to give her without water. How could she look to a future without water? How could she raise children and teach them the values her mother taught her? There wasn't a dry eye in the place when she finished. Afterward, a woman came up and pressed a twenty-dollar bill into Kayla's hand, leaving the young girl puzzled.

That evening as they ate dinner, Trish had to excuse herself. She was sick again. Elaine worried because she had watched Trish grow sicker over the past few months. Doctors told her she had Crohn's Disease, but still she kept going.

On May 7, Trish was deposed in connection with the *Bragg* case. Pat and Joe had insisted that it not be at Jackson Kelly—so it was at a court reporter's office. Because her deposition was set for the afternoon, she and Elaine went to lunch with Joe, Pat, and Suzanne at Blossom's Restaurant, near Joe's office. The attorneys tried to prepare Trish for the barrage from the coal attorneys. "As long as they don't ask what color my underwear is," she joked, "I won't be offended." Then she became serious. "Okay, what questions are going to upset me?"

"There will be a lot about mountaintop," Joe said.

"They just aren't doing a good job of enforcing the regulations," she replied.

"Be matter of fact, and don't make faces," Joe said. "And be glad Pat's not doing the deposition." Everyone laughed.

"They do know I'm sick," Trish said.

"Yes," Joe said. But the only way they could have kept her from the deposition was to write the judge.

"You should tell them your illness is aggravated by stress," Suzanne suggested.

Oddly, the deposition room was not office grey—but lavender. There were upholstered chairs covered in coarse-weave purple fabric, pale lavender paint. "Isn't this pretty," Trish remarked. A few minutes later, Joe took stock of the setting. "It's ugly—it's purple," he pronounced.

Trish abided most of the questions—until the DEP attorney's turn. He kept asking about her job, Dewey's job, and when Dewey had worked last. *It's like he's trying to form a case against us,* she thought. *Those poor ignorant people on welfare.* He asked Trish if the drainage pipe from her house runs into the creek. She wasn't going to lie. "We don't have public sewer up here," she told him. By the end, Trish wanted to walk around the table and bash one of the attorneys on the head. "Ten years ago, you would have had to get me out of jail," she told Joe later.

Attorney Bob McLuskey told Joe afterward, "I heard her testify at some hearing, and she was full of vim and vigor. She isn't feeling well, is she?"

Before the deposition, Trish and Elaine had visited John Ailes at DEP. Arch had applied to expand the longwall mining under Pie. Trish was trying to stop the permit, pointing out that Eli McCoy had promised no mining on her side of Pigeon Creek until public water had reached Pie. The water was coming, but it wasn't there yet. Trish had constructed an agreement on paying for water replacement that she wanted to present to Arch. After consulting several water companies, she estimated a cost of $28,800 for each of forty families, enough for twenty years of water. First, she wanted John Ailes to review it.

It turned out that he wanted some changes in a couple of paragraphs. That was because DEP planned to use Trish's proposal as a model for water replacement and reimbursement in other communities.

As the meeting ended, Elaine asked Ailes, "Did you know Trish is in the honor society "Is that honorary or ornery?" quipped Joe Parker, an assistant chief for mining.

As Ailes and Parker accompanied Trish and Elaine up the rabbit's warren of cubicles to the front door, Parker paraphrased the verse from the book of Isaiah that Dr. Martin Luther King Jr. had used in his "I Have a Dream" speech: "The mountains shall come down, and the valleys shall come up. Does that mean there will be valley fills?"

"No," Trish shot back. "It means we will be equal with the coal companies."

Now there was a new legal team in the ballooning group of players. Shortly after the Haden ruling, Governor Underwood had hired Ben Bailey and his younger partner, Brian Glasser to handle the *Bragg* case. Bailey and Glasser were not coal experts, but Glasser, a tall man in his early thirties, had just won a big mining case for James "Buck" Harless, a timber and coal baron in Mingo County and a staunch Republican supporter. Glasser was a Democrat and had run Lloyd Jackson's brief campaign for governor in 1996. Bailey, in his late forties, was a Republican and had been a well-respected assistant U.S. attorney. Actually, he was the one Governor Underwood had hired; Glasser came with the package.

The two men struck an immediate rapport with Joe Lovett. Like Joe, Ben Bailey and his family lived without television, being devoted readers instead. Brian Glasser, immensely personable, had graduated summa cum laude from West Virginia University, gotten his law degree from Harvard, and was the state's most recent Rhodes Scholar. He had known Joe when they were growing up in Charleston and had been friends with one of Joe's stepbrothers. More recently, Joe and Brian had become casual friends within the Charleston legal community.

Lack of mining expertise didn't worry Glasser. Being a trial lawyer, he was used to immersing himself in new subjects, then moving on to another field when the trial ended. At Harvard, he'd already chosen to be a trial lawyer, spending as much time as possible outside of class and representing legal aid clients. Normally, he would have twenty or thirty clients at a time. But the *Bragg* case consumed him; he put all his other cases on hold in April and May as he and Bailey studied mining regulations. Comprehension took a while—you couldn't drop into this maelstrom with instant understanding, Glasser realized.

Not one to waste time, Glasser jump-started settlement discussions on May 3 while the lawyers were gathered at DEP. Pat had just finishing deposing one of the officials in preparation for trial of *Bragg*. Joe, Jim, Pat, and Suzanne had expected Haden to decide the buffer-zone and Approximate Original Contour issues. In fact in late April, they had asked him to issue a summary judgment (a decision based on briefs filed by attorneys, without a hearing) on these two most important points. Other claims, including hydrologic impacts and contemporaneous reclamation, could be settled.

Early on, Glasser had determined that the DEP permitting staff interpreted buffer zone, reclamation, and AOC inconsistently, partly because permits were reviewed at four different DEP regional offices. Those were easy fixes—train staff and develop universal policy. As for the more difficult matter—the size of valley fills—suggestions were flying at Bailey and Glasser. Glasser met with Terry Vance of the UMWA and the Coal Association.

He was spending ten hours a day at Jackson Kelly while also trying to line up witnesses in case the major issues went to trial before Haden.

He realized that negotiations would go better if it was just Joe and him—and a third lawyer from Jackson Kelly. In one of those improbable twists, like the ones that had brought Arley Johnson and Judge Haden to Trish Bragg and this case, Terry Sammons, that third lawyer, appeared associated with the coal industry—but had a heart for the people of the coalfields. Now in his late forties, Sammons, one of four sons of a UMWA miner, had grown up in a coal camp at Mud Lick near Gilbert. With a degree from Berea College in Kentucky, where kids from the coalfields can work to pay for their tuition, Sammons took a teaching job in Gilbert. When timber and coal baron Buck Harless saw Sammons maximizing his time with other jobs pumping gas and delivering newspapers, he decided he must hire this industrious young man. To environmentalists, Harless seemed an "antichrist," the power behind Governor Underwood, as Harless retorted after an article in the *Charleston Gazette*. But in the coalfields, he was often seen more as a rags-to-riches story. He had, furthermore, funded a home for foster children (his wife had been one), built a grand community center in Gilbert, and even turned his multimillion-dollar timber business over to employees. After fourteen years with Harless, Sammons became wealthy with his own business of coal-testing and advising on environmental permits. Selling the company assets, he embarked on further education, with first a master's program in environmental science and then law school. On a whim he had applied to Harvard as well as to a half dozen average schools—and was accepted by Harvard. Now he had taken his Harvard degree to Jackson Kelly just in time to join the *Bragg* defense team.

Sammons had one objective in the negotiations: to help the people of southern West Virginia. He loved the people—they were friendly, caring, and genuine. After a century of scratching out a living, scrunched in narrow hollows surrounded by coal mines, these people deserved something better. Already chairman of the Mingo County Economic Development Authority, Sammons decided the weed-infested flat land on mined-out mountains could be used for homesteading. A family could have a vineyard and make a decent living. His own father had been laid off from the mines in 1962 and had gone to Chicago looking for work. Sammons told

Joe and Glasser that in the end it was the miners who would be hurt by this case—not Joe, not Glasser, not himself.

Nearly every evening in late May and early June, Joe, Glasser, and Sammons could be found sitting on the porch, either at Joe's rented house deep in the woods above Charleston, or at Sammons's elegant home along Virginia Street in the heart of the city. By the end of the first week of June, they had devised a plan that would shift the burden of proof for blasting damage to the coal companies—just what WVOP had asked for originally the year before. Joe had come up with the concept of a land trust mostly in the middle of the state for recreation and capture of carbon dioxide emissions from coal power plants. For each acre of valley fill, coal companies would have to put 1.25 to 3.75 acres in trust, depending on the size of the fill. In addition, valley fills would be smaller. Hardwood forests would be replanted on mined land.

There was just one catch—the plaintiffs would have to give up their buffer-zone claim, and the Dal-Tex mine would proceed behind Weekley's house.

The environmental community went into a tailspin, as word of the deal filtered out. This was their one chance to stop mountaintop removal. Pat doubted that would happen, since the law specifically allowed mountaintop removal when in compliance with regulations. First Haden would have to rule in their favor, then they'd have to win the appeal at the Fourth Circuit, the most conservative court in the nation, and possibly win again at the Supreme Court. In case they won all these, Congress could still pass a law eliminating the buffer-zone rule. Even Cindy Rank disagreed with Joe; she wanted to go to court. Her fear was that the land-trust money would be diverted elsewhere, just as she'd seen mitigation paid for large valley fills spent outside of southern West Virginia. Trish, as usual, agreed to whatever Joe thought best.

Since the West Virginia Highlands Conservancy was a plaintiff, President Frank Young called a special board meeting for a vote on June 10. The board was clearly divided. Pat, who represented Highlands, gave the bottom line: a settlement would reduce mountaintop removal somewhat and benefit coalfield residents. Even victory with the buffer zone would do far less.

"I don't want reform, I want it to go away," said Julian Martin, a miner's son who had taught school in Lincoln County for many years and had fought against strip mining in the 1970s. "I don't see making a deal with people I don't trust."

"One of my problems," Cindy Rank said, "is that for years DEP has been accepting mitigation money from coal companies, filling streams in southern West Virginia and spending that money to restore damaged streams in other parts of the state. The idea of purchasing land in the middle of the state in exchange for filling valleys in the southern coalfields is just more of the same and not at all fair to all the communities where mining is destroying their lives. Furthermore if we do settle, a lot of people out there on the fringes will think the problem went away." Pat and Suzanne weren't sure the environmental community had been that strong in the past few months. They realized that they should have emphasized that the West Virginia Highlands Conservancy didn't take miners jobs—the problem was that DEP had failed to obey the law. Pat said, "There's no reason the environmentalists can't ratchet up publicity and make DEP's ineptitude a big issue."

Judy Rodd, who, with her husband, attorney Tom Rodd, had dealt with acid mine drainage issues in the northern part of the state, suggested that Highlands should put up a lot of money for a media campaign. "We need a whole lot of stuff happening," she said. "The coal industry has spent an amazing amount of money trying to convince the public mountaintop removal is okay."

John McFerrin, who was also on the WVOP board, had been leading the debate. "My experience has been that lawsuits don't eliminate industries," he said. "We don't have the power in the court system to stop the whole strip mining industry. The only way I've ever seen anything succeed in court is to worry it to death. The route I see to eliminate mountaintop removal is to raise the cost and make it uneconomical. If they have to buy land in the reserve that is an expense. If they have to do AOC (instead of leaving flat land), that is an expense. I can only support the settlement if we pledge to each other that we are going to soldier on and will fight on and make the message that this is the beginning of our campaign to end mountaintop removal."

At 6:52 p.m.—after four hours and twenty minutes of debate—the board voted. Before the yeas and the nays were given, Frank Young said that, as president, he would vote only if there was a tie. "My head says to

support the attorneys," he said. "My heart goes with the mining committee chairwoman. Cindy I love you."

The vote was nine to seven in favor of the settlement. Cindy, nearly in
tears, had voted no.

For five days the case was settled. Then it wasn't. The ever-shifting debate hit a sinkhole. Blair Gardner wrote a letter for Arch Coal, slamming
the settlement. Although Arch had always seemed uneasy with the land-
trust idea, Glasser was puzzled. Since he knew Joe had already gone home,
he hand-delivered the letter to him. Oddly, Joe seemed pleased—perhaps,
Glasser thought, because it meant the buffer zone and the Spruce Fork
permit would go to trial. For a few days, Glasser thought the pressure
from top government officials might change Arch's position. But then
OSM called to say it was starting rule-making to clarify the buffer zone.
Now it seemed impossible for Joe to deal away his buffer-zone claim.

Negotiations resumed for another month. So consumed was Joe that
he would wake up in the middle of the night and think of a word to
change—then worry about what Glasser would think. Finally a new agreement was hammered out. Gone were the land-trust and blasting restrictions. What remained were smaller valley fills, replanting hardwood forests on mountaintop mines, and homesteading. The new design for reduced valley fills quickly came to be known as AOC+ or the "Castle formula" because Mike Castle, a special assistant at OSM and a mining engineer, had created the design, with help from John Morgan. A few months
later Castle was named head of DEP.

There was some good news for Joe on the Spruce Fork mine. The
Corps of Engineers had withdrawn its approval of the Spruce Fork mine
under Nationwide Permit 21 for Section 404. Arch then was forced to
redo the permit and submit it for individual review—and it now was governed by the December 1998 settlement requiring individual review of
fills larger than 250 acres.

The West Virginia Highlands Conservancy board easily approved the
new settlement. Trish supported whatever Joe thought best. Burr Hatfield,
the Madison attorney, had withdrawn shortly after Haden's ruling, saying
his sons were being harassed. Joe expected the other four plaintiffs to agree.
Only James and Sibby Weekley remained a question mark.

James and Sibby came to Joe's office on July 12. He left saying only
that he would think about the agreement. When Glasser called to say the

Graffiti painted on a new bridge near Blair during the summer of 1999.

Coal Association had agreed, Joe told him Weekley had, too. The next day, he sent two law students, interning with Joe for the summer, down to Blair with the agreement for Weekley to sign.

Just as Joe was hurrying out of the office around 5:00 p.m., the phone rang. "He won't sign," one of the students said.

"Be patient," advised Pat, who was in Joe's office with Suzanne. "You should have gone down to talk to him. You need to hold his hand."

"Law would be great without clients," Suzanne joked. "Tell him," Suzanne whispered, "that all the other clients have agreed."

Joe was talking to Weekley now, rocking in his chair, holding his car keys in his left hand: "Have we protected your interest? Have we saved your land? And we will keep fighting against that permit. It's time to let it go and move on. You need to take care of yourself."

On the side of a new bridge near Blair, someone had painted "Fuck You Jim Weekley," "Fuck Carlos Gore," and "Fuck Vicky Moore." Tommy soon painted over Vicky's name. Weekley said he had received phone threats. "Have you taped any threats?" Joe asked. "If you have a tape, we will call the police."

After about twenty minutes, Joe gave up. He was late for dinner at his mother's. As he reached the sidewalk by his office door, he paused, looking thinner and frail, and said to Pat and Suzanne: "What I've learned about negotiations is that if other people aren't there to see the incremental steps, they get upset. They don't see the rationale behind each decision."

Two days later, Weekley had disappeared. No one answered the phone when Joe called. The next day, Friday, July 16, one of the law students called all the Weekleys in the phone book, finding one related to Ulysses S. Grant, but none to James. Before she started searching for his sisters, she walked into Joe's office and heard him on the phone with James. He had gone up into the woods to think. Firmly, Joe told him they weren't going to trial. Judge Haden would think him crazy if he walked in asking for a trial while the defendants came in with a settlement.

"Dealing with my clients is worse than dealing with the coal companies," he told Pat and Suzanne. "I'm going to have a little environmental law firm and do clean air cases. That's what I wanted to do and I got sidetracked."

Just as Weekley decided not to settle, Trish began getting phone calls. People from environmental groups didn't want her to agree, either. She felt sorry for Weekley; he had been through so much. These people were just confusing him, telling him this part and that part of the settlement weren't good. Her answer was that she listens to Joe.

Another week passed. By Wednesday, July 21, Weekley still hadn't signed. But Joe thought there was hope. Trish and Dewey and Cheryl Price, a plaintiff represented by Pat and Suzanne, gathered in Joe's office waiting for Weekley. Cindy and Carlos Gore were on speaker phone.

"Cindy," Trish began, "Let me ask you a question. Now that Highlands has made a decision, do you stand behind it?"

"Yes," Cindy replied.

"I don't want to make a decision," Gore said.

"I think a lot of my hesitations of a few weeks ago are less because this settlement doesn't include the buffer zone," Cindy offered. "If I were in your shoes, I would vote for it."

"You aren't the ones who sit down here on a keg of dynamite," Gore replied. "All hell might break loose."

"What happens at Blair doesn't ride on this consent decree," Cindy said. A consent decree is issued by the judge after the parties to a suit have agreed on a settlement. "If the judge comes up with a ruling supporting the buffer zone, it will apply to Arch because they have to get a new permit. Whether Arch goes to Wyoming or starts mining in Blair tomorrow doesn't depend on this." Then she added, "The things we are talking about in the consent decree won't stop Pigeonroost."

"And that is what Jimmy is worried about," said Gore.

"That's outside the consent decree," Cindy said.

"That's where you lost Jimmy," Gore added. "He wants to stop mountaintop removal."

"I've explained that to him many times," Joe interjected. "I know you are all under pressure. I hear it in your voice."

"Didn't you say the consent decree would go forward without Jimmy?" Gore asked.

"I think it will," Cindy answered.

"That doesn't mean squat to Jimmy," Gore said. "Last night he told me do what you want. Jimmy is headstrong. He will bite off his nose to spite his face."

"The whole problem is I don't want him to cut off my nose," Trish said.

"Well, honey, you better get ready," Gore said.

Then Gore put his wife, Linda, on the phone.

"I don't understand a whole lot," she said. "Where's that extra dirt going to go if not in valley fills?"

"What they will do is pile it back on top or in valley fills, so they are actually restoring the mountains closer to the original shape," Joe explained.

"Isn't there anything coming out of this suit for the people of Blair?" Gore asked, referring to the years of dust, blasting, and burning houses. "We can't get lawyers to work on personal suits. I get sick and tired of dealing with lawyers who can't fight coal companies."

Gore had hit the nerve of the problems in the coalfields. Joe and other environmental lawyers and green groups saw the situation in terms of environmental laws. Pat and Suzanne, though they had sympathy for coalfield residents like Trish and Gore, felt that most blasting and other nuisance cases would be difficult to win before juries in the coalfields. Few other lawyers had stepped forward to take cases.

Joe was boxed in by the rules of litigation. "One thing: we are not afraid to fight coal companies," he said. "We beat that permit across the road. That's what we promised to do—and we did it. When bringing suit against the state and federal government, we can't sue for past actions."

"Why can't we have a clause in here so we don't have to get out here and fight [blasting and dust] all over again?" Gore asked.

"I agree with everything you say," Joe said. "We should stop these people from doing this."

"Joe is right," Cindy said. "In this particular case, we can't get into this."

"What if another company comes in here," Linda asked, "Can this stop them?"

Joe held up his hands in frustration. "We would have to go in and try to beat them down."

"Well, Linda what do you think?" Gore asked his wife.

"If it's as good as it's going to get," she replied.

Joe gave a thumbs up and grinned.

"You got your answer, Joe," Gore declared.

"Carlos," Joe asked, "What should we do about James?"

"God help you if you can change his mind," Gore answered. "He tells one person one thing and another person another thing."

———

Harvard Ayers of Appalachian Voices was at Weekley's house the next evening. Whether he had formed Weekley's thoughts, no one could know. But Weekley was firm. "We will win," he declared. "The judge will stop mountaintop removal. And they will go back to deep mines. They will get the coal here [in Blair]. There's a 32-foot deep seam under here."

For miners like Bob Schultz, thoughts of going back to the far more dangerous underground mines would bring shudders. Environmentalists would cheer. Would Weekley prove to be a seer or a lunatic?

———

On Friday, July 23, Joe awoke at 4:00 a.m. obsessing about Weekley. This had to stop. At 9:00 a.m., he called the Weekleys to say he could no longer represent them if James persisted in opposing a settlement other clients wanted. In fact, Joe told them, if Weekley continued his opposition, Joe would be unable to continue representing any of the clients. He would have to quit the case. Sibby hung up on Joe.

Pat and Suzanne decided to drive down to Blair and confront Weekley and anybody there who might be confusing the issue. After a few miles, they thought better of the idea and drove around Charleston for awhile before ending up back at Joe's office. They devised a plan. Jim Hecker's research had shown that Joe could have Weekley sign an agreement waiving any conflict of interest he may have had with other clients. Weekley could also get a new lawyer to continue in the case. What was so frustrating for Joe was that he had tried to make it clear that the case was not being completely settled. The buffer zone—the most important SMCRA claim—would be decided by Haden.

They decided that more neutral people had better deliver the letter to Weekley. Chuck Norris, a stream expert working on the case, and Walt Morris, who had brought a case over cumulative hydrologic impact for a group of residents along Island Creek in Logan County, were in Joe's office. So they went to Blair. Pat and Suzanne decided to follow. Only their car wasn't on the street where they had parked it. Pat had forgotten cars had to be moved by 3:30 p.m., opening another lane for rush hour. An hour later, they finally found the towing lot and retrieved their car. They set off for Blair at 4:45 p.m.

"Are you wearing a bullet-proof vest?" Weekley asked when they drove up. Pat and Suzanne realized that Harvard Ayers and Shireen Parsons were inside. Pat and Suzanne perched on the porch steps while Weekley stood on the other side of the porch gate. Pat told him he wanted James to hear from him that the settlement agreement was going ahead. There wouldn't be a trial.

The reality grabbed Weekley. His body language changed, and his eyes were blinking rapidly. Pat realized that Weekley understood—for the first time. Trying to soften the blow, Pat looked around Weekley's yard at the edge of Pigeonroost and said, "It's so beautiful here. I've never seen it in the summer. That's why we wanted to save it."

Upon returning to Charleston, Pat and Suzanne joined Joe and his boss, Dan Hedges, for a drink at Mulligan's restaurant near their office. "I hope you don't spoil your children like you spoil James Weekley," Pat said.

"You have to be paranoid from now on," Hedges interjected. "Those people from North Carolina will be taping you every time you talk to James."

Pat parodied the ethics complaint: "Mr. Lovett harassed Mr. Weekley."

"First case, first victory, first disbarment," Pat joked.

At 4:00 a.m. on Friday, July 30, fierce lightening bolts lit up the sky above Charleston. By 10:30 a.m., the sky had cleared to a thick comforter of hot air as the city faced its twenty-third day of ninety-plus-degree heat that month. Already the stainless steel railings along the steps to the federal courthouse were nearly too hot to touch. Mobile units from all three local affiliates of media networks were parked along the street to cover the consent decree hearing.

Joe and Glasser had filed the consent decree just before the courthouse doors were locked Monday afternoon, July 26. The next day, the provisions were laid out in Ken Ward's story:

—AOC: Environmental groups, regulators, and the coal industry will develop a plan to "optimize" the amount of dirt and rock put back on the mountains. Variances from AOC will be granted only if coal companies show that there is an economic need for flat land.

—Commercial Forestry: The parties to the lawsuit will work together to assure commercial tree growth, with help from two forestry experts from Virginia Tech that DEP will hire as consultants.

—Homesteading: By October 15, DEP will propose new regulations to make homesteading an approved postmining land use. West Virginia residents with less than sixty thousand dollars in household income would be eligible.

—Hydrologic Reclamation Plans: By October 15, DEP will propose new regulations on reclaiming streams affected by mining, as well as how to restore, protect, or replace streams to premining conditions.

—Contemporaneous Reclamation: DEP will start to enforce stronger rules requiring reclamation soon after mining.

—Bonding: By October 15, DEP will write rules to prevent coal operators from getting bond money back before all reclamation is complete.

—Permit Review Committee: A five-member permit quality advisory committee will evaluate and improve mountaintop-removal permitting. Two members will be appointed by Mountain State Justice, two by the coal industry, and one by OSM.

—New DEP Positions: DEP will hire a qualified engineer and a qualified biologist to oversee implementation of the new AOC and post-mining land-use rules.

—Attorneys' Fees: DEP will pay 75 percent of the plaintiffs' legal fees, estimated at $650,000. [This money went not to Joe or Jim, but to Mountain State Justice, the firm Joe worked for, and to Trial Lawyers for Public Justice. Pat and Suzanne did receive their share.]

Joe and Glasser had asked Haden to rule on the buffer zone based on briefs they would submit in the next couple of weeks.

Now at the hearing Joe—and everyone else—would learn what Haden thought of the consent decree. Trish wasn't there. She had spent much of the week dealing with the birth of her sister-in-law's baby and helping care for the other two young children. She didn't have enough money for gas to go to Charleston, either. Joe hadn't reimbursed her for her last trip to discuss the settlement, and Dewey's disability check didn't come until August 3. James and Sibby Weekley were in court, though. As usual, the attorneys' tables on the defendants' side overflowed with lawyers. Joe again wore the gray suit that he kept in his office. Roger Wolfe was suave in a tailored navy suit.

After some discussion between Wolfe and Haden about the status of the Dal-Tex Spruce Fork permit behind Weekley's house, Haden drew himself up and began. "I have a few things to express concern about. I felt the filing of the papers after 5:00 p.m. and the media releases by the parties indicated this case was settled and no trial was necessary. And then the following releases that this will not change coal mining, contrasted with the statement that there was a major victory. I and the general public have not been acquainted with the settlement. There is less here than meets the eye, and things have not been resolved and settled. We are a long way away.

"I ask first who claims not to be bound by the proposed decree: Hobet, the UMWA, the coal lessors, the Coal Association will not be bound. Nor will the United States and its agencies, the Corps of Engineers, the director of DEP who was Michael Miano until yesterday will not be bound now but he agrees to be bound after the public comment period concludes. The West Virginia Legislature, which at some point must approve the regulations, is of course a non-party. Only the plaintiffs are bound to perform the proposed consent decree. I also suggest the public will be bound by the resolution of past issues if the court adopts the proposed consent decree.

"I read something in the media last week that struck me as true. An editorial in *The Daily Mail* suggested the entire case was tried and settled and the public does not know what's in the agreement. I think that's true. I think the public ought to be brought up to speed and given the ability to comment as to whether it should be approved, rejected or sent back to the bargaining table."

Haden took the unprecedented step of asking the public to comment on the settlement over the next forty-five days. He promised to read every submission.

The media converged on the lawyers as they stepped out onto the red-hot sidewalk. Ben Bailey asked, "Is every case going to be decided by a plebiscite now? Only 30 percent of the people vote."

"This is the best possible thing that could have happened," Pat declared.

Chapter 15

The Environmental Impact Statement

During the forty-five days of public comment on the consent decree, the study for the Environmental Impact Statement was actively proceeding. The EIS was one of the benefits gained from settling the Section 404 portion of *Bragg*, in December 1998.

In the middle of August 1999, Jim Green, in knee-high camouflage-colored waders, squatted in a sun-spattered stream deep in the woods, scrubbing wet rocks with a pot brush. The residue contained tiny stream-dwelling macroinvertebrates, which he dumped into plastic sample jars. In a few minutes, Green picked up a thin metal rod about four feet long, attached by a wire to the yellow battery hung from his shoulder. He stuck the probe in the water and read off the speed of the water flow. Next he used a small, hand-held device to measure conductivity, pH, and temperature.

Nearby, Maggie Passmore sat on a rock, ready to write down Green's readings. She guessed the pH would be about 8.5—then reduced her guess to 8.1 when Green said the stream had no algae. It was 8.1599, more alkaline than acidic and thus capable of sustaining life.

A little later, Passmore resumed her sampling, dropping a large white net into the stream. Gently she lifted it and shook out water. Then she plucked a large invertebrate with pointed clawlike protrusions from the net and dropped it into a sample jar, grinning at this treasure: a hellgrammite, the carnivorous larvae of the dobsonfly often used as fish bait.

Green and Passmore, field scientists, were the entire stream team for EPA Region 3, and to them fell responsibility for the stream-study portion of the Environmental Impact Statement. The entire study for the EIS took in most of eastern and southern Kentucky, small sections of north central Tennessee, and southwestern Virginia, as well as southwestern West Vir-

Jim Green (left) gathers macroinvertebrates from a stream in the coalfields as J. Bruce Wallace watches. Maggie Passmore is out of camera range.

ginia. Green and Passmore were based at the Wheeling, West Virginia, EPA laboratory with a support team of a geographic information specialist and two laboratory assistants. Green had worked for EPA since 1967, Passmore since 1990. Their work would be reviewed by Bruce Wallace, a professor at the University of Georgia, who was one of the experts for Joe and the plaintiffs.

Today was the last of six days of sample-gathering in the second of five rounds of sampling streams below existing valley fills, as well as streams in unmined areas. They had sampled in the spring of 1999, and later rounds were planned for November and February and the spring of 2000. Samples were being taken from 37 streams in five watersheds: Spruce Fork near Blair, Mud River near Hobet 21, Island Creek in Logan County, Clear Fork near Whitesville, and Twentymile Creek in the counties east of Charleston. Among those sites, 9 were unmined, 15 were below valley fills, 6 had both valley fills and residences, 4 had past mining other than fills, 2 had past mining and residences, and 1 was in a sediment-control pond. Although they were sampling streams in unmined areas, the reality, Green said, was that there were no virgin streams in West Virginia. Every area had been logged once or twice and then mined, and some areas had gas wells.

This day they were at Hughes Fork, deep in the woods below the Cannelton mine about twenty miles southeast of Charleston, near the Fayette County border. As usual, the fills were far from the mine entrance. Green joked that more of their time was spent driving than in streams. And once they parked, there was still a half-mile hike through the woods to the test site. As the first mountaintop mine, begun in 1977, it was a logical choice for study. Cannelton was designed before mountaintop mines had a few very large fills. Instead, nearly a dozen small fills were scattered in small hollows along Hughes Fork.

Green explained that Kentucky mines tended to the multiple-small-fills design. By the end of 2001, Kentucky had 4,995 fills, nearly five times as many as West Virginia's 1,147. But the average size was just ten acres, compared to twenty-two acres in West Virginia. Kentucky tended to have smaller mountaintop mines because often more rock and dirt covered the coal seams on the mountains, making it too expensive to remove more than a few seams. By contrast, West Virginia had coal seams closer to the surface, allowing for bigger mines and removal of as many as eighteen seams. Permit sizes were also limited because Kentucky mines had to be patched together from many small surface landowners. Green thought they might find different kinds of macroinvertebrates below the two kinds of fill designs, thus helping federal agencies choose the best size of valley fill.

There was quite a crowd along the stream that day. In each watershed, the DEP inspectors, who had helped them choose sites, usually drove Green and Passmore to the sampling spots. For much of the study, Green and Passmore were shadowed by two or three stream researchers from a company hired by the coal industry. Later the coal-industry research leader would go to work with Green and Passmore at the EPA laboratory in Wheeling. The industry wanted to replicate the EPA study in order to judge the validity of the findings.

Generally, Green and Passmore spent about five days in the coalfields, then took the jars of samples back to the lab in Wheeling. Two lab technicians randomly plucked one-eighth of a sample and placed it a white enamel pan, making sure they got at least one hundred organisms. Then the tedious work began. Using dental picks, they pulled out each tiny creature, identified it under the microscope, and logged it in a ledger.

Their entries were later transferred to a computer database. This procedure was called picking. One sample jar could consume a half day—or as many as four days if it had a lot of debris. Once the technicians finished, Green and Passmore would recheck 10 percent of what the technicians had worked on, for accuracy. Most of the creatures—the benthic (bottom-of-the-stream) macroinvertebrates—were immature and not terribly hard to identify to the family level. Since he had more years of experience, Green did all the identification for the 206 samples in this project, because they were sure their findings would be challenged.

"It's a major investment," Passmore said. "People didn't realize that when they wanted us to do 125 samples." In the end, they did nearly twice that number. So overwhelming was the first brainstorming session on the EIS in April that neither Passmore nor Green ate much for a few days. Then they decided they could do only so much—and they'd do it the best they could. In their premountaintop days, one of their proudest accomplishments was a map of the ecoregions of EPA Region 3, which includes West Virginia, Virginia, Pennsylvania, Maryland, and Delaware. They spent ten years on the map, grabbing funding anywhere they could. Now they could drive down a road, and Green would pipe up: "We just went into 67C [one of the ecoregions]."

Their weeks in the coalfields weren't without adventure. Green and Passmore had seen their share of trash dumped in streams, and one morning late in October, they came upon a broken aquarium and a pink hobbyhorse lying next to a stream. They had also seen a number of sewage pipes discharging straight from houses into streams. Even though Passmore tried to eat her lunch before sampling sites contaminated by human waste, she still developed a bad gastrointestinal disorder and wondered whether it was from the stress of the study of contaminated water. J. Bruce Wallace, Joe's stream expert, noted on one trip with Green and Passmore, "Ninety percent of the county needs to learn how to recycle. They should use the mitigation money to remove sewer lines from the creeks."

To Passmore's relief, they met the end-of-2000 deadline for their portion of the study. Their 150-page report was filled with data tables and technical formulas. For the layman, their most important findings concerned benthic life and conductivity. They found most of the streams below valley fills less healthy than those in unmined areas. Each stream was given a

Muddy runoff from a new valley fill at the Hobet 21 mine joins Mud River in 1998.

Stream Condition Index score based on the variety of benthic life. Over the five sampling periods, at least three-quarters of the streams in unmined areas scored Very Good—between 78 and 100 on a scale of 100. By contrast, less than one quarter of the streams below valley fills scored Very Good, while at least half scored Fair (46–70). The worst streams were those impacted both by valley fills and by housing (often with sewage running into streams); none of those scored Very Good.

Conductivity is used to estimate the amount of dissolved solids in water. Land development, including mining and logging, generally hike up the percentage of dissolved solids, which make water running off valley fills muddier than that of the clear streams it joins. High conductivity often means there are more solids in the streambeds. Streams below valley fills had the highest conductivity—generally ten times higher than those in unmined areas. Green and Passmore also found increased minerals, such as calcium, below valley fills. The flow rate of the streams below the fills, however, was higher than in unmined areas. This supported the coal industry's contention that the fills did not impede stream flow. Actually, Passmore believed that more water was not necessarily better water, especially since the water quality was impaired. In addition, merely having water in ephemeral and intermittent streams didn't prove they supported benthic life.

————

Although Green and Passmore weren't asked to calculate the percentage of ephemeral streams, they did find that intermittent and perennial streams started much closer to the head of the hollow than anyone expected. Before the scientists came to the streams, the best measure was the blue lines on the U.S. Geological Survey topographical maps. Green and Passmore found that streams began farther upstream than the maps showed. This would please Joe—but not coal companies, since the December 1998 settlement had promised that the buffer-zone rule would be clarified so that valley fills would be allowed only in ephemeral streams.

Considerable time was spent just trying to define intermittent and perennial streams, as opposed to ephemeral streams. There was the biological definition: where conditions are such that benthic life forms requiring water more than six months a year can complete the aquatic stage of their life cycle. Or the physical one: where water flows most of the year rather than only as a result of rain or snowmelt. For Passmore, the biological definition upheld the intent of the Clean Water Act: "We are supposed to protect, preserve and maintain biological, physical and chemical integrity. The biota integrate the physical and chemical and are the ultimate measurement of 'aquatic life use' and biointegrity."

Calculating the length of ephemeral streams in the coalfields was crucial if Haden ruled to uphold the buffer zone. Preliminary estimates of the length of ephemeral streams had shown that they might allow only 35-acre fills. Valley fills might be restricted to these small areas at the heads of the hollows. So EIS scientists set about predicting fill sizes based on what kinds of streams could be filled. Computer modeling of an actual mine site, assuming that 65 percent of the spoil returned to the mountaintop, gave 20 fills at 250 acres, 27 fills at 75 acres, and 49 fills at 35 acres.

However, even limiting valley fills to 250 acres would significantly reduce the amount of coal that could be mined in some counties. Unlimited fill size would allow mining of 1.9 billion tons—or thirty-one years' worth of surface mining at the current rate. Limiting fills to 35 acres would make 700 million tons unminable—or cut the amount of surface coal left in the state to twenty years' worth, according to the studies.

————

Green and Passmore's study, though it was the most scientifically defensible, was just one of a half dozen, including some by coal companies, that the EIS would cite in trying to clarify the impacts of valley fills on streams. The studies asked whether there was an impact from losing part of the stream, changing the water temperature below the fill, and increasing amounts of sediment. The short answer was yes, valley fills impact a variety of stream characteristics. Yet at the end, the EIS concluded that more study was needed before the impact of valley fills on streams would be fully known.

For Bruce Wallace, Joe's stream expert, however, the impacts were clear. Now age sixty in 1999, he had devoted much of his life to understanding first- and second-order streams. These tiny trickles, which are the first buried by a valley fill, can provide 80 percent of the chopped-up leaves and other nutrients to some downstream species of creatures.

"I hate to think about the future," he said in the summer of 1999 when Green and Passmore were sampling streams. "The eastern deciduous forest is being overwhelmed by fossil fuel extraction. We are in the process of altering the landscape and burying headwater streams, and we don't know what is going to happen in a hundred years."

———

The stream study was one of a dozen planned sections of the EIS—but probably the most comprehensive and a key to the future of valley fills. For example, there would be sections on terrestrial habitat on reclaimed mines, the economic impact of mountaintop removal, the stability of fills over time and in storms, how to streamline the permitting process, and impacts on the community. Not only West Virginia would be studied, but also mountaintop-mining areas of Kentucky, Tennessee, and Virginia. The EIS was expected to cost between $2.4 million and $4.2 million.

Bringing together the four federal agencies involved was like keeping peace between in-laws at Thanksgiving dinner. There was the military-minded Army Corps of Engineers, personified by Rodney Woods, a member of the National Rifle Association, who pointed to Dan Ramsey as an aging hippie with a gray ponytail—confirmation that the people in the Fish and Wildlife Service were all tree-huggers. David Densmore, supervisor of the Pennsylvania office of the U.S. Fish and Wildlife Service, didn't hold out much hope for the EIS, expecting it to become another tower of paper in his office. Like Green and Passmore, EPA was scientifically oriented and a bit liberal. OSM tended to be more bureaucratic, its role reduced to reactive oversight rather than proactive innovation.

W. Michael McCabe had chosen as EIS leader Rebecca Hanmer, former head of EPA Region 4, who had also served as deputy assistant administrator and acting assistant administrator for water in EPA headquarters in the 1980s. She immediately incensed Joe when she put the EIS in terms of preserving miners' jobs. Joe banged his fist on the table: "It isn't only about jobs, it's the future of West Virginia after the coal companies leave."

"We have feelings, too," Hanmer said later. "And those of us who sat through those public meetings were touched by people who said their mortgages were in jeopardy. We have worked so hard under the Clean Water Act to do some kind of balancing."

In early meetings, Hanmer saw the most crucial problem as the lack of thorough monitoring of benthic creatures in the streams below valley fills. Coal officials kept telling her nothing was wrong with the streams—an assertion Green and Passmore would disprove. Hanmer had dealt with point-source pollution at EPA, but she soon realized that ecological disruption in streams is far more complicated. Bruce Wallace and his colleagues at the University of Georgia were recognized experts in this field, and she was glad he was on board. Already the coal industry had protested the validity of the study design for streams below valley fills.

She asked the scientists to help EPA. "In the regulation game, we cannot stand there and say the Clean Water Act prohibits you from touching any part of the stream," she said. "Section 404 envisions development." At a discussion on headwater streams in March 1999, Hanmer asked how many headwater streams could be lost before affecting the integrity of the entire basin. One stream specialist responded, "You ask us is it okay to rob a bank for $10 and wrong to rob for $1,000. We're not going to do that." She pressed on; EPA would have to make a decision. Sounding much like Ben Stout describing stream ecology to Haden, she explained: "The thing we talk about is nutrient transport. Shredders eat oak leaves, and in their waste turn harsh organic matter into fine organic matter. The question is do you need all those first order streams to do it? If you have 50 percent of the streams left, will that be enough?"

The answer could take nine years to determine, Wallace replied. EPA doesn't have nine years—or enough money, she pointed out.

Steven Handel atop a mountaintop removal mine.

Hanmer was particularly interested in using a watershed approach. Pioneering work was being done at Canaan Valley Institute in the northeastern part of the state, which had made presentations to the EIS team. Stakeholders depending on a watershed—including industry and citizens—worked cooperatively to both develop and preserve this area that sustains them. Perhaps the EIS could explore how mining operations could be sequenced within a watershed so as to preserve the hydrologic balance. This concept touched on cumulative hydrologic impact, the concept Pat McGinley had eloquently argued before Judge Haden. Hanmer knew the idea was used in more developed areas, and a few years later invoking the watershed would seem to have been prescient.

———

Steven Handel, a professor of plant ecology at Rutgers University in New Jersey, was Joe's expert on terrestrial habitat. Wearing a N.Y. Yankees cap backward and with a camera around his neck, Handel joyfully bounced across mountaintop mines.

A short man with a salt-and-pepper beard, Handel liked the challenge of restoring wrecked landscapes. He had spent the past six years helping New York City's sanitation department figure out how to grow native

One of Steven Handel's students gazes at a tree on the hill beyond James Weekley's home on Pigeonroost Branch.

plants and trees on its soon-to-be-closed Fresh Kills landfill on Staten Island. As he viewed the coalfields, he marveled at the dozens of kinds of trees in Blair. Everywhere he went, he reeled off names of plants and trees, then plucked samples, carting them back to New Jersey in plastic bags. At least plants were smaller than the rack of elk antlers, caribou heads, and stuffed marlin he had collected on previous field trips.

The next spring and summer, several of his students researched plants and trees in fifty-five areas on and near ten surface and mountaintop mines six to twenty-four years old. They sampled both on the mine and from nearby unmined slopes and forests. And they gathered herbs on the slopes near nineteen of the sites sampled by Green and Passmore. One of the sample sites was a hillside along the headwaters of Pigeonroost Branch beyond Weekley's house, very close to where Haden had stood watching Ben Stout scoop out macroinvertebrates.

Students Kate Burke and Amy Long were there now, in July 2000. A light breeze lifted the tree leaves, with Pigeonroost Branch gurgling background music. A lone "wheet wheet" sounded in the distance. So steep was the hill that they had made staffs from fallen branches to keep them from sliding right to the bottom.

"This is the first place I've seen grown yellow birch," Burke commented.

"This place has done pretty well to save itself," Long surmised. She had already studied more than four dozen sites. "The Zapata mine had wonderful growth," she continued, referring to the oldest part of the strip mining around Blair, done in the 1970s and 1980s.

"We were really surprised," agreed Burke. "Reading the study, we thought this just couldn't be."

"They used smaller equipment then, and the fills were different," Long explained.

The study concluded that the old mines, such as Cannelton, had rich flora, with nearly as many native species as the unmined areas. They found very few of the native species of the forests in the newer mined areas. According to their report, "the poor invasion and growth of native vegetation support the conclusion that these lands will not return to premining vegetation for much time, and will not afford habitat to many preexisting animal species. Less soil compaction, smaller mining areas, healthy soil profiles, and native plant material all would support a healthier ecosystem returning."

After the Surface Mining Control and Reclamation Act was passed in 1977, mines began to compact the soil on mined areas in order to prevent runoff and slides. Rarely was topsoil set aside in the original deforestation—even though the law required doing so. Tree seedlings struggled mightily to grow with few nutrients, trying to spread roots into ground as hard as cement. However, the soil on the finished mines would be more tree-friendly because of the July settlement hammered out by Joe, Brian Glasser, and Terry Sammons.

Commercial tree farming was expected to be one of the most popular choices under the stricter definition of acceptable postmining land uses following mountaintop removal, as required under the same settlement. Using the land for pasture, as grassland, or merely as support for fish and wildlife was no longer acceptable. SMCRA had decreed higher and better use.

Since tree-growing was an essential part of terrestrial habitat, a seeming multitude of agency personnel and lawyers involved in the EIS, including OSM director Kathy Karpan—who had insulted Vicky Moore at

James Burger, forestry professor and expert for the plaintiffs in Bragg v. Robertson, explains how well trees can grow on mined land if the soil is prepared properly.

OSM in Washington—trooped off to the experimental forest on an old surface mine at Powell River in the southwestern tip of Virginia. Here James Burger of Virginia Polytech Institute had been trying different ways to grow trees on mined lands.

"This is what coal mining is all about," Burger told the crowd as they stood among two-foot-wide tall trees on a flawless September day. "This forest is about 80 years old. Each of us uses two trees this size a year."

"What would it take for trees to grow on mines?" John Ailes asked. "Are there sufficient amounts of top soil 10 to 15 feet down to store and then once they [the mines] get it move on?"

"That would be the best way," Burger replied. "The best material is the top 20 to 30 feet, and that always goes into the valley fill or pit where coal was removed."

"It's easier to save something at 10 to 15 feet than go down and get something at 40 feet," Ailes agreed.

The pine trees in sandstone in the test plots were six times as tall as those in ground-up rock shale. "The message," Burger said, "is you've got to create top soil selected for trees, not for groundcover." Trees have different soil tastes than plants.

The crowd expanded as more than a hundred people settled down for grilled steaks under a picnic pavilion. Kathy Karpan was the dinner speaker. Growing up in a mining family, she had learned three things: coal is essential to the economy; it's dangerous (her grandfather had black lung and her father broke his back); and mining does bad things to the environment. The town where she grew up was the subsidence capital of the coalfields.

The *Bragg* case had been the bane of her existence for the past year. But some good had come out of it, she said. "For all the anguish, we've seen redemption. We've seen the heartbreak of people not thinking coal was mined properly. The public is raising the bar—now they want reclamation you can't see. It also means we must work with the coal industry to have the kind of discussions we had today.

"I think there are some win-win situations. Trees are wonderful things. They break the wind and provide building materials. Just wish we didn't have to have a couple of people from West Virginia sue us to get there."

Chapter 16

Unbelievable

We're about to get smashed, Joe thought. He had just learned that Haden had ruled in his favor on his sole remaining claim—no mining within the one-hundred-foot buffer zone for intermediate and perennial streams.

Actually, Joe had thought he had a fifty-fifty chance of winning. He should be thrilled, he thought; Haden had bought all his arguments, Section 404, Section 402—everything. Though it was no longer part of the case, Haden had actually rendered an opinion on 404: "The Court finds and concludes that overburden or excess spoil, being a pollutant and waste material, is not 'fill material' subject to Corps authority under Section 404 of the [Clean Water Act] when it is discharged into waters of the United States for the primary purpose of waste disposal. The Corps' 404 authority to permit fills in the waters of the United States does not include authority to permit valley fills for coal mining waste disposal."

For one brief moment—and it will be brief—we shut down the whole coal industry, Joe thought.

———

"Wednesday, October 20, 1999, may go down as the bleakest day in the recent history of West Virginia." So began Governor Cecil Underwood at the following morning's press conference. "The federal court decision places thousands of families at risk. The decision extends far beyond the coal industry. It potentially affects all forms of mining. It also affects construction of highways and building development."

DEP must halt all valley fills in intermediate and perennial streams, Underwood said, spreading panic through the industry and miners like Bob Schultz. The state budget must be cut by 10 percent to make up the loss of $100 million in taxes on coal that wouldn't be mined.

Already 370 of the 399 miners at Dal-Tex had been laid off. Bob

Schultz had a couple more months of work before the preparation plant finally shut down. Laid-off miners were getting $1,200 in unemployment compensation instead of the $3,000 a month they made at the mine. Arch had also threatened to shut down Hobet 21 and the Ruffner mine along Rum Creek, over the mountain from Blair, laying off 612 more miners.

That afternoon Underwood and his entourage went down to rally the coalfields at the Logan County courthouse. More than one hundred stirred-up local residents, including Raymond Chafin and Rick Abraham, squeezed into the courtroom. Associated Press reporter Martha Hodel, who had grown up in Jeffrey, a coal camp near Blair, was pushed to the floor and bruised.

"New schools, the ability to build sewers are all at risk," Underwood declared. "People in the southern coalfields are faced with the specter of having to leave. Miners go to work, spend their time and take home their paycheck. None of us will stop until this has been solved. It's the fight of our lives."

On behalf of DEP, Ben Bailey and Brian Glasser immediately asked Haden to stay the ruling. Underwood, the coal industry, and coalfield government officials planned a march on Washington and a plea to President Bill Clinton and Congress to immediately change the buffer-zone rule.

———

Trish heard the news from a reporter. "Great," she said. But she had something else on her mind—something bringing her struggle full circle. Piled high in her living room were documents on Arch Coal's new underground permit. Despite those assurances in 1995 that DEP would not allow more deep mining in Pie—on her side of Pigeon Creek—before public water was in place, DEP had granted the permit in June. Public water lines were being laid along Pigeon Creek—but the system wasn't in place yet.

Trish had known about the permit since the spring of 1998. She and Freda Simpkins had spent a few hours looking at the maps in the Logan DEP office. The mine would stretch from Beech Creek, where Freda lived, under a mountain to the other side of Pigeon Creek—impacting 262 houses and going directly under 14. That day Trish had said to Nick Schaer, hydrogeologist in the Logan office, "When we have problems, they will tell us it is the surface mine and the surface mine will tell us it is the deep mines."

"What happens," Freda asked, "if the road collapses and someone falls in?" She wasn't exaggerating. The previous winter, a teenage girl living on Beech Creek had fallen about ten feet into a mine when the earth in her yard had suddenly collapsed.

"They will have a funeral, fill the road in with dirt, and the mining will keep on going," Trish answered, only half joking. Then she added, "Pretty soon all the mines will be joining together."

"They are," replied Schaer, ominously. Schaer was creating a master map of valley fills and mining. His data was the basis for the map of valley fills and mountaintop-removal mines that Cindy Rank had created—and which was a prominent display in the courtroom during the February hearing.

Trish had protested the new Arch mine at permit hearings and had made many calls to John Ailes and Larry Alt—as had her neighbors. All to no avail.

In June, she and Susan and Elaine and neighbors Deb and Herbie Hatfield had met with Blair Gardner at the Jackson Kelly law office to discuss her proposal that Arch reimburse residents for the cost of public water. Joe was there to provide support. Trish had carefully researched the cost of public water in other communities. Her report, "Public Water for Pie," was bound in spiral notebooks and given to all the Arch Coal officials at the meeting.

A family of four would use 400 gallons a day, plus another 50 gallons if they had chickens or horses. Their monthly bill would start at $16 and double over the next twenty years. Therefore, she was asking for $28,800 for each of forty families' water bills over twenty years, a total of nearly $1.2 million.

Blair Gardner turned her down, not imagining the possible consequences. So now she was making one last attempt at stopping the new permit. She was going to represent herself before the Surface Mine Board in two days, on Friday, October 22. Unlike Vicky Moore three years earlier, Trish had lots of support. Joe would be there, as would supportive DEP inspectors.

Trish was attending West Virginia State College now, driving nearly two hours to the campus near Charleston in order to finish her bachelor's degree in psychology. After her classes ended the day of Haden's momentous ruling, she had spent time in Charleston preparing for the hearing with Rick Eades, a hydrogeologist in his forties who had returned to West

Virginia a year earlier after working as a consultant to the federal government cleaning up hazardous waste sites. Tired of the stress, he had gone back to his home state to help out. More than many environmentalists, he would help coalfield citizens with technical issues as often as he worked with environmental groups.

Trish was feeling pretty confident after talking with Eades. "You don't know how powerful you are," he had told her.

A DEP inspector had informed her that an agency attorney was concerned about the hearing. "What is it with them?" she had asked him. "Why are they so threatened by a little fat woman? They told me this thing with the hearing Friday could escalate into something like what I did with mountaintop removal. I said I didn't do anything with mountaintop removal—it was the Logan DEP that did it to themselves."

Joe wanted to be sure Trish was well prepared. He didn't expect her to win—but he did want to get some facts in the record. He had a plan. So the evening after the biggest court ruling of his brief career, he and a mining consultant and a DEP inspector on Trish's side met with her in a conference room at the Ramada Inn in South Charleston for several hours.

At 9:10 p.m., Trish started the two-hour drive back to Pie because she didn't have the money for a hotel room. She arose at 4:00 the next morning and picked up Elaine near Logan. The navy blue sky was still speckled with stars when they arrived at the Nitro DEP headquarters. Shortly before the board's 7:00 a.m. start time, Trish walked in and sat down in the tan chair reserved for the appellant. John Ailes and Nick Schaer were among the DEP staff across the table.

Trish told the board she'd like to make an opening statement but apologized because she was very nervous. "Because of the devastation of my community," she read, "it is very important to bring attention to Mountaineer Mine Number 2 because we have already lost water once. I can't understand why DEP is allowing another mine in the same area. I have been damaged by that same mine, suffered water loss, stream loss up Nighway Branch. It took my right to enjoy the community. I have lost property value."

DEP attorney Tom Clarke countered in his opening statement. "Two times before it had been found that this mine destroyed underground water flow. That is not a reason to deny the permit. By its very nature, mining is going to change the hydrological balance. A water replacement statute exists as the mechanism after the permit is issued to require replacement of water supplies." He explained that DEP had reasserted the 1995 promise in conditions on the mine: no mining could occur west of Route 52 and north of Route 44 until a permanent water replacement system was in place for all property owners within one hundred feet of the edge of coal being mined.

Trish turned to John Ailes and asked, "Are you happy with the condition of replacement water?"

"Not particularly," Ailes answered. "We haven't resolved the issue of a permanent replacement water supply."

Trish called Nick Schaer, the hydrologist from the Logan office, to the witness chair. "Can you tell me where the water loss will be from this new permit?"

"You're asking me to play the role of psychic," Schaer replied.

"You are the hydrologist on this permit, and you don't know how many wells will be lost?" Trish pressed.

"I don't think we'll lose 31 wells all at once like we did before," he replied.

"Nick, do you know that the Hatfields's new well is 300 feet deep and goes dry after 12 minutes?" she asked.

Schaer searched the papers in his files for a minute before answering, "No."

"Nick, do you know the average woman's shower is 20 minutes?" Trish paused. "Nick, do you take showers?"

Everyone laughed.

When Trish took her turn in the witness chair, the Jackson Kelly attorney representing Arch asked, "Are you the named plaintiff in the mountaintop removal case?"

Trish gave him a steady stare and replied, "Yes."

———

At 6:30 a.m. Tuesday, October 26, Joe's second son, David, was born. The day before, what Joe had expected had happened. West Virginia's three representatives and two senators, all Democrats, had begun drafting a rider nullifying the buffer-zone rule to attach to an appropriations bill. Even worse, he had heard that Clinton would support the rider—even though he had vetoed one bill in part because it included a provision exempting

Alaska salmon fishing from the Endangered Species Act. The sponsor of the rider was Robert C. Byrd.

Actually, Haden had addressed the option of changing the law when he wrote: "However, if application of the buffer zone rule, a regulation under federal law, prevents surface area coal mining or substantially limits its application to mountaintop removal in the Appalachian coalfields, it is up to Congress and the Legislature, but not to this Court to alter that result."

Riders—clauses added to a legislative bill but dealing with subjects often different from those in the original bill—had increasingly become a way to weaken environmental laws. By attaching them to popular spending bills, members of Congress, often Republicans, could open wilderness areas to logging or weaken clean-air laws.

Word of this rider put a cattle prod to the environmental community. Their nerve center was the Citizens Coal Council's cramped space in half an office in a brownstone near the Capitol. The group had begun in 1989 because coalfield residents thought SMCRA enforcement was missing. Starting with seven member groups, it had grown to fifty-two, including WVOP. Carolyn Johnson, a veteran of the original battles over SMCRA, had flown in from the Denver office to help Jane Kochersperger, who spent most of the day with her ear glued to the phone. Johnson had mobilized contacts from the original SMCRA debates, careful to add surface mining to mountaintop removal since they would be able to identify with that.

———

On Friday, October 29, Haden stayed his ruling, saying he wanted to "attempt to defuse invective and diminish irrational fears so that reasoned decisions can be made." Now valley-fill permits could proceed in the review process, and operating mines could continue.

Still, West Virginia's delegation pressed ahead with the rider—even though the stay of the ruling was reason enough for the White House to withdraw support.

On Wednesday, November 3, Joe was in Washington for a press conference in a small upstairs room at the Willard Hotel. Finally, the national environmental groups had taken on mountaintop removal, he thought. Brent Blackwelder, president of Friends of the Earth, described mountaintop removal as "a sort of Armageddon visited on the state of West Virgin-

Carol Jackson talks with a reporter about her stream graveyard.

ia." "Today," he continued, "we want to send a very clear message to the President to veto any anti-environmental riders."

That night, nearly two dozen folks from West Virginia arrived in Washington, set to lobby their Congress members the next day. They had ridden twelve hours from Charleston on a Cardinal bus, the same company that Rick Abraham had used to bring miners to Charleston. "You're a lot nicer," the driver told them. "The miners got drunk and rowdy." The bus driver recognized Carol Jackson, the artist who had made the graveyard of streams that was first displayed at the EPA hearing in Logan a year earlier. He remembered watching a miner kick down the graveyard at an EPA meeting on the Environmental Impact Statement in Charleston. Tomorrow, she would set up her largest graveyard on the lawn of the Capitol.

Their first meeting at Senator Jay Rockefeller's office did not go well. He rushed in while they were talking to staffers, said he supported the rider, and apologized for having to rush to a meeting.

They didn't have much luck with the press, either. About seventy-five reporters and television crews were at the other side of the East Lawn, waiting for Vice President Al Gore to emerge from the Capitol. Even an invitation from environmental-group staffers couldn't entice more than a handful of reporters to the cardboard stream graveyard.

Rumors were zipping through the group. They had heard the rider would be on the foreign appropriations bill. "Good," said Blackwelder. "We will send a message to the world that they don't need to bomb us; we are doing it to ourselves."

Their next appointment was with Brad Campbell of the President's Council on Environmental Quality at the Old Executive Building near the White House. Although Clinton wasn't supporting the rider, Campbell was noncommittal about whether Clinton would veto it. "The difficulty we are in is," he said, "if we say something about this rider, it means we don't think the other 20 riders are important."

Only after they had left the building did they get the first encouraging news. "We got the Republican letter," Courtney Cuff, a young woman from Friends of the Earth started screaming, waving her cell phone. "This is really big." Twenty independent Republicans, led by Chris Shays of Connecticut, had written a letter opposing the rider.

"We need to take time to celebrate our victories," Carolyn Johnson said. "If we don't, God won't give us anymore." So they did a group cheer.

The group returned to West Virginia that night, but Joe stayed until the end of the week. Despite manic strategy sessions and many calls to EPA and White House staffers, Joe didn't think they'd made any progress in stopping the rider. *Byrd knows the Senate better than anyone,* Joe thought. *And he wants this more than anything I can remember. I've never seen him go out on a limb like this. He's staked his reputation on it.* The 2000 election was complicating the struggle. Joe had heard that Al Gore didn't want to come out against the rider because he could lose the support of the AFL-CIO, closely aligned with the UMWA. In fact, the only senator willing to stand on the Senate floor and oppose Byrd's rider was Paul Wellstone of Minnesota. He said, "I can speak certainly from what I have seen in eastern Kentucky, and it is pretty awful when that leftover rock and earth gets dumped in the streams."

Oddly, Joe was enjoying the spectacle. *It is really intriguing,* he thought. *I'll never have another case like this. Either good will triumph over evil or evil will triumph over good.*

———

Trish was trying to keep her mind on college while controversy swirled around her. She watched an interview with Terry Vance, the UMWA leader at the Dal-Tex mine, on CNN and felt sorry for him. They had made him look like a poor illiterate coal miner.

Some of Trish's neighbors had stopped talking to her. She felt like a leper in her community. A woman from her church had blamed her for her husband's being laid off. Then she said she'd tell the newspaper Dewey got a disability check. Trish told her that Dewey had worked very hard in the mines. Trish thought, *I've been to the altar so many times and prayed for her.* Elaine told Trish to let the answering machine take the calls. "Let it go. You know what you did, and you did it for the right reason."

Members were calling the WVOP office to cancel their membership. Many were related to miners and thought WVOP had sided with the environmentalists. A leaflet about the case was handed out at Elaine's church. The woman next to her said she'd hate to lose her union medical card. Elaine responded, "I would hate to lose my medical card, too. But I work with people every day who drink bad water because of the mines."

For a week ads ran on television, recruiting miners to march on Washington. On Tuesday, November 9, Bob Schultz and a thousand other miners and coalfield politicians stood on the broad plaza in front of the Capitol. Behind them, soaring toward the crystal blue sky, was the Washington Monument. "People ask why we march," intoned Cecil Roberts, president of the UMWA. "Look at history. Martin Luther King marched, Jesus marched, Moses marched. They didn't just send email or a Fax. Moses had to see the government. We believe our cause is just and our cause is right. We don't ask for a lot today. Just the opportunity to mine coal and burn it."

Senator Byrd, the constitutional conscience of the Senate, stood before the throng, his white hair waving in the wind. He said, "As one who grew up in a coal mining home, ate from a coal miner's table, one who knew the joys and sorrows of coal mining, as one who married a coal miner's daughter, as one who has helped to bear coffins of coal miners up the steep hills of West Virginia, as one who has never turned you down.

"On many instances, I have brought to the floor legislation of interest to environmentalists." Nonetheless, he continued, "I also believe in balance. When God drove Adam and Eve out of the garden, he gave the edict to earn bread with the sweat of their brows.

West Virginia miners rally at the nation's capital.

"This is a crucial time. Your voices must be heard. You at the other end of the avenue [the White House] hear these people. You have been listening to the voices of the other side [environmentalists]. Now listen to these voices. Coal is vital to this country; coal turns on the light in that capitol, coal turns on the light in the White House." Still, Byrd knew hope was fading. Congress was supposed to recess the next day. "We're not giving up, but we've only got two days left. Let our voices be heard."

The crowd began to chant: "Save Our Jobs. Save Our Jobs."

When the rally ended, Rick Abraham and a group of West Virginia politicians walked back to Union Station. "I wonder what Jefferson would think today," Abraham said to the others. "It's amazing how the balance of powers works." Upon Abraham's request, a trumpet player struck up West Virginia's unofficial anthem, John Denver's "Take Me Home, Country Roads."

On the lawn on the southeast corner of the Capitol, the environmentalists were holding their own press conference. Representative Chris Shays was speaking, "I worked with Rahall [Nick Rahall, representative for southern West Virginia] to prevent the rider on mining out west. All of us, including Democrats like Rahall, have been opposed to environmental riders for five years. To negate environmental laws would be derelict."

That day, Byrd released his hold on the Foreign Appropriations Bill, thus giving up his right to insert a rider. He seemed to have surrendered—but environmentalists worried about eleventh-hour amendments.

After the press conference, the environmentalists talked strategy. Perhaps Doonesbury would do a cartoon, or Herblock at the *Washington Post* would. All the major groups, including the Natural Resources Defense Council, Environmental Defense, the U.S. Public Interest Research Club, the Friends of the Earth, the Sierra Club, the Audubon Society, the National Wildlife Federation, and the League of Conservation Voters, were involved. But Joan Mulhern, of the legal group Earthjustice, had taken the lead.

As soon as she read about the Haden ruling, Mulhern knew Congress would attempt a rider. She had come to Washington after working as program director of the Public Interest Research Group in Vermont—a state that didn't blow up its mountains, she liked to say. Earthjustice, which had been the legal defense arm of the Sierra Club before becoming independent, had represented more than five hundred environmental groups. About seven years earlier, it had opened a Washington office to try to prevent weakening of federal environmental laws and, if possible, to strengthen them. She and associates had been able to block a number of environmental riders. The buffer zone fit that mission, quickly becoming one of the biggest rider issues of the past few years.

She had begun work with a conference call involving Joe and others on October 26. Quickly, she got the attention of the *New York Times* and the *Washington Post;* both ran stories October 30 and editorials a few days later. Getting the Republican support was most important—and actually a little easier because they were now battling the Democrats, instead of their own leadership, the usual source of environmental riders. All the environmental groups marshaled members, who swamped Congress and the White House with e-mails.

Mulhern and Courtney Cuff spent many hours in the halls of the Capitol—especially outside S128, the Senate Appropriations room in a lower floor of the Capitol. Even in those pre-9/11 days, security was tight; only members of Congress, staff, and the press were allowed. Somehow Mulhern and Cuff slipped through the warren of Capitol tunnels to the door of S128. There they were joined by Louise Dunlap, who had been a young lobbyist like Courtney Cuff when SMCRA was being debated.

Dunlap enjoyed trying for the sun—just as she'd done in the 1970s. "These laws can only be protected if you are vigilant," she said to a reporter. Dunlap perked up when she saw the chief of staff for the appropriations committee, who had been helpful twenty-five years earlier during the SMCRA battle. Ironically, one of the mass of journalists and cameramen outside S128 was Dave Hess of Knight Ridder, who had covered SMCRA for the *Akron Beacon Journal.*

Outside S128 was the place to be, the evening of November 10—when Congress was supposed to adjourn. It was a lovely part of the Capitol, with Corinthian half columns set into pale-green walls and a floor of black and white tiles arranged in a diamond pattern. The ceilings were curved, with nineteenth-century landscapes. The mass of press waited for appropriations committee members, shouting questions as members rushed by. At about eight o'clock, Representative David Obey appeared. "Four or five issues stalling negotiations, mountaintop removal," he tossed over his shoulder.

"There's Byrd," Dunlap exclaimed as he strode toward the men's room. Seven reporters gathered, waiting. After five minutes he emerged to a question about mountaintop removal. "Remember the story about old stone face last summer," he said cryptically. "I'm old stone face."

"Do you know if it will come up tonight?" a reporter pressed.

"I don't know" was the only reply.

"Will you finish tonight?"

Again he said "I don't know," as he escaped.

The next few days passed anxiously. Mulhern and Cuff spent the weekend at the Capitol lobbying anyone they could find. With no word, many reporters thought Joe's side had won.

Suddenly on Monday, November 15, Dunlap heard that the White House had crumbled. It was sending compromise language. Maybe something that would eliminate the buffer-zone protection for two years while a compromise law was devised. She knew people should have stayed fired up. Late in the afternoon, she rushed toward S128, only to be barred by the guards. Instead she got reports by cell phone.

Outside S128 was Representative Bill Young of Florida, chairman of the House Appropriations Committee. "We agreed to eliminate the riders," he told the reporters, then added that one rider they dropped was Byrd's.

"Has Byrd signed off?" asked a reporter.

"Best I know," Young replied.

Afterward, a CNN reporter joked with another reporter. "They gave Byrd a state. The good news is there isn't a rider. The bad news is now Virginia is part of West Virginia." Well-known around the Capitol was Byrd's proclivity for obtaining funds for buildings and roads in West Virginia—then getting them named after him—not to say the projects hadn't benefited the economically depressed state.

Dunlap wasn't ready to declare victory. Byrd was in West Virginia for a fund-raiser on Tuesday, November 16. He returned on Wednesday and spent hours with the appropriations committee—lecturing it on mining, Dunlap heard.

The White House was caving again. Byrd was going to do them some favor in the budget. In fact, Brad Campbell called Joe Wednesday morning to tell him the White House was considering another compromise for Byrd. Joe heard a click on the phone and realized Campbell had switched the call to his cell phone while walking to Byrd's office. Joe suddenly understood that this was a done deal. Joe called Mulhern, and they conferenced on Campbell's cell phone, with Joe screaming, "Stop!" even as Campbell was in Byrd's office. Byrd rebuffed the offer, and an hour later, Campbell called Joe, a bit bewildered at the outcome—but it was great news for Joe.

Everyone's head was spinning. Chris Shays rushed back from National Airport, where he was about to board a plane home to Connecticut, because he thought Byrd was going to pull something.

The next night, however, it was over for Byrd. Nonetheless, his Senate colleagues allowed him to save face—and created even more panic among Joe, Mulhern, and their associates. The Senate voted 56–33 to attach Byrd's amendment to a continuing resolution to keep the government running through November 23 without a budget. However, the House refused to take up the legislation, both houses having passed a bill to fund the government through December 22. Still, the vote set the stage for one of Byrd's grandstanding speeches on the floor late Thursday afternoon. "Fie on the White House. Fie," shouted Byrd. "Peter heard the cock crow three times—thrice. He denied the Lord three times, and then hung his head in shame. White House, hang your head in shame."

Trish had prayed to Jesus. She watched Byrd's speech, feeling a bit sorry for him. She'd always enjoyed listening to his eloquence. Now he seemed shaky, old. Too bad that people had suddenly forgotten all the great things he had done for the state. Joe figured they had beaten the rider because they were just lucky. Now they'd have to wait a year and a half for the Fourth Circuit Court of Appeals to rule. At this most conservative court in the nation, Joe was sure they'd lose. The near certainty of loss at the court of appeals was precisely why he had recommended that his clients settle the buffer zone claim.

As Joe expected, in April 2001 the appeals court overturned Haden's ruling. The court did not rule on whether the buffer zone was valid. Instead, the three-judge panel deemed that the case belonged in state court and that citizens did not have the right to sue state regulators over failure to enforce SMCRA.

On December 24, 1999, the preparation plant at Dal-Tex had shut down. Two hours before leaving, Bob Schultz cut off the tip of his index finger. At least he'd allow himself time to heal, for he was out of a job for the first time in his adult life. He tried working on road construction and went to a lot of interviews, but he didn't want to be retrained like some of his fellow miners—one had become a chef, another a farrier. In May 2000 his union seniority landed him a job driving a bulldozer at Arch's Hobet 21 mine. He just wanted to provide for his family, see his two sons go to college and away from the mines.

For Trish, more adventures lay ahead.

Chapter 17

The New Era

By 2006 Trish felt not sadness at defeat before the appeals court, but joy in other victories that had come from her efforts. The case and Trish's own struggle had changed the coalfields for the better in significant ways. Those who stare in horror at mountaintop removal for the first time in 2007 may not realize how much the coalfields have moved forward since Joe Lovett met Patricia Bragg in 1998.

Because of several deep-mining and flooding disasters that occurred in the early 2000s, tougher laws are in place and are enforced. Lawyers, inspired by Joe Lovett and Pat McGinley, have taken—and won—a number of nuisance cases over water, blasting, and dust. Valley fills are smaller, thanks to the new Approximate Original Contour formula. Most mines have chosen to restore the original peaks; the few flattened hills have been replanted with native hardwoods.

Just as the woes coal brought to Pie and Blair were closely intertwined with the downtrodden economy and sometimes corrupt political system, progress in the struggle with coal couldn't come without bringing other industry to the coalfields and giving politicians a shot of courage. The 1977 surface mine law was supposed to allow mountaintop removal only if the flat land was used for economic development. The conversion of thousands of acres to little more than barren grassland was attacked both in the *Bragg* case and by Senator Lloyd Jackson in the 1999 Governor's Task Force report. As a result, Mingo County set the example, creating a master plan for land that would be flattened by mining, bringing in industries ranging from wood flooring to fish farms.

Progress in the coalfields is closely tied to integrity on the part of politicians. Arley Johnson opened the new century, finally standing to his full height against a corrupt legislative handout, courage he attributed to Trish and WVOP. Down in Mingo County, the sheriff—the county's most powerful elected official—campaigned against vote-buying, giving that county its first hope of truly free elections.

As the struggle for better mining continues, it is well to look at a few people, inspired by the *Bragg* case, who cared enough to make a difference. For if they can try, others can, too. Anyone searching for inspiration can look to Trish herself. To be sure, the battle for equality with coal may well continue. But the scales are tipping toward balance.

Disasters and Their Effects

Those who grew up in the coalfields have the specter of the 1972 Buffalo Creek Flood etched into their psyches. Every heavy rain, they fear another flood, another slurry impoundment collapse. From 2000 to 2004, the deluges never seemed to end. Coalfield disasters had always spurred better regulations and oversight. Yet, the intensity of the focus during this period and the dedication of a few regulators were unprecedented.

On October 11, 2000, a large slurry impoundment near Inez, Kentucky, collapsed into the deep mine underneath. More than 300 million gallons of molasses-like black slurry spewed out into Coldwater Creek and Wolf Creek, which fed into the Tug Fork of Big Sandy River, on the state line between southern West Virginia and Kentucky. As the crow flies, Inez is about thirty-five miles northwest of Pie.

An estimated 1.6 million fish were smothered, including every one in the two creeks nearest the spill. Towns along the Big Sandy had to shut off water intakes from the river for weeks. Cleanup took several years and cost $46 million. The coal company also paid $3.45 million to Kentucky in penalties and fines, some for the purpose of restocking fish. About 450 people sued Martin County Coal, a Massey Energy subsidiary, most of them later settling for undisclosed amounts. EPA declared this the greatest environmental disaster east of the Mississippi River.

The huge spill realized fears that had for years haunted Freda Hudson Williams of WVOP. She and hundreds of other residents along the Coal River near Whitesville, West Virginia, lived in the shadow of three impoundments, including Brushy Fork. The Brushy Fork impoundment dam is expected to become the highest in the nation at 920 feet and to contain more than 8 billion gallons of slurry.

Freda's concerns were supported by federal and state governments' weak record of overseeing impoundments. After two impoundments had

Slurry impoundment above Rawl.

(Top) The creek is black near the huge slurry spill. (Bottom) Dried slurry covers a lawn at the house nearest the mine.

collapsed into deep mines in southern Virginia in 1996, dumping thousands of gallons of slurry into streams, the Mine Safety and Health Administration (MSHA) had reviewed all coal impoundments in the nation. There were 650 in all; 220 were built over deep mines, with 77 that could collapse into underground mines. Of those, 32 were in West Virginia.

Freda had been fighting coal companies even longer than Trish. In 1996 she and some neighbors had won a lawsuit to stop coal trucks from a Massey mine from speeding along five miles of Route 1 in Clear Fork in Raleigh County. She was an early member of WVOP and had helped lobby for the blasting bill that Arley Johnson sponsored in the 1998 state legislature.

So it was not surprising that Freda Williams would testify before a committee of the National Academy of Sciences during a study that Congressman Nick Rahall requested after the Inez disaster. The Brushy Fork impoundment and the one near Inez had been designed by the same engineer, she told the scientists. And like the Inez impoundment, Brushy Fork was constructed over a deep mine, because the Massey mine had gone beyond its permitted area. Based on thorough examination of the inspection reports on Brushy Fork, she told the scientists there was a crack sixty feet wide under the impoundment. "It's not a question of if the dam will break, but when," she emphasized to the panel. "We have no evacuation plan. If you live on Route 3 [along Coal River] and read some of these reports, it will give you sleepless nights."

Freda told the committee that several alternatives were already being used at other coal operations. These include filtering water out of the coal and drying the solids into blocks. Coal companies were suggesting injecting the slurry into old deep mines, but leaks had developed in some cases, sending black slurry into adjacent streams.

As Freda knew, the coalfields were pocked with old deep mines from the early decades of the twentieth century. No agency had completely accurate maps of preexisting mines, so it was possible that a huge impoundment could exist over a deep mine filled with water. In 1977 MSHA had issued an advisory that any impoundment built less than one hundred feet above a deep mine was unsafe. Nonetheless, a DEP engineer informed the panel that there were a number of active facilities as little as fifty feet above a deep mine. He was especially concerned about room-and-pillar deep mines where pillars ten to fifteen feet wide are left supporting the roof of mined-out areas.

In October 2001, a year after the Inez disaster, the committee issued its report, urging OSM and MSHA to set a minimum width for the barrier between an impoundment and a deep mine. In addition, it urged development of alternative methods of disposal of slurry, as well as research on the health effects of the chemicals in the slurry. In December 2003, West Virginia received a $1.2 million federal grant to create digital maps of old deep mines.

The Inez disaster also prompted Davitt McAteer, a West Virginia native who was head of the MSHA in the Clinton administration, to establish the Coal Impoundment Project at the National Technology Transfer Center at Wheeling Jesuit University. The Web-based project lists the safety status of all impoundments in West Virginia, Kentucky, and Pennsylvania and is helping local communities develop evacuation plans.

No impoundments have failed in West Virginia yet. What did come were floods worthy of Noah. For four years straight, beginning July 8, 2001, aberrant downpours swept off valley fills, old mines, logging roads, and clear-cut hills, washing away homes and lives. All told more than a billion dollars of damage resulted.

The pattern of storms over the four years confirmed what climate scientists had been predicting: with global warming would come more isolated heavy storms—they just couldn't predict where the storms would hit yet. There had been 2 to 4 percent more heavy precipitation events in the Northern Hemisphere since the 1950s. Data since 1948 for Pineville in Wyoming County, near the center of the 2001 deluge, showed that 1999 through 2003 had sixteen days with rainfall over 1.5 inches, the most intense period of precipitation in a half century.

Trish actually had a trial-run flood Labor Day weekend of 2000, when water rose over the steep banks of Nighway Branch, reaching as far as Susan's house, next to Trish and Dewey's. A DEP inspector told Trish the valley fill hadn't been reclaimed as fast as regulations required, so there was not vegetation to slow the water runoff. New managers from the Arch deep mine got an earful when they arrived on Trish's porch. "All I wanted was water," she began. "What do you want?" one manager asked her, "that the mines buy everyone out?"

In 2001, floodwaters ripped apart hundreds of homes. Photograph by Robert Gates.

"No," she replied, then pointed down the creek to the fancy house below hers and Susan's. "See these houses. You have a mansion, a country cottage, and a shack. And you know who will fight the hardest. I will be here to the end. This is the only thing I've ever had in my name."

The next summer, in 2001, the state had a new governor, and DEP had a new mine director, Matthew Crum. Crum had grown up in Roanoke, Virginia, and had graduated from Virginia Polytechnic Institute and from law school at Washington and Lee University. He had been on the job just eighteen days when his phone rang early Sunday morning, July 8, as pelting rain covered an area stretching seventy miles north-to-south and thirty miles east-to-west: from Fayette County east of Charleston to McDowell County in the southern tip. Losses totaled more than $700 million. At least one-fifth of the area's one hundred thousand residents were displaced or suffered severe damage.

For the next two weeks, Crum spent twelve-hour days flying over the flooded areas and driving up narrow hollows, frequently stopping to talk to distraught residents. When he came home and watched the television news stories, he knew the devastation was far worse than reporters could convey. He was touched personally and vowed to do something. Moved, too, were John Ailes and Ed Griffith, who often accompanied Crum. Ailes, who was now special assistant for mining to the secretary of DEP, was called into duty with the National Guard and sent to help clean up the flooded coalfields.

Many residents blamed mountaintop removal and logging for exacerbating the damage. Four years earlier, on June 1, 1997, a woman and a teenage boy had died along White Oak Creek in Artie, near Freda Williams's home. When a torrent of water swept down the valley fill at a mountaintop-removal mine, the tiny stream became so violent that it swallowed the two as they tried to get from their car to their homes. White Oak Creek flooded again July 26, 2001—again from the valley fill.

In July 2001 other land disturbances had contributed as well. Old piles of waste coal eroded, washing coal into people's yards. Roads to gas wells had become causeways for storm water, as had dirt roads cut to logging sites. Old deep mines had caved in, letting loose their water. To be sure, land disturbances weren't the only problem. Debris dammed streams, spreading water out into nearby communities. Floodplain regulations had not been enforced, leaving many homes in dangerous areas. Residents didn't even know they lived on floodplains, because the maps from the Federal Emergency Management Agency hadn't been updated for two decades.

Hearing residents' charges, Governor Bob Wise called for a study of whether mining and logging had contributed to the flooding. Freda Williams, Elaine Purkey, Cindy Rank, and Rick Eades, the hydrogeologist who had helped Trish, were on the study task force. Using computer modeling on three valley fills, the Environmental Impact Statement from the *Bragg* case had already determined that one of the fills could increase flooding as much as 13 percent. A U.S. Geological Survey study of two years of storm runoff in two watersheds, one mined and one unmined, also part of the EIS, concurred: during heavy storms, runoff increased from the fills, while the fills actually absorbed water and slowed runoff in lighter rains.

Unfortunately, it took another year—and another round of terrible floods—before DEP finished its study in mid-June 2002. Did mining and timbering worsen the flooding? The simple answer was yes, by much as 21 percent at one place in the three watersheds studied.

DEP's computer study of Scrabble Creek, in Fayette County, and Seng Creek, near Whitesville, produced new insights into how flooding happens in the southern West Virginia coalfields. Storms that start at the top of a mountain and move down, as happened on July 8, 2001, increase flows in the hollows. Short and narrow watersheds have less room to slow down the runoff. North-facing slopes, which receive less sun, have less vegetation to slow runoff. The depth and the type of soil are also very important because those factors determine how much water can be absorbed and not run off.

The percentage didn't matter to mining director Crum or to Ailes, who wrote most of the recommended rule changes. Absolutely no increase in runoff from mining or timbering should be allowed. DEP called for valley fills to be built from the bottom up so they would not melt down in heavy rain. Even more importantly, new mining would not be permitted to increase runoff in a watershed. In what DEP called its Storm Water Runoff Analysis, the condition of the entire watershed would be reviewed before creating a new valley fill.

DEP had no authority over logging. Still, the study stated that timbering should be limited by the steepness and soil conditions of a watershed. Previous forest fires could also limit the amount of logging activity. Cut treetops and branches should be removed from roadways so as not to be washed out in storms. Proposed logging sites would be reviewed by inspectors before cutting began.

Crum personally ushered the recommendations on mining through the 2003 legislature. He'd had to compromise with the coal companies on valley-fill design: if topography prohibited bottom-up design, mines could slow rushing water with a long runoff area at the bottom of sediment ponds. Actually, Crum considered the provision that barred increased runoff from new mining his most important accomplishment. As for logging, the legislature did nothing to control potential flooding.

The two years from the summer of 2001 to the summer of 2003 were a brief golden period at DEP. The *Bragg* case was on Governor Bob Wise's radar when the former congressman took office in 2001. He immediately elevated the Division of Environmental Protection to cabinet status and hired as secretary Michael Callaghan, an assistant U.S. attorney, who had been the criminal chief for the southern district of West Virginia. Callaghan, a West Virginia native, was charged with making the agency a tough enforcer. "We want to end the polarization that has taken place over this agency," Wise said at the February 2001 press conference introducing Callaghan. "We want to take on mountaintop mining and get this settled once and for all. It has been described as 'environment vs. jobs.' But we can have both. If we don't have both . . . nobody wins."

To clamp down on mines, Callaghan chose his acquaintance Matthew Crum. After a brief stint as an attorney for the state and DEP in the early 1990s, Crum had spent three years in the Clinton Department of Justice working on environmental cases, especially Superfund hazardous waste sites. When he heard that Callaghan had taken over DEP, he contacted him. They quickly decided mining was the division where Crum could do the most good, since the problem seemed to be lack of enforcement of the laws. John Ailes was moved to special assistant for mining to Callaghan. Cynics would say he was shoved aside. In reality, DEP ended up with two dedicated mining regulators—as the response to flooding would show.

Crum brought to the job a quick grasp of issues combined with a sensitivity and integrity rare among mining officials. Twelve days into his new job, Crum quickly ordered a Massey mine shut down after black water from coal washing spilled into the nearby creek, something he did repeatedly as several more serious spills occurred at Massey mines in the next months. DEP inspectors quickly warmed to Crum, sensing support at the main office when they wanted to curtail illegal mining practices. At one of the first spills, Crum looked at the inspector for the mine and said there were grounds to go ahead and issue an imminent-danger cessation order to shut down the operation until fixes were made. The inspector gave him a strange look and asked, "Are you sure you want me to do that?" Crum told him, "Of course."

Crum wasn't afraid to confront the coal companies. He used DEP's biggest gun, show-cause hearings, on three Massey mines. If a mine has three violations of the same type, it can be shut down. In the past, this had rarely been done, as Vicky Moore had charged in relation to her dust problems. Later, the Surface Mine Board reduced the length of the suspensions, but the point had been made: Matthew Crum was tough.

Toughness didn't seem to satisfy environmentalists, though. In his first months, he wanted to hear from environmentalists, coalfield residents, and the coal industry. The industry marched right in. Crum quickly came to respect Elaine Purkey and Freda Williams and other residents

A concerned resident shows a handful of coal slurry after a spill from the Hobet 21 mine into the Little Coal River in 1997.

of the coalfields as devoted and well-prepared. By contrast, the Ohio Valley Environmental Coalition and the West Virginia Highlands Conservancy never responded to his invitations. Maybe, he mused, they feel they've been burned too often by previous DEP directors or fear their issues will be co-opted.

Before the environmentalists and Crum had a chance to come to terms, he was gone, fired in August 2003 by Stephanie Timmermeyer, the new DEP secretary, only two years out of law school. Michael Callaghan, who aspired to be governor someday, had gone on to chair the state Democratic Committee and ran a strong, but ultimately losing, race for Congress in 2006 against Shelley Moore Capito, the popular incumbent, daughter of former governor Arch Moore. Crum went to head the southwest Virginia office of the Nature Conservancy. He still kept close tabs on the coalfields, advising Freda Williams and working on a plan to grow hardwood trees on reclaimed mines as part of a national carbon sink to lessen air pollution and greenhouse gases. His name was at the top of the list to head OSM under the next Democratic president. John Ailes had gone to Kuwait to serve with the National Guard in the Iraq war. Upon his return, he would retire. Ed Griffith had already retired. What remained were a core of dedicated regulators quietly working among memories of a time of fearlessness inspired by the *Bragg* case.

Lawyers Take Courage

Billboards for personal-injury lawyers were hard to miss around Logan. But no attorneys were out soliciting clients whose homes had been damaged by the mines when Pat McGinley and Suzanne Weise joined Vicky and Tommy Moore's dust case. Lawyers didn't think they had much chance of winning a case against a coal company, and even a rare victory wouldn't net enough to pay expert witnesses.

Because of the *Bragg* case, the legal climate has changed in the coalfields, yielding an unusual convergence of honorable lawyers. When Brian Glasser had listened to depositions from Trish and other plaintiffs, he was shocked at the living conditions near the mine. So it wasn't hard for Joe Lovett to persuade him, or Ben Bailey, to take on what were known in legal talk as "nuisance cases." Carefully, they would try to figure out how to use civil courts to bring a measure of environmental justice to the coalfields. Joe Lovett would cocounsel on most of their cases. As for paying expert witnesses, Bailey and Glasser used some of the four hundred thousand dollars they'd been paid to defend DEP—a kind of just deserts.

Fittingly, Bailey and Glasser began with a case over the water loss in Trish's community of Pie. On October 18, 1999, just days before Haden's momentous decision, Joe and Ben Bailey met with Trish and three dozen of her neighbors, as well as Freda Simpkins and several of Freda's friends from Beech Creek. They gathered in the cafeteria-gym at Varney Grade School, where Joe had first seen Trish two years earlier when she gave a passionate speech about damages from the mine planned behind the school. Now that mine had already cut off parts of the mountain.

Bailey told the local residents that his firm had hired a hydrogeologist and had spent six days reviewing the mine records at DEP. The case would center on loss of water wells, loss of water in streams, and subsidence damage to houses. He was pretty confident he could win this case for Pie's water. "We are talking about money damages," Bailey said. "We are not trying to stop jobs. This is to make sure you are compensated for your damages."

The case could go to trial, but nine out of ten cases are settled, Bailey explained. Not that settling would make the case go much faster. As Bailey predicted, the case dragged on for several years. Having been through half a decade of mining troubles, Trish and her neighbors grew increasingly angry and distrustful of the lawyers. Trish told the attorneys that while they were fighting the case on paper, she and her neighbors were living it. When word of the case got out, Trish once again faced angry words from mining supporters.

"Best damn thing you can do is leave Mingo Logan [coal company] alone," a man told her while she stood in line at a local convenience store. "All you do is take jobs out of people's homes."

Trish turned around. "As long as I live and breathe, I am going to say what I think," she practically spit at him. "I lived with this five years. These mines aren't built right." Then she picked up her groceries and stomped out.

Judge Michael Thornsbury finally ordered the case settled in the spring of 2002. Trish's neighbors showed up at the Mingo County courthouse ready for a hearing. Instead, Judge Thornsbury called the attorneys into his chambers. "The settlement is generous," he told Ben Bailey and Joe. "Take it."

Joe and Bailey left the chambers and conferred with Trish's neighbors. She was at work, and Joe called to tell her. All the plaintiffs agreed. "Hooray for Jesus," said Brother Goodman, who had been at that meeting at Susan's house seven years earlier. Because the case was settled, the exact amount was never disclosed. But it was generous.

Thus began a series of nuisance cases in the coalfields for Bailey & Glasser. They won three more water cases, one in Wayne County and one for Trish's in-laws and a few of their neighbors. Their largest case was against a Massey Energy mine for 245 plaintiffs not far from Trish on Duncan Fork and Riffe Branch along Corridor G. People claimed the mine had taken their water in 2000 and 2001 and that replacement water in water buffaloes (plastic tanks) was frequently contaminated. A jury awarded the plaintiffs $1.54 million, ranging from nothing to $49,000 for the various plaintiffs, but refused to approve punitive damages for Massey.

Their best-known case was over coal dust in Sylvester, along the Coal River. The coal dust had become unbearable late in 1998 after DEP allowed the company to remove a slim ridge and use the fill material as a platform for a coal stockpile and loading area. Sylvester was downwind of the stockpile of coal. Vicky Moore, Elaine Purkey, and DEP inspector Bill Cook had been among the first to try to help the community. Vicky walked through the town and showed them how to video every time they got dusted. Cook tried every legitimate regulatory tactic he could imagine. This dust was wrong, he believed, just as blasting problems were wrong for Dickie Judy.

In October 2000 the Sylvester citizens, led by Pauline Canterberry and Mary Miller, won one of citizens' few clear victories before the Surface Mine Board. At an all-day hearing, the citizens helped DEP defend against Elk Run's appeal of a show-cause order over the dust.

"This came from my furniture," said Canterberry, an energetic gray-haired senior citizen, as she held up a glass jar filled with black dust. "There are people who have lived in Sylvester for 30, 40, 50 years, and now they find themselves on the brink of losing their homes. We have gone to meeting after meeting with the company. Screens have been constructed with no result. How can this happen in America?"

The board took only fifteen minutes to decide. "The company does not have the license to damage communities because they don't have the technology," Chairman Tom Michael said in upholding the show-cause order. "In this business, that's what we call a slam dunk," said John Ailes as the Sylvester residents cheered.

Unfortunately, the show-cause order wasn't enough. Soon after the 2001 floods, DEP mining director Matthew Crum had to deal with Sylvester. Citizens were very impressed when he examined their sooty community and met in their homes. Eventually, he ordered the company to build a dome over the piles of coal, move the piles away from the town, or close the preparation plant. The dome was built, but it was not as effective as the mining director had hoped. Crum was looking into alternatives when he was fired.

In December 2002 Brian Glasser began trying a case before a jury for about 150 of the town's residents in Boone County court, claiming that their damages included $3.9 million in lost property values. Joe Lovett had done much of the legal briefing for this case, though he didn't argue it. One witness Glasser couldn't call was Bill Cook. He had died while jogging in the Kanawha State Forest two weeks before the trial began. About a year earlier, he had left DEP to work as safety inspector for one of the Massey deep mines along the Coal River, thinking he could make things better from the inside.

The judge barred testimony regarding several dozen violations issued over the dust, but Glasser still won the case, though not as much money was rewarded as he had asked for. The jury found Elk Run negligent and awarded $473,000, with $4,300 on average to each plaintiff, but again did not require punitive damages from Elk Run. The greatest victory in the case was not monetary. It came three weeks later when the judge set up a court-overseen dust-control and dust-monitoring system for Elk Run. Included would be enclosure of the huge railroad loading area. Residents could go back to court anytime the dust got bad again. Pauline Canterberry was sad that Vicky Moore hadn't come to watch the trial. Finally, residents had had their day in court over dust.

This case set an important precedent on the award of legal fees to attorneys. Pat McGinley and Suzanne Weise helped Joe and Glasser use the "citizens suit" provision under the Surface Mining Control and Reclamation Act. Although lawyers used "nuisance" as shorthand for lawsuits over dust and water loss, Pat pointed out that the offenses included intentional trespass, negligence, and property damage caused by violation of the West Virginia Surface Mining Act. If plaintiffs prove these three causes, federal and state mining laws allow citizens to recoup the costs of lawyers and expert witnesses. The judge ordered Massey to pay $1.57 million in legal fees and $191,000 for expert witnesses to Bailey & Glasser.

Bailey and Glasser gained a new ally in 2004. When John Ailes returned from the Iraq war, he had reached the National Guard's mandatory retirement age of sixty. Mulling his options, he chose a consultant's job at Bailey & Glasser. Coal folks told him he'd gone over to the dark side. No, Elaine Purkey said, it was the right side.

Yet another attorney was called by conscience to the coalfields. Kevin Thompson, who grew up in Point Pleasant, north of Huntington, attributes his distrust of coal companies to his grandfathers, both retired state troopers. His first two cases were for two people Trish had met in 1998, James Bailey in Ragland and James Scott in Rawl. One of the few lawyers to take on the difficult-to-prove blasting-damage cases, Thompson settled a blasting case for the Baileys and about fifty other plaintiffs who were impacted by White Flame Energy, the mine that had consumed the mountain range between Varney and Ragland—and in the process had brought Trish back into the mining battle in 1997. In 2005 he started another case when White Flame blasting resumed, stronger than ever, near Bailey's home. Thompson also settled what had been a $2.5 million claim against Arch Coal for contaminating land supposedly reclaimed.

The Rawl case, Thompson jokes, is his *A Civil Action*—referring to the book of that title by Jonathan Harr. Here he is trying to prove that residents' illnesses are linked to well water contaminated by slurry injected by a Massey Energy mine into an old deep mine below the community. People in Rawl and nearby Lick Creek had lobbied for public water for nearly a decade. Mingo County finally found the money and built the water lines in 2006. Thompson has two other environmental-health cases, one against Massey on possible health effects of a sixteen-story coal silo looming over Marsh Fork Elementary School along Coal River and another on a school near Omar that is built near a dump used by coal companies in the first half of the twentieth century.

Like DEP inspectors and coalfield residents, Thompson has found that dealing with Massey is different from confronting Arch and White Flame. Those two companies have accepted that he has a strong case and even try to improve their mining. He has seen Arch improve its handling of waste oil, for example. But Massey has not responded to the allegations and in fact has sued him for defamation of character.

When the floods devastated the coalfields in 2001, Charleston attorney Stuart Calwell was incensed at what he believed the mines and timber companies had inflicted upon vulnerable people. Quickly he filed a case. Over the next five years, the case swelled to more than five thousand plaintiffs suing nearly four hundred land-use companies, including coal mines, timber companies, gas companies, and railroads. So large were the proceedings that the case was broken down into a series of trials by six watersheds and numerous sub-watersheds. In May 2006 Calwell, Scott Segal, Warren Randolph McGraw II, and other plaintiffs' attorneys won their first jury trial. This portion of the larger case involved nine hundred plaintiffs in two sub-watersheds of the Upper Guyandotte in Mullens and Oceana in Wyoming County, the epicenter of the 2001 floods. By the time the jury got the case, all thirty-one defendants except the two largest land companies, Western Pocahontas Properties and Western Pocahontas Corporation, had settled. In what could become a landmark decision, the jury found that the land companies helped cause the floods. However in March 2007 a judge vacated the jury decision; a retrial may be granted, depending on the outcome of any appeals.

The courageous step Brian Glasser and Ben Bailey took that October evening of 1999, accepting a nuisance case over water in Pie, did indeed show that courts could bring a measure of justice to the coalfields.

The New Economy

In the fall of 1998, Senator Lloyd Jackson had called for a frank discussion of how the coalfields would survive when all the coal had been mined. His report to the Governor's Task Force on Mountaintop Mining and Related Mining Methods formed the basis of SB 681, passed six months later. The *Bragg* case had both prompted the task force and then weakened the final outcome of Jackson's efforts. Yet his clarion call lived on in a series of steps away from the coal-based economy in Mingo and Logan counties.

Two other men were inspired by the *Bragg* case as well. The first was Terry Sammons, the Harvard-educated lawyer from Gilbert in Mingo County. Unfortunately, his dream of homesteading on mountaintop sites had not been chosen by any mines as a postmining use. Coal companies claimed that the guidelines developed by the architecture school at the University of Virginia were too onerous. Nonetheless, he found other ways to meld mining and the economy in Mingo County.

For a couple of years, he taught a course at Southern West Virginia Community College, where students learned a reality-based mix of environmentalism and the economy. "Corporations are rational economic actors—obligated to maximize shareholder value," Sammons told a half dozen students one May evening as a coal train echoed with a whistle. Yet corporations' best interests certainly can be harmful at times. Sammons drew a circle on the blackboard. "Remember the example of cigarettes," he told the students. "If you calculate the true cost, Medicaid has to pay $10 billion that's not borne by Philip Morris. In the environmental world, if a company can externalize costs, say if it can't reclaim a mine, and it paid a $100,000 bond—but it costs $500,000 for reclaiming?"

"The taxpayer pays," a student interjected.

"The true cost of coal" is a phrase that gained credence as global warming came to the forefront of public opinion in the second half of the 1990s. "Coal is $25 a ton," Sammons said. "But the true cost is $90 a ton.

That $65 difference goes for pollution control, breathing problems, contamination. If I sell that product, I should bear those costs. If the industry paid for those external costs, we would pay 20 cents a kilowatt hour, instead of 5 cents we pay now. Maybe we should use hydropower, wind generators, insulate our homes, drive less."

Then Sammons drew the discussion to a conclusion. "How we are going to make a difference is by us. The politics of the past have been too old-boy network. The internet gives us the ability to find information, to challenge. What I want you to remember is always to focus on the dream. We are fortunate to live in southern West Virginia. Do we talk differently? Yes. Do we act differently? Yes. We want to see progress. But we want to keep that unique thing that makes us good alive."

Sammons and his wife, Penny, lived what he preached. By the summer of 2005, besides his law office in Gilbert, he had a frame shop, a geotechnical firm, a rental business, and a coal-testing business. Penny Sammons had a coffeehouse with tall sunlit windows, a pressed-tin ceiling, free wireless Internet access, and a reading library upstairs.

As president of the Mingo County Redevelopment Authority, Sammons dreamed big, too. He and Mike Whitt, the capable executive director, created a master plan for the county, intertwined with existing and planned mountaintop-removal mines—just as SMCRA decreed nearly thirty years earlier. "Compared to five years ago, this is real," Sammons said in 2005. "This is not a field of dreams. The *Bragg* case accelerated development. It's the reason for post-mining land development."

At a 2001 meeting with the governor's development director, Mike Whitt made his position clear: "We can sit here and blame everyone for the past. What we need to do is have people tell us how to solve problems. We can look at the person in the mirror and ask what have you done you done to solve problems. Ninety-nine percent of the people in the county have done nothing to solve the problems."

The redevelopment authority has done quite a bit. It purchased and developed 650 acres of an old Arch Coal mountaintop mine on the Logan-Mingo border. There a wood-flooring plant employed two hundred people at more then ten dollars an hour, with benefits. Authority board member Buck Harless put together a consortium of his and three other companies to invest in machinery, because he wanted to bring value-added lumber-finishing jobs to the coalfields. The industrial park was named

James H. "Buck" Harless Wood Industrial Products Park. Harless's International Industries transferred its ownership share to Columbia Forest Products of Portland, Oregon, the nation's largest flooring manufacturer, which had partnered with International, at the end of 2003. Harless's company continued to supply wood to the plant.

Other economic-development projects included a fish hatchery that used water from an old deep mine, just up the road from Trish's house, where arctic char were hatched and then sent to a grow-out facility near Man. The fish were targeted for dinner plates at swank East Coast restaurants. There was a demonstration agriculture site with cows and vineyards on an old Arch Coal mine above Ragland. And White Flame had agreed to build several miles of the new four-lane King Coal Highway that will cross the mountains near Trish's house. White Flame and Arch Coal built the Twisted Gun Golf Course on their mine above Gilbert. On the drawing board were plans for upscale housing, as well as an airport, for executives at the new industries that Whitt and Sammons hoped would be set up in Mingo and for the possibility of a Federal Express hub on the White Flame mine above Varney.

Mingo was the first coal county to adopt a master plan so that coal companies could plan ahead for industrial development on mountaintop mines, knowing what development the county wanted. The plan also spelled out what roads and power lines the mines had to leave on the land when they departed—an unprecedented step toward coal leaving something good behind.

Fifteen other coal counties had similar master plans by the end of 2005, thanks to the Office of Coalfield Community Development established by Jackson's SB 681. The office had also helped develop a vineyard and winery as a cooperative to be maintained by a family on-site in Logan County, a dam for a recreational lake at Fola Coal in Clay County, northeast of Charleston, and a housing project for flooded-out families at Bluestone Coal in McDowell County. Administrator Paul Hardesty had lived through the height of the *Bragg* case as Logan County administrator and a school board member, seeing the county budget drop from $5.5 million to $4.2 million when Arch shut down the mine in Blair. The son of a safety director at Island Creek Coal and the grandson of a UMWA representative, Hardesty knew all too well the double-edged sword of coal and was happy to find a way to make the coalfields a better world.

Another man who helped bring the coalfield economy into the twenty-first century was drawn to the challenge both by his ancestry and by his rare ability to give a damn, and then act. Leff Moore was the great-great-grandson of William Madison Peyton, namesake of Madison, the county seat of Boone County. A historical marker stands at the town of Peytona, honoring the man who built the locks and dams to float coal down the Coal River to Charleston.

A century ago, Moore said one April afternoon in 2000, those who recognized the value of the coal in the mountains bought the rights. "This land ownership pattern exists. And you can say it shouldn't have, or you can say government should have stepped in, but it exists. I'm not a defender but a pragmatist who says it is what it is. If I could have been around 100 years ago and been a benevolent dictator, I might have seen it differently. The question becomes, if you are a pragmatic realist, what do you do?"

Moore's own vision dawned one day at an old western town in Arizona where he watched a gunfight, staged for tourists. "What do the southern coalfields have besides coal, gas and timber?" he wondered. "They have beautiful mountains and forests and a heritage that fascinates the rest of America." His dream expanded: the major attraction would be a trail network for all-terrain vehicles, motorbikes, mountain bikes, and even horseback riders. He'd gotten the idea from guides for riding mountain bikes in western states. A study showed that one state had gained $3.2 billion from this kind of tourism. So was born the Hatfield-McCoy Trail.

Now the big obstacle was the land companies, which would have to grant permission for thousands of strangers to ride across fields fraught with liability potential. Moore, a respected liberal lobbyist, figured he'd show the land companies what was in it for them, because that's the only approach that succeeds in the corporate world. The land-company owners lived by a mantra: never sell the land, because someday it might be needed for a coal-processing plant, or more coal might be discovered. But land companies were also subject to the same boom-and-bust cycles as mining. "If land companies can see a win-win situation," Moore said, "where the land is managed by someone other than themselves, they've got the benefit of a diversified tax base as the population leaves Appalachia. And there are more businesses to contribute to health-care costs."

It took years and the involvement of several federal agencies, including the Bureau of Land Management. Concerned about a future Demo-cratic governor who hated coal companies, the land corporations would deal only with the federal government. So Moore conceived a Hatfield-McCoy oversight board of land and coal companies and redevelopment officials. BLM guidelines would be followed in establishing the trails. This would be world-class, the authority decreed. Buck Harless wanted the trail to be as monumental as the community center he had recently built in Gilbert—not just four pieces of plywood with spray-paint graffiti.

And world-class it has become. The Hatfield-McCoy Trail is now said to be the largest tourist draw in West Virginia, with seventy-three thou-sand user permits sold in the past five years, 81 percent to out-of-state rid-ers. The trail now encompasses five hundred miles in five counties. Local service businesses have sprung up, including four outfitters and fifty-two motels, bed-and-breakfasts, and campgrounds. "Will Hatfield-McCoy save southern West Virginia?" Moore asked. "No. But is it a paradigm shift? Just sit in the office and answer the phone."

Moore dreamed, too, of drawing tourists to the history of the coal-fields. Amazed, he had watched a group of ATV riders drink in history from a local resident during a trial run of the trails. "This old guy is selling hot dogs, and he had all these stories," Moore recalled. "It was like 50 chil-dren hanging out at Santa Claus' feet. But guess what, the tipple has been torn down now. Now what's in it for me. We have lost lots of heritage icons. The coal company store got torn down, the mine portal no longer exists, the coal camp is gone. The reason is if it's sitting there, it's a liability, they can be sued."

Hopefully, the demolition will slow and the restoration begin. Unfor-tunately, Moore died in 2004. But thanks again to West Virginia's mem-bers of Congress, eleven southern counties were designated a National Coal Heritage Area in 1996, one of eighteen National Heritage Areas. Coal Heritage signs dot the roads along Route 52 from Bluefield to Welch, then north to Pineville and ending in Beckley. Corridor G has its own tourism committee, with historic markers and signs that point to nearby attractions sprouting between Charleston and Williamson. When the res-taurant at Chief Logan State Park moved to the new lodge on Corridor G, a coal museum opened in the former building. A group of Logan citizens are installing historical signs with names of dozens of coal camps and communities, many of which no longer exist. And the state has nominated the battleground on Blair Mountain as a national historic site. In fact, a 1991 study had suggested establishing a coal-mining-life museum in Dobra, near Bob Schultz's home, a railroad interpretive center, and a historical trail along the battle path.

The more people who give a damn, the better life in the coalfields can be.

My Vote Is Not for Sale

"What is courage? "It is daring to attempt things that are good—when everyone else says it's impossible—you've got to try." Arley Johnson strode from side to side in front of the pulpit, looking over a rainbow of ladies' hats as he spoke to the Raleigh County chapter of the National Association for the Advancement of Colored People in honor of Dr. Martin Luther King Jr.'s birthday in January 2000.

As Arley spoke, he was living a profile in courage as he battled House Speaker Bob Kiss over the budget digest—that approximately $35 million in leftover funds that were doled out to delegates by Kiss and the leadership in the House but, in the Senate, split evenly among senatorial districts. Arley's fight embodied political freedom—and engagement—all too rare in the coalfields. Media and activists lauded his efforts, and a few political officials followed in his path.

The point of contention this first month of the new century had begun a few months earlier when it had appeared Kiss would be appointed to the state Supreme Court of Appeals—a promotion denied by a lawsuit over the legislature's vote for the justices' pay raises. However, Arley had already circulated a letter among delegates slamming the budget digest as his candidate, judiciary chairman Rick Staton, vied for the Speaker's seat. When Kiss lost, he made short work of Arley, kicking him off the judiciary committee and stripping him of his vice chairmanship of the insurance committee. "Last Friday," began the *Charleston Gazette* editorial, "We published a cartoon of the Legislature's returning House Speaker Bob Kiss as Genghis Khan, ready to put the heads of his enemies on spikes. Welcome to the spike, Arley Johnson."

As the legislature went into session in January, Arley was front page news. Not only had he been demoted, but now House finance chairman Harold Michael was supposed to have called him "boy." He'd had "the boy" up in his office for an hour and a half for a lesson on the budget digest. For Arley, as for many other African Americans, "boy" brought up the image of slavery.

Finally, on January 24, everyone had had enough and came together in the semblance of a group hug. Harold Michael rose on the floor of the House to declare: "I would extend my friendship to the Delegate from Cabell and pledge to work together for betterment of the state." Then Michael walked down from his seat in a back corner and shook hands with Arley, who picked up his microphone and stood: "I think we are going to have a better House, better government. I still intend to speak out if I see an injustice. I will do so with respect and with dignity; I think that is how we move forward, how we grow, how we allow our minds to be expanded and let our spirits run free."

Kiss returned Arley to the judiciary committee and his vice chairmanship. As Arley walked back to his office, Bill Raney stopped him and shook his hand. Later that year Arley brought a lawsuit over the budget digest, winning small reforms but not abolishing it. Another case was brought in 2004 by Dan Hedges, Joe Lovett's mentor. Early in the 2006 session, when it appeared that case would force the House to reveal how the digest was divvied up, Kiss pushed through the House a bill eliminating the budget digest. With regret, the senators agreed. Finally, the budget digest was history.

Arley left the legislature in February 2001, when he was appointed executive director of the Governor's Workforce Development and Investment Board by newly elected Democratic governor Bob Wise. Arley's older children were starting college, and the salary increase would help his family. He stayed on when Democrat Joe Manchin was elected governor in 2004, trying to make a difference for the needy as his office administered four federal grant programs to the sixteen community-action agencies around the state. When the time was right, he expected to run for state Senate.

Senator Lloyd Jackson left the legislature and lost to Joe Manchin in the 2004 primary for governor. He was considered too "white bread" compared to Manchin's down-home manner. Senator Jeffrey Kessler fulfilled his promise as a rising star when he took over the judiciary chairmanship after a Christian Right Republican defeated the long-time chairman.

Although two of them were gone from the legislature, all three—Arley, Jackson, and Kessler—would be noted in history for their courage to do what was right for the coalfield residents.

That spring of 2000, an equally important battle for political freedom was being waged in Trish's county of Mingo. Sheriff Tennis Hatfield had taken on the ingrained political practice of vote-buying. "Let's show them Mingo County is not for sale. The ball is in your court, voters," Hatfield thundered in a radio ad Monday, May 8, the day before the primary. Though the incumbent, Hatfield was considered the underdog among the three candidates and was sure he was going to lose. Buck Harless, timber baron and political boss, backed another candidate. People in Gilbert had told Hatfield they'd love to vote for him—but Buck knows how you vote. If we don't stop these political agendas, we'll kill this county, Hatfield thought.

At the *Williamson Daily News*, editor Melody Kinser, sports editor Chuck Carter, and news editor Audrey Carter (no relation) agreed. In the weeks before the election, they covered election fraud in personal columns. "Mingo County has a reputation when it comes to politics and it's not a good one," wrote Audrey Carter. "Think about it—some of our politicians have spent time in jail because for them it didn't matter what the cost, they wanted the position so-o-o-o bad. I continue to live in Mingo County because I love this county and want to see it prosper and move ahead. But I know when it comes to politics, we have a problem and some of the deals being made behind closed doors may have a far-reaching effect."

Whether Mingo could cross the millennium was answered late Tuesday night in the courthouse, the command center of political life in the county. Peggy Hatfield sat at a table tucked in a corner of the narrow entrance to her husband's office. A happy woman, she'd recently been diagnosed with cancer. Her blond wig was a little askew, but she didn't notice as she kept the precinct tally on a yellow legal pad, jotting down each result announced on the local radio news. Tennis had secluded himself in his office, certain of defeat. Just today a woman had called and told him, "They told me how to vote." Yet, he still liked to hear Peggy shout when he won a precinct. He could tell how he was doing by the decibel level.

The Williamson Field House precinct came in: Tennis 213, Cline 85. Peggy waved her hand: "Thank you, Lord. We need a good lead." At 10:45 p.m., 15 precincts had reported. Tennis 1,374, Jeff Cline 983. At 20 precincts it was Tennis 1,743, Cline 1,395. But within minutes, a hush spread across the group. Thirty precincts in: Tennis 2,553, Cline 2,520.

"It's a dog fight," Peggy said.

What precincts remained? Everyone searched Peggy's sheets. Delbarton, bad for Tennis. Chattaroy would be good. Lenore—very bad. Usually, the most corrupt precincts reported last.

At 10:40 a man had run up from the downstairs room where votes were being counted. Halcy Hatfield, the good-government group's candidate for county commissioner, had won, defeating the incumbent. Everyone started shouting.

Then the word came: Tennis was tied. Then another dispatch: Tennis had won.

"They can't buy Mingo County," said chief deputy James Pack, with a fierce pride.

Not until 2005 was vote-buying curtailed in Logan and Lincoln counties. After several years of federal investigation, thirteen politicians in those counties pleaded guilty to vote-buying, including Logan County clerk Glen Adkins and a member of the powerful Stowers family in Lincoln County, a force Arley had to deal with in his elections.

"Vote buying in Logan County was symptomatic of the large scale corruption existing in the two counties," said Booth Goodwin, an assistant U.S. attorney who worked on the investigation. "The ability to commercialize the vote permits 'them' to keep the power. It leads to less engagement in political power and political debate."

The challenge would be to carry forward the courage demonstrated by Arley Johnson and Tennis Hatfield, for the coalfield citizenry to become engaged in the political debate and to make their own futures better.

Mining Becomes More Responsive

The election of 2000 reversed the balance of regulatory power. Instead of a Democrat in the White House, a Republican ruled the land, while a Democrat took over the West Virginia statehouse. Heavily Democratic West Virginia surprised the nation by giving George W. Bush its five electoral votes in the general election of 2000; cast otherwise, they would have given Al Gore an uncontested victory. Bush's election opened the way for weaker federal oversight of mining and kept Joe Lovett busy in the courts. The Bush administration weakened oversight of mining, but balance was maintained under the Democrats in West Virginia, who enacted many of the regulations decreed by the *Bragg* case.

By early 2006, mountaintop removal continued, but it was considerably better controlled than nine years earlier. (Deep mining, however, suffered several deadly accidents, beginning with the death of twelve miners in an explosion in the middle of the state. These deaths finally brought national attention to the dangers of deep mining and spurred stronger safety controls.)

Roger Calhoun, head of the OSM regional office that oversees DEP, had seen improvement since the 1999 Haden ruling in the *Bragg* case, and many of the changes came directly from the 1999 settlement. Many more mountaintop mining sites were slated to return to native hardwoods under the commercial-forestry provision of the settlement. The state, Calhoun said, seemed to be adhering to the flood regulations Matthew Crum had pushed through in 2003, requiring the coal companies to prevent any additional runoff during storms.

Most of the permits for new mountaintop mining granted between January 2000 and April 2006 were for mines that would return the mountains to Approximate Original Contour, according to the Department of Environmental Protection. Of the fifty-four mines, only ten were granted variances that would permanently lower the mountain instead of restoring the Approximate Original Contour. Eight of those chose commercial forestry as the postmining land use. One land use, near Charleston, was industrial, while an expansion of Arch's Samples mine had mixed uses, including commercial forestry, fish and wildlife habitat, and recreation. These mines, many of them extensions of existing mines, such as Hobet 21 and Samples, would cover 50,478 acres, or seventy-eight square miles. But if regulations are followed, the topography will mostly return to those original cone-shaped mountains in a few decades.

These fifty-four mines planned 477 valley fills. The vast majority were shorter than a half mile. Only 25, just 5 percent, were larger than 250 acres. The two largest were at Massey Energy's Independence Coal: 1,300 acres and 900 acres. By comparison, between 1993 and 1998, 10 percent of the 379 fills were larger than 250 acres.

Blasting appeared a bit less of a problem but still bothersome. Early in 2006, Dave Vande Linde, a longtime DEP employee who had worked on the Environmental Impact Statement, took over as head of the blasting office. He felt that he had come full circle, since his father had been the first head of the state environmental agency in 1963. His father had been inspired to curtail mining abuses after he judged an art show at a school in

265

Danville. The water in every child's picture was black: streams, lakes, and even oceans. That was all kids saw, because coal slurry colored the rivers so black that one retired miner once said it seemed like you could dip your pen in and start writing.

The blasting office had a staff of sixteen, including seven inspectors who dealt only with blasting complaints. Blasters had to be recertified every three years and took regular refresher courses to help them do a better job. Unfortunately, modified blast designs to lessen nuisance and shaking of homes were still rare. However, a new mine on a mountain along the West Virginia Turnpike between Charleston and Beckley was required to limit its blasts so as to keep rocks from falling on vehicles on the highway.

Regulators would have to hang tough as coal boomed in 2006. Prices had more than doubled in the past few years, hitting nearly fifty dollars a ton. New companies were reopening marginal mines. As of mid-March 2006, there were 195 active surface and 206 active underground mines in the state.

Electricity use was expected to grow by 50 percent between 2004 and 2030, according to the federal Energy Information Administration. As many as 120 coal-fueled power plants were being planned across the country, and they would produce enough electricity for more than 70 million homes—though protests could block a significant number of plants. Spurred by deregulation, the nation's power grid was modernizing and expanding. With eased federal regulations on placement of giant 765-kilovolt lines, American Electric Power planned to stretch power lines from the John Amos plant near Nitro to the Northeast, thus bringing more cheap coal electricity to an area traditionally powered by the more expensive natural gas and oil.

Coal had become an integral part of the national security program, with incentives in the Energy Policy Act of 2005 for development of pollution controls at power plants and research into conversion of coal to liquid fuels. "The challenge," President George W. Bush said when signing the bill, "is to take advantage of our coal resources while keeping our air clean." West Virginia jumped on the bandwagon for coal gasification, and in December 2006 the Mingo County Redevelopment Authority joined Colorado-based Rentech to develop a clean transportation-fuel plant in Mingo. Using its patented Fischer-Tropsch method, Rentech planned to extract carbon from coal, synthesize it to a gas, and convert the gas to ultraclean fuel. Mike Whitt of the Redevelopment Authority, at the announcement of the plan, called it "a vital step that West Virginia is taking in its efforts to further national energy independence and security while utilizing our resources in an environmentally sensitive manner."

Depending on your view, the good news is that coal production will probably stay about the same in Appalachia for the next few decades. Future coal production will continue to shift to the West, according to the federal Energy Information Administration. With the cheapest coal, western production is expected to double between 2004 and 2030. Already approximately twenty power plants east of the Mississippi have switched to coal from the Powder River Basin in Montana and Wyoming; that coal costs about one-third of the price of Appalachian coal but has lower heat value. Total coal production is expected to rise about 40 percent by 2030.

By 2030 most of the coal on the state's mountains may be nearly gone. In 1996 the Energy Information Administration predicted that the state had 2,800 million more tons of surface minable coal, or 49 more years' worth at the current rate of mining. There were 16,800 million tons of underground coal, or enough to sustain mining for another 144 years. Interestingly, Kentucky had 5,600 million tons atop mountains, more than three times as much as remained underground. Tennessee and Virginia were more evenly split, with 300 million tons underground and 200 million on the surface left in Tennessee and 900 million tons underground and 500 million remaining on the surface in Virginia.

At least one member of the Schultz family could be in the deep mines when mountaintop coal is gone. Although Bob succeeded in getting his younger son, Nick, to airplane mechanic school in North Carolina, the hollows drew him home and into a union deep mine. Bob told him he'd either love it or hate it. Nick loved it. Bob's elder son, Rich, a top mechanic at a large car dealer along Corridor G, was a popular participant on the PBS *Junkyard Wars*. In 2006 Bob Schultz still drove a bulldozer at Hobet 21. In January of that year, he had to start all-night oxygen treatments. The black lung came from the mines and the preparation plant, the asbestosis probably from ripping apart diesel engines in the 1970s without protective masks. His wife, Debra, wished he'd retire, but he was several years away from union health protection—and he felt he had to keep supporting his family.

Deep mining was all but ignored by environmentalists until a tragic series of accidents early in 2006. Trish already knew of the need for tough regulation of deep mines, but it became painfully apparent to everyone when twelve miners perished in the January 2 explosion at the Sago Mine near the middle of the state; the thirteenth miner miraculously survived. Within the next month, two miners (including a distant cousin of Trish's husband) died in a fire at a Massey Energy mine near Logan. And two others died on February 1, one in a deep mine and the other at Massey Energy's Elk Run mountaintop mine near Dickie Judy's home. Within months the West Virginia Legislature and Congress passed tougher safety regulations mandating better emergency communication and tracking devices and more oxygen supplies underground. Sadly, investigators found the Sago miners close to safety, but rescuers had had no way to talk with them.

Environmentalists were disheartened by President Bush's weak efforts at controlling power-plant pollution. Most importantly, he seemed to have reneged on a promise to reduce carbon-dioxide emissions, which make up the biggest part—60 percent—of greenhouse gases. These emissions have risen 20 percent just since 1955. And emissions from power plants increased 9 percent from 1995 to 2003.

Coal-fired plants produced about 36 percent of the carbon dioxide, 64 percent of the soot-forming sulfur dioxide, 26 percent of the smog-forming nitrogen oxide, and 41 percent of the mercury. In the end, states may bring the tough controls into being. Connecticut, Delaware, Maine, New Hampshire, New Jersey, New York, and Vermont joined a proposed Northeast Regional Greenhouse Gas Initiative that would freeze carbon-dioxide emissions at current levels by 2009 and reduce emissions by 10 percent beginning in 2015.

The Environmental Impact Statement—supposed to be finished by the end of 2000—dragged on until the final report was issued late in 2005. The heads of the four federal agencies announced that more research was needed for definitive answers, and for that research there was no money. Instead, efforts would focus on making permit review more efficient—which the agencies believed should lead to better environmental protection. Whether that happens remains to be seen. The EIS did produce tens of thousands of pages of the most complete data ever seen on mountaintop removal.

Perhaps the greatest blow to protection of the streams came when the Bush administration altered Section 404 of the Clean Water Act in May

2002. Now valley-fill waste met the definition of filling waterways for development. The administration had put out rules for comment on altering the one-hundred-foot buffer zone, the OSM regulation that was Joe's winning chip. But as of early 2006, that change had not been finalized.

As coal boomed and the Bush administration found ways to help the coal industry, the struggle for responsible mining fell, as always, to the citizens and the lawyers. Joe Lovett continued on with other cases based on legal arguments similar to those in the *Bragg* case. Some months, he would rock back in his office chair and say, "We lost." Then he'd talk about doing clean-air cases. But coal always drew him back. After the *Bragg* case, he had several more major victories in federal district court—only to see them overturned by the same three-judge panel of the Fourth Circuit Court of Appeals in Richmond, Virginia.

Joe and Gretchen moved to Lewisburg, a quaint city surrounded by rolling fields two hours east of Charleston. They have three sons now and live in a new energy-efficient, environment-friendly house. Joe has set up his own public-interest law firm, the Appalachian Center for the Economy and the Environment.

Just five days after the Bush Administration snatched away Section 404 protection, Judge Haden upheld the Section 404 protection in Joe's case over an eastern Kentucky mine. "The Court does not rule in a vacuum," Haden wrote. "It is aware of the immense political and economic pressures on the agencies to continue to approve mountaintop removal coal mining valley fills for waste disposal, and to give assurances that future legal challenges to the practice will fail." Again the Fourth Circuit Court of Appeals overturned Haden.

Joe and Jim Hecker won another case in July 2004, when they argued that the Corps of Engineers, hiding behind Nationwide Permit 21, had failed to do individual reviews of fills exceeding 250 acres. The result was that permits covering twenty-six miles of stream at seventeen mines were voided. Again, the ruling was overturned. Trying another tack, Joe and Jim filed another case over Nationwide Permit 21, this time concerning mines in Kentucky. The appeal was going to be heard by the more liberal Sixth Circuit Court of Appeals in Cincinnati.

With the continuing lawsuits, the Corps was actually doing individual reviews on fills in southern West Virginia. Forty-three fills had been released as of March 2006, and forty-five were pending. The Corps had found that many of the mines in its region, which includes Kentucky and Ohio, were already asking for individual permits even though they weren't a requirement. Nationwide Permit 21, which had given blanket approval for valley fills since 1986, was renewed in March 2007.

In that month Judge Robert C. Chambers, in the Huntington district of federal court, issued an opinion that Joe believed could radically limit—or completely stop—mountaintop removal. Joe, with lawyers from Earthjustice, had filed the case in September 2005 over the new mountaintop permit planned on the southwest side of Blair by Massey Energy, near the site of the 1921 Battle of Blair Mountain. Plaintiffs included the West Virginia Highlands Conservancy, the Ohio Valley Environmental Coalition, and Coal River Mountain Watch. Joe later expanded the case to several other mines, including Elk Run's Black Castle, the one that so troubled Dickie Judy and swathed Sylvester in dust. Attorneys argued that the Corps did not examine the harm valley fills did when obliterating headwater streams—and that attempts to "mitigate" by recreating streams were insufficient. Chambers agreed, sounding like Joe's stream expert in the Bragg hearing when he wrote: "Headwater streams, such as those at issue here, are typically found in forested hollows. . . . Trees often produce a canopy covering portions of the stream, shading the water in the summer and providing organic matter. This organic matter is collected within the headwater streams, broken down and transported downstream where it supplied much of the energy and material which support life and other ecological functions." His ruling blocked permits for the Massey mine near Blair, the one near Elk Run, and two others.

Joan Mulhern of Earthjustice, who had lobbied against the congressional rider after Judge Haden's 1999 ruling, predicted that Joe would eventually prevail. Judge Chambers's ruling could be the time. She and Joe have higher hopes of winning at the Fourth Circuit Court of Appeals. One reason is that J. Michael Luttig, the conservative judge who presided over all three of Joe's appeals, resigned, after being passed over twice for the U.S. Supreme Court. In December 2006 the Fourth Circuit, for the first time, upheld a ruling by Judge Chambers in a 2003 case over a mine near Hominy Creek in Nicholas County. Though Joe was not an attorney on this case, it involved a principle of the *Bragg* case. Chambers stopped DEP from weakening the rule on cumulative impact. Joe believes he has a good chance with the Fourth Circuit in the March 2007 case because there were six days of fact-based testimony. Therefore it would be harder for appeals judges to find a reason for reversal. If the case stands, it will have sweeping impacts, since at the time of the ruling the Corps had more than forty individual permits for mountaintop mines pending in the region, which includes Kentucky.

Nearly eight years after the Haden ruling, the Corps finally granted the redesigned permit for the mountaintop mine in Blair in January 2007. The size had been reduced by nearly one-third, to 2,278 acres. The valley fill remained behind James Weekley's home, but much farther away. James and Sibby still lived in their home on Pigeonroost and still took their grandchildren up the hollow. Unfortunately, Sibby died in January 2007. Vicky and Tommy Moore had moved close to Madison in 2004, with Dustin due to start college in 2007 and planning to be a doctor. Joe is hoping Judge Chambers's ruling will also halt the Spruce mine.

Chances for curtailing global warming got a big boost when Democrats took control of both houses of Congress in the 2006 midterm election. Barbara Boxer of California took over the Senate Environment and Public Works Committee and quickly vowed to curb greenhouse gases, taking the lead from her own state's goal of lowering emissions to 1990 levels by 2020. As head of the Senate Energy and Natural Resources Committee, Jeff Bingaman of New Mexico was expected to push to have as much as 10 percent of the nation's electricity generated from renewable resources by 2020. Indeed, the nation's awareness of the energy crisis and climate change seemed to reach a tipping point in 2006, with films, documentaries, and a continuing series on the successes and failures of alternative energy in the New York Times.

However, Jim Hecker and others saw little likelihood that mining would be curtailed, as Nick Rahall of southern West Virginia was in line to chair the House Resources Committee and Rick Boucher from just across the border in southern Virginia could take over the Energy and Environmental Initiatives Committee. Boucher hoped to pass a bill to develop liquid fuels from coal, thus encouraging more mining. The southern West Virginia coalfields should benefit, though, because Senator Robert Byrd took back his former post as head of the powerful Senate Appropriations Committee.

Rahall did bring huge help to the West Virginia coalfields in another way. At the end of 2006, he finally succeeded in revamping the Abandoned Mine Lands program. Now the old hills of coal waste and other dangerous abandoned mines from before 1977 will finally be cleaned up—binging new jobs as well. The $1 billion-plus allotted to AML will no longer be subject to annual federal budgetary whims. West Virginia could get $40 million in 2007 and $70 million a year after that. Some AML money will still fund health care for retired coal miners. In January 2007 Governor Joe Manchin announced that much of the new AML funding would bring public water to more than seven thousand West Virginians in nineteen counties, including the communities of Dingess and Ragland in Mingo County and Amherstdale and Holden in Logan County.

The 2006 elections brought changes in the West Virginia legislature, as well, with Democrats gaining back two Senate seats and four in the House. Speaker Bob Kiss chose not to run for reelection. Early in December 2006, Delegate Rick Thompson, who is more liberal, won a contested Speaker's race. He quickly promised more open debate and appointed fresh faces as committee chairs, including a woman for judiciary and Mike Caputo, who had led the coal-truck legislation, as majority whip. It seemed the legislature was moving toward the true democracy Arley Johnson had tried to forge.

———

After the *Bragg* case, Arch Coal became more environment- and citizen-friendly, according to former DEP mining director Matthew Crum and Arch's own Larry Emerson, who oversaw environmental issues at all the Arch mines. "Some things we need to think about," Emerson told Shepherd University students at an April 2005 forum, include "putting something back in these sites and incorporating sustainable concepts. We must use mining as a means to achieving an end and leave something the community can use." He had made similar comments four years earlier after a meeting in Logan on the Spruce Fork permit in Blair. "We used to think we were there to mine coal," he had mused. "Now we realize we are a neighbor. But we had to be kicked to realize it."

In fact, when Arch began work on a new deep mine between Sharples and Blair, it established a committee of local citizens and held an informational open house. In 2006 Arch paid much of the cost for extending public water two miles to Sharples. Local residents welcomed Arch's offer of cooperation. However, the deep mine certainly altered a community already shrunken by the mountaintop mining of the 1990s. The elementary school had closed and both school buildings had been replaced by settling ponds for the slurry before water drained into Spruce Fork. A bridge fit for a four-lane highway took the rerouted Route 17 over double train tracks that would carry out the coal.

Unfortunately, Arch got rid of nearly half of its West Virginia mines in 2005, merging three of its largest surface mines, including Hobet 21 and Samples, with four large deep mines owned by a Boston investment firm. Arch would own just 37 percent of the new company. It would keep the yet-to-open mine in Blair, but the majority of Arch coal would be mined in Wyoming and several other western states, where coal seams were a fat fifty feet or more thick and mines were in the middle of nowhere. Arch's largest mine in Wyoming produced about 100 million tons of coal a year, compared to about 6 million tons a year for the company's largest West Virginia mine.

Massey Energy is now the largest coal company in the state. As DEP inspector Bill Cook had said eight years earlier, Massey is no Arch. Chief Executive Don Blankenship made news in the *Wall Street Journal* and *Vanity Fair* for his notorious meddling in state affairs. He had spent $6 million of his own money to make the state more business-friendly. His television ads and campaign contributions had successfully elected an unknown lawyer to the state Supreme Court, dumping the most liberal justice, Warren McGraw. Blankenship also helped persuade voters to veto Governor Joe Manchin's plan for a $5.5 million bond to rescue the state employees' pension plan.

Yet in Mingo and Logan, Blankenship was known more for his hardscrabble life story and millions of dollars in good deeds. For several summers, Massey has held a picnic in Logan, drawing more than thirty thousand employees and friends. Massey's charity has included Christmas parties for kids, sponsorship of high school sports tournaments, scholarships, and restoration of the athletic fields at the high school in Matewan. In 2003 Massey sponsored a series of television ads blaming economic decline and school closures on the outward migration of former miners in search of work.

Interestingly, just as the coal company holdings were changing hands, so too had the ownership of the mineral itself. By 2007 Corbin "Corby" Robertson Jr. had become the largest owner of coal in West Virginia, after the federal government. Robertson, an heir to one of Houston's best-known and most philanthropic oil families, controlled about 20 billion tons of coal, equal to nearly twenty times the annual coal production in the United States.

———

Activism in the coalfields has changed since Trish began fighting for water in 1994. Unfortunately, WVOP died in June 2002 for lack of money and membership. Foundations had chosen instead to fund more sophisticated groups opposed to mountaintop removal. OVEC received a large Ford Foundation grant.

Actually, large foundations had been increasingly reluctant to support community organizing. The National Network of Grantmakers, which includes many of the nation's most progressive foundations, found that its affiliated groups gave just 10 percent of their funds for citizen participation in 1994. "There have never been many funders with a commitment to or even an understanding of the importance of community-based efforts," stated a Southern Empowerment Project report in 1992. However, community groups themselves hadn't always made their best case, the report noted. "This is particularly important now when institutional funders seem to view community organizing as adversarial and unfocused instead of understanding it for what it is—empowering and community building."

Appalachian Voices, the North Carolina group that worked with James Weekley during the settlement negotiations, had established Coal River Mountain Watch in Whitesville with help from Freda Williams and a couple of other local residents. Freda had left the group; in 2006 it was headed by Judy Bonds, a gray-haired dynamo who had burst into the mountaintop-removal battle in 1999 when she joined James Weekley and a dozen others as he recreated the 1921 march of the miners to Blair Mountain.

Bonds became a powerful voice. Living right next to Massey's Marfork office building near Whitesville, she had seen her creek repeatedly polluted by black-water spills from the mine. Finally fed up, she sold her home to the coal company and left the hollow. "I envision people in West Virginia finally rising up and speaking in one voice," she said in a 2000 interview published in the West Virginia Highlands Conservancy newspaper. "I hope the coal miners will join with us and say the coal companies need to comply with the law. They [the coal companies] need to be better neighbors, they need to be kinder to the environment." The larger envi-

Part of James Weekley's re-creation of the march to the Battle of Blair Mountain comes through Blair early in September 1999. Judy Bonds is second from left, Shireen Parsons third from left.

ronmental groups persuaded the Goldman Prize to give Bonds the world's most prestigious—and valuable, at $125,000—environmental activist award in 2003. Quickly, she became the face of coal activism, quoted and filmed by dozens of media outlets. At the awards ceremony, Jim Hecker was glad for the attention to mountaintop removal but wondered why the award hadn't gone to Trish Bragg or Cindy Rank.

In the summer of 2001, the UMWA made peace with mining opponents and joined against a common enemy: Massey Energy. Although the UMWA hoped to begin unionizing Massey mines, a horrific coal-truck accident early in September 2001 caused the campaign to focus first on coal-truck safety. Coal trucks weighing 160,000 pounds regularly hurtled along narrow coalfield roads, blatantly violating weight limits of 65,000 pounds. The effort to enforce the weight laws took a path though the legislature much like that of the blasting law. Delegate Mike Caputo, a UMWA representative, kicked it off with a passionate speech reminiscent of the one Arley Johnson gave for the blasting bill—though he didn't lose his job. After the coalition succeeded in blocking the industry bill to raise the weight limit in the 2002 session, a task force was appointed. But the next year, the election had taken away a significant number of allies in the legislature, so the increase to 120,000 pounds sped through, but at least it was accompanied by tough safety regulations. No one has been killed in a coal-truck accident since.

A new kind of activism came to the coalfields in West Virginia, Kentucky, Tennessee, and Virginia with Mountain Justice Summer in the summers of 2005 and 2006. In West Virginia, one group worked along Coal River while another worked in Rawl gathering information on water polluted by the slurry injected into the underground mines. Mountain Justice Summer leaders educated young people in mining laws and how to read permits and maps. Born out of United Mountain Defense in Tennessee, Mountain Justice Summer stated in its Web site that it was part of the growing anti-mountaintop-removal movement. Early in 2006, United Mountain Defense had—remarkably—persuaded Tennessee to enforce the one-hundred–foot buffer zone around streams, thus barring large valley fills. The Tennessee group is also trying to get a bill passed that would completely ban mountaintop removal, hoping that eventually this would lead to similar efforts in the three neighboring states.

The more sophisticated environmental groups have successfully drawn more national attention to mountaintop removal. Appalachian Voices funded the Appalachian Treasures project that sent a paid staffer and many volunteers, including Larry Gibson and Judy Bonds, around the country talking to small groups at colleges and rotary and other clubs. Audiences were urged to write their members of Congress asking them to support the Clean Water Protection Act, which would make valley fills absolutely illegal under Section 404. Chances for passage got a boost when the Democrats took over Congress in November 2006, though the bill would still face a veto by President Bush.

Yet, most of the activism focused just on mountaintop removal. Not much interest in the political and economic conditions was evident. Nor did many residents of the coalfields, except for a few dozen along Coal River, attend the environmental group gatherings. If life in the coalfields is going to truly improve, if coal can be mined safely, those who live near the mines and work in the mines must lead the way.

Paul W. Eubank of Amhertsdale, along Buffalo Creek, wrote in a letter to the *Logan Banner* after the 2006 mining accidents: "Was the miners

Larry Gibson (left) shows the mountaintop removal behind his family's home place on top of Kayford Mountain.

afraid to report an accident that was about to happen? Or an unsafe situation that could lead to problems later on. Were they afraid to report such things to the Mine Management because they might have been told they would be fired? Were they told that if they didn't do their job that there was others waiting to take their place?"

No one in the coalfields should fear for his or her job or home. Trish's hope was that a group like the Organizing Project could be born again—the need was so great. In many communities residents remained befuddled by mining regulations—just as Trish had once been. Nevertheless, ·such a group needed broader goals, for coal was certainly not the only problem in the coalfields, where drugs were rampant and most of the hollows still lacked public sewers. Trash marred many lovely streams and hollows that could be potential tourist attractions.

The importance of Saul Alinsky's bottom-up approach to change was resurrected during the 2008 Democratic race for the White House. In their youth, Hillary Rodham Clinton and Barack Obama had studied Alinsky principles: Hillary in her senior thesis at Wellesley College, and Obama as an organizer for an Alinsky-related group on the south side of

Chicago. Though the two have somewhat differing opinions of Alinsky's theories, both believe that the most impacted citizens must help solve the problems, rather than waiting until change is dictated from on high—the philosophy that so infused everything Trish had done.

Trish believed that "Appalachians need to know they can change things." Her own life and the improvements in mining, regulation, and politics show that change indeed is coming to the West Virginia coalfields.

Epilogue

"The first thing I want you to know is that I'm not a public speaker. I am a housewife—and I'm very proud of that, too." Trish stood at the podium in a ballroom at a Montreal hotel, speaking at the annual meeting of Trial Lawyers for Public Justice in July 2001. Her blond hair swept across the shoulders of her forest-green-and-cream pantsuit. On the dais behind her sat TLPJ president Peter Perlman and Morris Dees, the legendary crusader against the Ku Klux Klan.

Jim Hecker had introduced the *Bragg* case to the audience of three hundred. "We've already achieved several goals: We stopped the largest mine, stopped the state from rubber stamping permits and won an injunction to stop dumping in streams."

As she spoke, Trish took the audience mentally down to Pie. "When I came into West Virginia as a young bride at seventeen, my first experience was with my bridal shower. My husband is from a family of ten and that's just a small family to them," she paused as the audience laughed. "When I got to that bridal shower there were 75—and then I was really overwhelmed." The audience laughed along as Trish smiled. "They brought me gifts and didn't even know my first name." She added that even today all of those present would eagerly respond to "any kind of whim and need" that she might have, if she picked up the phone and called them.

TLPJ president Perlman and Morris Dees were spellbound.

"When we started having all the trouble," Trish continued. "I just knew I was one housewife who saw a situation coming that was going tear up everything I came to West Virginia to find. The little community I lived in for over 20 years was going to be destroyed by mountaintop removal."

Trish pushed her prepared speech aside and looked straight at the audience. "Could you imagine getting 25 or 30 calls a day? I did. Older

Trish and Dewey in a park above Montreal after Trish spoke to Trial Lawyers for Public Justice.

people didn't have any water, or their bathtub fell through the floor. You're talking about people who live on limited income, six hundred dollars a month. How are they going to fix those damages? More importantly why should they?" Trish looked at Jim Hecker and smiled, then took a sip from a bottle of water.

"You can imagine how refreshing it was to run into Trial Lawyers for Public Justice. Because lawyers hadn't been real nice to me. You don't have any idea how it feels to know that somebody believes in what you are doing and it's right and it's okay for you to fight back. You gave us that right," she said, addressing the TLPJ representatives. "And why? It wasn't for money, thank God, because I didn't have any. It was because you believed in the American Way."

The entire audience rose into a standing ovation—rare at a TLPJ conference.

"Trish," TLPJ president Perlman told her, "I don't know how many great trial lawyers there are in this room. But none of them could have put it as well as you did as to what kind of difference you can make."

Trish had spent the year and a half since Haden's momentous ruling finishing college while struggling with serious illness. Early in 2000 she had passed out in a restroom in Chapmanville on her way to college. It was the fourth time in a month she had been sick. An EKG showed heart trouble. Already she had ulcers, and doctors thought she should have a hysterectomy. Refusing to quit, she was back in college in a few days.

In May 2001 she graduated from West Virginia State College—summa cum laude. Only in Spanish did she achieve less than an A. To younger students, she had become a bit of a media star, occasionally granting requests for an autograph on a newspaper article. Her family gave her a remodeled bathroom as a graduation present—all white fixtures, bright and new. Dewey was so proud of her accomplishments. As she walked across the stage to accept her diploma, surrounding her were the helping hands of many people.

Soon she had a full-time job at a nonprofit in Logan that supervised child-care providers. Despite ill health, Trish still tried to help others with mining problems. A few weeks after her hysterectomy early in 2003, she went to a new group in Delbarton that was trying to curtail a slurry impoundment at a Massey mine. In August 2005 she watched proudly as Mingo officials came to a meeting at the new firehouse she had worked so hard to get for Pie. As soon as the fire truck and volunteers firefighters arrived, her neighbors could qualify for lower home insurance rates.

Kayla graduated from high school in 2006—planning to go to college in Tennessee and hoping to be a nurse. Doctors, she said, are too impersonal. "I created a monster, and I mean that in the very best sense," Trish would say of dragging her to all those rallies and government offices. Connie, a nurse, and her husband, Robert Hager, bought Susan's house, the one whose well had gone dry in 1994 (by now piped-in water served many houses in the community). In March 2005 Alexandria Glennisa Hager, Trish's first grandchild, was born. Trish quit her job to help care for "Lexie" and worked as a substitute teacher several days a week. Robert had been an accountant for Massey but moved to Arch the week his daughter was born. Arch gave him full medical benefits from the start and that first week off. He was being trained to take over accounting for West Virginia operations.

In the fall of 2004, Trish and her family moved into the new home she thought she'd never have.

In 2004 a dream, seemingly impossible a decade earlier, came true. As the trees on Trish's beloved hills shed their autumn finery, Trish, Dewey, and Kayla moved into their brand new home, sheltered under a sky-blue metal roof and warmed by porches front and back.

That others in the southern West Virginia coalfields will have their spirits raised as high is the dream Trish hopes her struggle will someday realize.

Appendix

The *Bragg v. Robertson* Case

The West Virginia Division of Environmental Protection, by its actions in approving mining permits, had violated its duties under the federal Surface Mining Control and Reclamation Act. The U.S. Army Corps of Engineers, by its actions in approving permits to fill streams with mining waste, had violated its duties under the federal Clean Water Act and the federal National Environmental Policy Act. The violations were related primarily to the valley fills created by mountaintop-mining operations.

Date Filed: July 16, 1998.

Plaintiffs:
Patricia Bragg
Carlos and Linda Gore
Harry "Burr" Hatfield
Jerry Methena
Cheryl Price
James and Sibby Weekley
West Virginia Highlands Conservancy

Primary Defendants:
U.S. Army Corps of Engineers
West Virginia Division of Environmental Protection

Attorneys for the Plaintiffs:
Jim Hecker
Joe Lovett
Pat McGinley
Suzanne Weise

Presiding Judge: Charles H. Haden II

Progress of the Suit:

Temporary Restraining Order hearing, February 3, 1998 (TRO granted).

Preliminary Injunction hearing, February 4–19, 1998. Favorable ruling, March 3, 1998.

Settlement 1, December 23, 1998. The part of the case against the U.S. Army Corps of Engineers, pertaining to filling streams under Section 404 of the Clean Water Act and requiring the preparation of an Environmental Impact Statement under the National Environmental Policy Act, was settled at this time.

Settlement 2, July 26, 1999. The case against the West Virginia Division of Environmental Protection, except for the issue of whether DEP's permits for valley fills complied with the buffer-zone rule under the Surface Mining Control and Reclamation Act, was settled at this time.

Summary Judgment, October 20, 1999. Judge Haden granted summary judgment for the plaintiffs and ruled that the West Virginia DEP's approvals of the burial of streams with mining waste from valley fills violated the buffer-zone rule under the Surface Mining Control and Reclamation Act.

Summary of Outcome:

Settlement 1 resulted in the federal Environment Impact Statement, an extensive study of mining impacts; a two-year moratorium on mountaintop removal so that the buffer-zone rule could be reworked; and a ruling that every valley fill over 250 acres would get intensive individual review by the Army Corps of Engineers.

Settlement 2 yielded gains related to restoring mountains to Approximate Original Contour after mining, replanting mined areas with trees, encouraging homesteading on flattened mountains, reclaiming streams after mining, and improving the processes of mining permit approval and mining oversight.

Aftermath:

Judge Haden's ruling on the buffer-zone issue was overturned by the Fourth Circuit Court of Appeals. The court dismissed the buffer-zone claim for lack of jurisdiction, without reaching the merits. The U.S. Supreme Court declined further review. Nevertheless, several improvements remained: for example, mining permits were more carefully considered, native hardwood forests were planned for replanting after mining, and valley fills were less frequent and better designed. In addition, the Corps withdrew its permit to Arch coal for the enormous Spruce No. 1 mountaintop-removal mine near Blair. Further mining on that tract was delayed for eight years pending preparation of a separate Environment Impact Statement and downsizing and reconfiguration of the mine to reduce its environmental impacts.

Bibliography

For various materials relating to the events reported in this book, the reader may consult the Archives and History Department, Division of Culture and History, West Virginia Archives and History Library, Cultural Center, in Charleston, WV.

Newspapers

Beckley (WV) Register-Herald, 1997–2006.
Bluefield (WV) Daily Telegraph, 1997–2006.
Charleston (WV) Daily Mail, 1997–2006.
Charleston (WV) Gazette, Charleston, WV, 1997–2006.
Huntington (WV) Herald-Dispatch, Huntington, WV, 1997–2006.
Logan (WV) Banner, 1908–1914 (the "King Case" over ownership of mineral rights), 1997–2006.
Mountain Monitor. A publication of West Virginia Organizing Project, Logan, WV, 1995–2000.
Reporter. A publication of Citizens Coal Council, Washington, DC, 1997–2006.
Williamson (WV) Daily News, 1997–2006.

Newspaper Coverage of Selected Topics

Blair History, *Logan (WV) Banner,* 1937–1939.

"Valuable Rum Creek Land Once Sold for $3 per Acre." December 9, 1937.
"'Five Block,' Located between Blair and Sharples, Was Thriving Community during War Days." March 2, 1939.
"First Logan County Coal Shipped in 1903 from Stone Branch Mine above Big Creek." April 17, 1939.
"Sovereign Was Once Thriving Mining Town." May 31, 1939.

Election 2000, Mingo County, *Williamson (WV) Daily News,* **April–May 2000.**

Carter, Audrey. "Only You Can Change the System." April 13, 2000.
Carter, Chuck. "Political Favors: What About Me?!" April 22, 2000.
Kinser, Melody. "Something to Think About." April 30, 2000.
"A New Day Dawns on Our County." April 27, 2000.
"Voting Is a Right and a Privilege." May 7, 2000.

Vote Buying Trial. *Logan (WV) Banner,* **January–October 1971.**

"U.S. Jury Indicts 4 County Officials, Sen. Smith." January 13, 1971.
"Napier Repeats Testimony That Tomblin Paid Him Money." August 30, 1971.
"Sheriff Urged False Poll Slip Be Used, Jury Told." September 1, 1971.
"U.S. Winds Up Case against 5 Local Men." September 2, 1971.
"Trial of 5 Local Men Moves into 10th Day." September 8, 1971.
"5 Logan Countians Given 10-Year Terms." October 14, 1971.

Law

Surface Mining Control and Reclamation Act of 1977, 30 U.S.C.

Lawsuits, Depositions, and Hearings

Bragg v. Robertson (S.D. W.Va. 1998).
Kentuckians for the Commonwealth, Inc. v. Rivenburgh. 204 F. Supp. 2d 927 (S.D. W.Va. 2002), vacated, 317 F.3d 425 (4th Cir. 2003).
Moore v. Hobet Mining, Inc. No. 97-C-266-0 (Cir. Ct. Logan County, W.Va. July 1998).
Ohio River Valley Environmental Coalition, Inc. v. Norton. No. Civ.A. 3:04–0084, 2005 WL 5188120 (S.D. W.Va. Nov. 22, 2005), aff'd sub nom *Ohio Valley River Coalition, Inc. v. Kempthorne,* 473 F.3d 94 (4th Cir. 2006).
Ohio Valley Environmental Coalition v. Bulen. 410 F. Supp. 2d 450 (S.D. W.Va. 2004), aff'd in part and vacated in part, 429 F.3d 493 (2005).
Ohio Valley Environmental Coalition v. U.S. Army Corps of Engineers. ___ F. Supp. 2d ___, 2007 WL 902097 (S.D. W.Va. March 23, 2007).
West Virginia Coal Association v. Reilly (S.D. W.Va. 1989).
Deposition of James Weekley, *Bragg v. Robertson.*
Deposition of Donald Mueller, *Moore v. Hobet Mining, Inc.*
Deposition of Terrence Irons, *Moore v. Hobet Mining, Inc.*

Hearing for the Temporary Restraining Order. February 3, 1998, federal district court (S.D. W.Va. 1998). Transcript available from the court in Charleston, WV.

Hearing for the Preliminary Injunction. February 4–19, 1998, federal district court (S.D. W.Va. 1998). Transcript available from the court in Charleston, WV.

Other Sources

Abramson, Rudy. "A Judge in Coal Country." *Alicia Patterson Foundation Reporter*, 2003.

Alinsky, Saul. *Rules for Radicals*. New York: Vintage Books, 1971.

Associated Press. "Bucking the Trend: Harless Stays Put, Amasses a Fortune." August 13, 2000.

Baldwin, Justine Aleshire. "A Pictorial History: Blair." Unpublished document, 1998.

———. "A Pictorial History: Sharples." Unpublished document, 1998.

"Boone County Coal Corporation." *West Virginia Review* 20, no. 9 (1943): 32–36.

Borgos, Seth, and Scott Douglas. "Community Organizing and Civic Renewal: A View from the South." Virginia Organizing Project, Charlottesville, VA, 1998.

Brown, John M. "Timbering and Flooding in Fayette County, West Virginia." Timber Reform Research Project of the West Virginia Highlands Conservancy, Morgantown, WV, 2002.

Burton, Mark L. "Coal and the West Virginia Economy: Issues for the Coming Century." *Regional Economic Review*, Center for Business and Economic Research, Marshall Univ., Special Edition,1999.

Campbell, Shirley Young. *Coal & People*. Parsons, WV: McLain, 1981.

Caudill, Harry M. *Night Comes to the Cumberlands: A Biography of a Depressed Area*. Boston: Little, Brown, 1962.

Chafin, Raymond, and Topper Sherwood. *Just Good Politics: The Life of Raymond Chafin, Appalachian Boss*. Pittsburgh: Univ. of Pittsburgh Press, 1994.

Chircop, Jeanne. *Facts about Coal*. Washington, DC: National Mining Association, 1998.

Coalfields Expressway Authority. "The Way Home for West Virginia." Pineville, WV, 2001.

Coghill, Kenneth L. *The Lawmaking Process in West Virginia: A Study in Legislative Ethics*. Parsons, WV: McClain, 1970.

Cohen, Stan. *King Coal: A Pictorial Heritage of West Virginia Coal Mining*. Charleston, WV: Pictorial History, 1984.

Colarusso, Dan. "In an Energy Fog, Coal Starts to Shine." *New York Times*, April 29, 2001, 6.

"Community Organizing: Democratic Revitalization through Bottom Up Reform."

In *Foundations in the New Era, a NCRP Special Report*. Washington, DC: National Committee for Responsive Philanthropy, 1995.

Conley, Phil, and Boyd B. Stutler. *West Virginia Yesterday and Today*. Charleston, WV: Education Foundation, 1966.

Constantz, George. *Hollows, Peepers, and Highlanders: An Appalachian Mountain Ecology*. Missoula, MT: Mountain Press, 1994.

Corbin, David Alan. *Life, Work, and Rebellion in the Coal Fields: The Southern West Virginia Miners, 1880–1922*. Urbana: Univ. of Illinois Press, 1981.

Couto, Richard A., and Catherine S. Guthrie. *Making Democracy Work Better: Mediating Structures, Social Capital, and the Democratic Prospect*. Chapel Hill: Univ. of North Carolina Press, 1999.

Davis, F. Keith. *West Virginia Tough Boys: Vote Buying, Fist Fighting, and a President Named JFK*. Chapmanville, WV: Woodland Press, 2003.

Dietz, Dennis. *The Flood and the Blood*. South Charleston, WV: Mountain Memory Books, 1988.

Dotson-Lewis, B.B. *Sago Mine Disaster (Featured Story): Appalachian Coalfield Stories*. West Conshohocken, PA: Infinity, 2006.

Dotson-Lewis, B.L. *Appalachia: Spirit Triumphant*. West Conshohocken, PA: Infinity, 2004.

Eades, Rick. "Timber and Mine Sites and Their Relationships to July 2001 Flood Damages in Fayette County." Prepared for Fayette County Commission, Fayette, WV, 2001.

Eilperin, Juliet. "U.S. Faces 'Pivotal Moment' on Clean-Air Regulations." *Washington Post*, January 27, 2005.

Epstein, Paul R., Sarah Meginness, John Rich, Roger Swartz, Jean McGuire, and John Auerbach. *Urban Indicators of Climate Change*. Boston: Center for Health and the Global Environment, Harvard Medical School, and Boston Public Health Commission, 2003.

"Final Report." Governor's Task Force on Mountaintop Removal and Related Mining Practices, Charleston, WV, November 1998.

Fisher, Stephen L., ed. *Fighting Back in Appalachia: Traditions of Resistance and Change*. Philadelphia: Temple Univ. Press, 1993.

Fitzgerald, Tom. "How to Protect Your Land and Water from Underground Mining." Citizens Coal Council, Washington, DC, n.d.

Flood Analysis Technical Team. "FATT Runoff Analyses." West Virginia Department of Environmental Protection, Nitro, WV, 2002.

Giardina, Denise. *The Unquiet Earth*. New York: Ballantine Books, 1992.

Gillespie, William H., Mary Beth Adams, Jim Kochenderfer, and Joe McNeel. "Forests and Floods: A Review of Pertinent Literature on the Impact of Forests on

Floods with Observations on the Flooding That Occurred in Southern West Virginia during the Early Summer of 2001 and Eastern West Virginia during the Fall of 1985." Prepared for West Virginia Division of Forestry, Charleston, WV, 2001.

Gleick, Elizabeth. "No Way Out." *Time,* December 23, 1996. Regarding the murder of Jackie Weekley.

Goodall, Cecile R. "The Legislature in Action." *West Virginia Review,* February 1933, 138–140.

Harless, James H. "I'm Not the Antichrist, Mingo's Buck Harless Says." *Charleston Gazette,* April 1, 2001.

Heilprin, John. "Democrats to Stress Environmental Issues." Associated Press, November 14, 2006.

House Committee on Interior and Insular Affairs. *Compilation of Selected Laws concerning Minerals and Mining with Amendments through the 101st Congress.* 102nd Cong., 1st sess., 1991.

Hufford, Mary. "Tending the Commons: Folklife and Landscape in Southern West Virginia." http://memory.loc.gov/ammem/collections/tending/ack.html.

In Memory: Hon. Charles H. Haden II, 1937 to 2004. Private brochure for memorial service, March 2004.

Jehl, Douglas. "On Environmental Rules, Bush Sees a Balance, Critics a Threat." *New York Times,* February 23, 2003, 1.

Keith, Bruce, and Ronald Althouse, eds. *Inside West Virginia: Public Policy Perspectives for the 21st Century.* Morgantown: West Virginia Univ. Press, 1999.

Kenny, Hammil Thomas. *West Virginia Place Names.* Piedmont, WV: Place Name Press, 1945.

"King Coal Highway, Draft Environmental Impact Statement." West Virginia Department of Transportation, Division of Highways, Charleston, WV, 1999.

Lee, Howard B. *Lost Tales of Appalachia.* Parsons, WV: McClain, 1977.

Little, Elbert L. *National Audubon Society Guide to North American Trees.* Vol. 1, *Eastern Region.* New York: Alfred A. Knopf, 1980.

Lockard, Duane. *Coal: A Memoir and Critique.* Charlottesville: Univ. Press of Virginia, 1998.

Loeb, Penny. "Deluge without End." *Southern Exposure,* 2004, 50–67.

———. "The Coalfield Communities of Southern West Virginia." http://www.wv-coalfield.com.

Loughry, Allen. *Don't Buy Another Vote, I Won't Pay for a Landslide: The Sordid and Continuing History of Political Corruption in West Virginia.* Parsons, WV: McClain, 2006.

Massay, Glenn F. "Legislators, Lobbyists, and Loopholes: Coal Mining Legislation in West Virginia, 1875–1901." *West Virginia History,* April 1971, 135–70.

Mauer, B.B., ed. *Mountain Heritage.* Parsons, WV: McClain, 1980.

McGinley, Patrick C. "From Pick and Shovel to Mountaintop Removal: Environmental Justice in the Appalachian Coalfields." *Environmental Law* 34, no. 1 (2004): 21–106.

McGraw, Darrell V., Jr., and Jan L. Kesling. "Background for Public Policy-Making in West Virginia: Proceedings of West Virginia Pre-Legislative Conference." Bureau for Government Research, West Virginia Univ., December 1968.

"Mingo County Land Use Master Plan." Mingo County Redevelopment Authority, Williamson, WV, 2001.

Moffat, Charles H. *Ken Hechler: Maverick Public Servant.* Charleston, WV: Mountain State Press, 1987.

Montrie, Chad. *To Save the Land and People: A History of Opposition to Surface Coal Mining in Appalachia.* Chapel Hill: Univ. of North Carolina Press, 2003.

Morris, Joe, and Paul Nyden. "Oil Heir Buying W. Va. by the Ton." *Charleston Gazette,* February 4, 2007.

National Assessment Synthesis Team. *Climate Change Impacts on the United States: The Potential Consequences of Climate Variability and Change.* Cambridge: Cambridge Univ. Press, 2000.

National Mining Association. *Facts about Minerals, 1999–2000.* Washington, DC: National Mining Association, 2001.

North, E. Lee. *The 55 West Virginias: A Guide to the State's Counties.* 2nd rev. ed. Morgantown: West Virginia Univ. Press, 1998.

Peyton, Billie Joe, Lee R. Maddex, and Michael E. Workman. "Cultural Reconnaissance Survey of Blair Mountain." Institute for the History of Technology and Industrial Archaeology, commissioned for West Virginia Humanities Council, Charleston, WV, 1991.

Peyton, Billie Joe, Michael E. Workman, Michael W. Caplinger, and Jeffrey A. Drobney. "Blair Mountain Cultural Resource Survey and Recording Project: Phase I Final Report." Institute for the History of Technology and Industrial Archaeology, Charleston, WV, 1991.

Photiadis, John D., and Harry K. Schwarzweller, eds. *Change in Rural Appalachia: Implications for Action Programs.* Philadelphia: Univ. of Pennsylvania Press, 1970.

Pollution on the Rise: Local Trends in Power Plant Pollution. U.S. Public Interest Research Group Education Fund. January 2005. Available in Report Archives at http://www.uspirg.org/home/.

Radcliffe, David, ed. *People's History: The Story of Hartford Areas Rally Together.* Hartford, CT: Hartford Areas Rally Together, 1995.

"Recommendations for Strengthening the West Virginia Legislature." Final Report of the Citizens Advisory Commission on the Legislature of West Virginia. Charleston, WV, December 15, 1968.

Regional Greenhouse Gas Initiative. http://www.rggi.org/agreement.htm.

Reporting on Climate Change. Washington, DC: Environmental Law Institute, 2003.

Rice, Otis K., and Stephen W. Brown. *West Virginia: A History.* Lexington: Univ. Press of Kentucky, 1993.

Rogers, Sam. "List of Explanations of Place Names in Logan and Mingo Counties." Unpublished document available at *Logan Banner,* Logan, WV.

Savage, Lon. *Thunder in the Mountains: The West Virginia Mine War, 1920–21.* Pittsburgh: Univ. of Pittsburgh Press, 1990.

Scott, Otto. *Buried Treasure: The Story of Arch Mineral.* Washington, DC: Braddock Communications, 1989.

Slevin, Peter. "For Clinton and Obama, a Common Ideological Touchstone." *Washington Post,* March 25, 2007, A1.

Smith, Wesley J. *Fighting for Public Justice: Cases and Trial Lawyers That Made a Difference.* U.S.A.: Fontana Lithograph, 2001.

Souvenir program. Seventh Annual West Virginia Coal Festival, Madison, WV, 2000.

Spence, Robert Y. *Land of the Guyandotte.* Detroit: Harlo, 1976.

Squillace, Mark. *The Stripmining Handbook: A Coalfield Citizens' Guide to Using the Law to Fight Back against the Ravages of Strip Mining and Underground Mining.* Washington, DC: Environmental Policy Institute, 1990.

"A Study of the West Virginia Coal Industry and Ways to Help It." Presented to the West Virginia Joint Committee on Government and Finance by the Subcommittee on Coal Mining. January 1975.

"Testimony and Report of the Legislative Bribery Committee of the Senate and House of Delegates." Charleston, WV, 1913.

Toothman, Fred R. *Great Coal Leaders of West Virginia.* Huntington, WV: Vandalia, 1988.

Tuckwiller, Tara. "The 'One-Man Political Machine': 'Everything He Touches Turns to Gold; He's Blessed and Very Thankful.'" *Charleston Gazette,* March 11, 2001.

U.S. Department of Labor. Mine Safety and Health Administration. *Report of the Secretary of Labor's Advisory Committee on the Elimination of Pneumoconiosis among Coal Mine Workers.* Washington, DC: Government Printing Office, 1996.

U.S. Department of the Interior. Office of Surface Mining, Reclamation, and Enforcement. "A Draft Report of the Beech Creek Watershed Hydrologic Investigation, Mingo County, West Virginia." Washington, DC, 2000.

———. *Surface Coal Mining Reclamation: 15 Years of Progress, 1977–1992: A Report on the Protection and Restoration of the Nation's Land and Water Resources under Titles IV and V of the Surface Mining Control and Reclamation Act of 1997.* Washington, DC: Government Printing Office, 1992.

U.S. Environmental Protection Agency. *Mountaintop Mining/Valley Fills in Appalachia: Draft Programmatic Environmental Impact Statement.* Washington, DC: U.S. Environmental Protection Agency, 2003.

Waller, Altina L. *Feud: Hatfields, McCoys, and Social Change in Appalachia, 1860–1900.* Chapel Hill: Univ. of North Carolina Press, 1988.

Warrick, Joby. "What Lies Beneath." *Washington Post,* January 21, 2007.

"Water and Wastewater." West Virginia Infrastructure and Jobs Development Council, Charleston, WV, 2000.

Watson, Traci. "EPA Lists Areas with Too Much Soot in Air." *USA Today,* June 30, 2004, 3A.

Weller, Jack. *Yesterday's People: Life in Contemporary Appalachia.* Lexington: Univ. Press of Kentucky, 1965.

"West Virginia Acid Mine Drainage Study: A Quantitative Inventory and Interpretive Review of Water Quality on Active Mining Operations in West Virginia." West Virginia Division of Environmental Protection, Office of Mining and Reclamation, 1999.

West Virginia Coal Association. *Coal Facts 1996.* Charleston, WV: West Virginia Coal Association, 1997.

West Virginia Division of Environmental Protection. Office of Mining and Reclamation. "A Quantitative Inventory and Interpretive Review of Water Quality on Active Mining Operations in West Virginia." Charleston, WV, 1995.

Williams, John Alexander. *West Virginia: A History.* New York: Norton, 1984.

Zuercher, Melanie A. *Making History: The First Ten Years of KFTC.* U.S.A: Brown and Kroger, 1991.